THE LIBERATING SPIRIT

The Liberating Spirit

Toward an Hispanic American Pentecostal Social Ethic

Eldin Villafañe

WILLIAM B. EERDMANS PUBLISHING COMPANY
GRAND RAPIDS, MICHIGAN

First published 1992 by University Press of America.

This edition published 1993 by Wm. B. Eerdmans Publishing Co.
255 Jefferson Ave. S.E., Grand Rapids, Michigan 49503

Printed in the United States of America

ISBN 0-8028-0728-3

ACKNOWLEDGMENTS

I am indebted to a variety of persons and contexts that over many years' time have contributed in one way or another to this book.

From that small store-front Hispanic Pentecostal church in the "barrio" of mid-Manhattan of the early 1950's, under the pioneering efforts of Rev. "Tony" Hernandez, to the large "Iglesia Cristiana Juan 3:16" in the Bronx, under the dynamic leadership of Rev. Ricardo Tañon (my spiritual father), the Hispanic Pentecostal churches have been the most formative context of this writer's spiritual pilgrimage. The many Hispanic Pentecostal churches in our "barrios" have been the major source of inspiration for this labor of love.

I owe a special gratitude to Dr. Paul K. Deats, Jr., and Dr. Robert Pazmiño, who supported and helped direct the research for this work.

My friends and colleagues at the Center for Urban Ministerial Education (C.U.M.E.) of Gordon-Conwell Theological Seminary in Boston have provided support and encouragement at many important points. Special thanks are in order to Rev. Efraín Agosto, Rev. Ira Frazier, Rev. Lorraine Anderson, Mrs. Nivia Ferrer, and Mr. Bruce Jackson and Mrs. Naomi Wilshire, who helped with the preparation of this manuscript.

Last but not least, grateful appreciation is here expressed to the members of my family, my wife, Margie and my children, Karen Ann, Eldin Lynn, and Dwight Louis for their untiring support and love through the years.

TABLE OF CONTENTS

INTRODUCTION

For many years now an overriding passion has motivated my research -- the construction of a social ethic for the Hispanic Pentecostal Church in the United States. This social ethic, though, must cohere with the Hispanic American socio-cultural experience as well as be consistent with Hispanic Pentecostalism's self understanding of ethics emerging from its experience of the Spirit. This has been the not too modest goal of this book. You, the reader, will be the judge whether I have made some contribution towards that end.

The historical origins and development in the 20th century of the Hispanic American Pentecostal Church have been among the poor and the oppressed.[1] This study rests on the following assumptions. In order for the Hispanic American Pentecostal Church to continue to minister *with* and *to* the poor and oppressed, and thus to be true to the Gospel as a prophetic voice both as a church and by its message, and in order to preserve its Hispanic cultural identity, it must construct a social ethic that affirms its cultural heritage, and it must do so coming to terms with its social status as a minority-sect church in the U.S.A. This self-understanding as a minority-sect church (the church of the poor and the oppressed) must have within it a liberated and liberating Gospel.

The Hispanic American Pentecostal Church also shares a theological heritage. It subscribes to the four basic principles of the Reformation: *Sola Gracia*, *Solo Cristo*, *Sola Escritura* and *Sola Fe*. Nevertheless, the Pentecostal church in its origins, and particularly the Hispanic Pentecostal Church in its origin and development, have their "spiritual ancestors" in the left-wing of the Reformation. This is true both as to its constituency - the poor and oppressed - and as to its theological and ethical formulations. John Thomas Nichol sees the close affinity of the Pentecostal churches in their origins to the left-wing of the Reformation:

---

[1]Juan Lugo, *Pentecostés en Puerto Rico: La Vida de Un Misionero* (San Juan, Puerto Rico: Puerto Rico Gospel Press, 1951; Roberto Dominguez, *Pioneros de Pentecostés: En el Mundo de Habla Hispana* (Miami, Florida: Literatura Evangelica, 1971); Renato Poblete and Thomas F. O'Dea, "Anomie and the Quest for Community: The Formation of Sects Among the "Puerto Ricans of New York," *American Catholic Sociological Review* 21 (Spring 1960): 18-36.

... the emphasis which are manifested by the Pentecostals would place them in the radical (left) wing of the Reformation. Like their spiritual ancestors, the Anabaptists, pentecostals declare (1) that the individual as well as the corporate body of believers should seek for and submit to the leading of the Spirit; (2) that there should be a return to apostolic simplicity in worship; (3) that believers ought to separate themselves from the world; (4) that believer's baptism replaces infant baptism; and (5) that believers should look for the imminent visible return of Christ who will set up his millennial reign.[2]

Thus there is a further critical assumption to consider. As a minority-sect church in the U.S.A. in the 20th century, the Hispanic American Pentecostal Church must not develop just a "community ethic" (an ethic for the church), but an authentic social ethic that takes seriously both reason and society, thus taking seriously its call as a church to be a "community of the Spirit" *in* the world and a "community of the Spirit" *for* the world, but not *of* the world.

The significance of this study can be noted on several fronts. First, it must be pointed out that Pentecostals in general have not produced any significant or scholarly work on ethics. Walter J. Hollenweger is still on target: "The Charismatic revival has so far made no contribution to the theme of ethical rigorism ... This is disappointing."[3] With regards to Hispanic American Pentecostals, this is true as well. Orlando Costas' statement still rings true, although we have had some serious works emerging among Hispanic Christians these past few years (please see bibliography):

Se puede decir, sin embargo, que en lo general a los hispanos, tanto católicos como protestantes, nos faltan trabajos serios que traten de los problemas de la experiencia de la fe cristiana en la diaspora hispánica estadounidence y propongan respuestas teológicas relevantes.[4]

---

[2]John Thomas Nichols, *The Pentecostals* (Plainfield, New Jersey: Logos International, 1966), p. 3.

[3]Walter J. Hollenweger, *The Pentecostals: The Charismatic Movement in the Churches* (Minneapolis, Minnesota: Augsburg Publishing House, 1972), p. 3.

[4]"It can be said, however, that Hispanics in general, Catholics as well as Protestants, lack serious works that deal with the problems of the experiences of the Christian faith in the 'diaspsora hispánica' of the United States and that propose relevant theological answers." Orlando Costas, *Predicación Evangélica y Teología Hispana* (San Diego, California: Publicaciones de las Americas, 1982), p. 15; Unless otherwise noted, all translations, Spanish to English and English to Spanish are by the author.

It is hoped that the subject matter of this study might serve to both stimulate and facilitate an interest in, substantive discussions of, and vigorous commitments to, this long neglected and critically needed dimension of the faith. It is hoped that at the "praxis" level the fruits of my labor will be most significant. The social conscience of the Hispanic church, and most of all the Hispanic Pentecostal church, must be challenged. Placed at its service must be tools of critical analysis and synoptic integration, which take seriously their socio-cultural reality and aspirations and provide historical projects of action in line with a liberated and liberating Gospel.

Perhaps, it has been too much to ask the Hispanic Pentecostal Church, a poor and oppressed group, one with limited access to education and other opportunities and resources in the greater society, at this juncture in its history, to have produced mature theological and ethical reflection of its "being and doing" for scholarly debate. It is hoped that this study will begin to address this need and make a significant contribution.

Special reference will be given to the North-Eastern United States given the author's knowledge of and experience with Hispanics and the Hispanic Pentecostal church in this area, the majority being Puerto Ricans.

In Chapters I and II of this study I draw from the relevant literature a multifaceted picture of Hispanic American life and culture and the complex religious web that gives hope and meaning to the "diaspora hispánica." In Chapter III I interweave the social science literature with contributions of Personalism, in locating and situating Hispanic Pentecostal reality. I note those personal and social forces which oppress Hispanics; giving special attention to identifying and critically evaluating the Hispanic Pentecostal church as it provides a liberating context consistent with Hispanic reality and its theological self-understanding. In Chapter IV I draw from the relevant literature (Scripture, theology and ethics) those relevant elements which are coherent with the Hispanic Pentecostal experience - particularly as it relates to the ministry of the Spirit - and informative in building and enriching the same. A Pneumatological Paradigm is presented. Chapter V is a constructive presentation of a social ethic for Hispanic American Pentecostalism. This ethic is consistent with Hispanic American Pentecostalism's self-understanding of ethics emerging from its experience of the Spirit. I conclude the chapter by drawing the implications for the life and mission of the Hispanic Pentecostal church of this social ethic.

CHAPTER I

HISPANIC AMERICAN REALITY

Hispanic Heritage

> There are times in the history of persons and
> peoples, particularly times of crisis ... when the
> awakening of a sense of heritage becomes a potent
> determinant of destiny.[1]

A sampling of articles in our print media highlights the emergence into national consciousness of a peculiar "pueblo" - the Hispanics.[2] This emergence into national consciousness has significantly challenged the political, economical, educational and religious structures and leadership of North American society.

The exponential growth of Hispanics in the United States is one of the critical factors, with its social implications, that makes for this significance. Hispanics are one of the fastest-growing minorities in the United States. According to the Census Bureau there are "officially" 22.4 million US Hispanics. The 1980 figures noted 14.6 million Hispanics. It is important to note that the 22.4 million 1990 figures ommitted approximately 3.5 million (population of Puerto Rico); plus the close to 2 to 4 million undocumented; plus undercount for improperly identified non-Hispanics, for an estimate ranging from 25 million to 30

---

[1]John A. MacKay, *Heritage and Destiny* (New York: The Macmillan Co., 1943), p. 1.

[2]"Hispanics Make Their Move," *U.S. News & World Report*, 24 August 1981, pp. 60-64; Thomas B. Morgan, "The Latinization of America," *Esquire*, (May 1983), pp. 47-56; "Hispanic Americans, Soon: The Biggest Minority," *Time*, 16 October 1978, pp. 48-61; Goeffrey Godsell, "Hispanics in the U.S.: 'Ethnic Sleeping Giant' Awakens," *Christian Science Monitor* 28, 29, 30 April and 1 and 2 May 1980; "Our Decade in the Sun," *Agenda (A Journal of Hispanic Issues)* 10 (January - February 1980): 2; John M. Wilson, "Hispanic Images Finally Reach the Big Screen," *The Boston Globe*, 2 January 1986, p. 43.

million Hispanics.[3]   Orlando Costas reminds us, "But Hispanics are not just numerically significant. They are also one of the most depressed minorities in the nation. A 'windshield' survey ... immediately reveals a socially marginated and economically oppressed people."[4]

It must be noted early that the name Hispanic is a collective designation of significant political utility which has emerged as a national umbrella for "Mexican," "Mexican-American," "Chicano," "Puerto Rican," "Cuban," "Cuban-American," "Dominican," "Latino," "Latin American" and other Central and South American national origin persons.[5] Pablo Sedillo in his article, "The Forum of National Hispanic Organizations - First Steps Towards Unity," expresses eloquently the significance of the term Hispanic:

> It is impossible to track and retrace the steps leading to just how the popularization of the term 'Hispanic' came about... for the Hispanic the term evokes a sense of presence, of a reality from whose magnetism none can withdraw. As members of a group that has survived in the Americas and evolved out of a distinctively Hispanic complex, they have found in the term the symbol or emblem which in one utterance gives them a self-identity cultured in all of its identifying aspects: ethnicity, language, customs, tradition, history, Christian upbringing, family and bloodlines. The term buoys their spirit to the edge of emotion and provides the opportunity to tell the world that they have arrived. The Hispanic's new voice will no longer be a Cuban's voice, or a Boricua's or a Chicano's in isolation. The new voice is a concert (a capella) ...[6]

---

[3]"Census Says Good Life Still Eludes Most of US Hispanic Population", *The Boston Globe*, April 11, 1991; see also, Joan Moore and Harry Pachon, *Hispanics in the United States* (New Jersey: Prentice-Hall, Inc., 1985), p. l; National Conference of Catholic Bishops, *The Hispanic Presence: Challenge and Commitment: A Pastoral Letter on Hispanic Ministry*, (Washington, D.C., U.S. Catholic Conference, 1984), p. 5.

[4]Orlando Costas, *Christ Outside the Gate: Mission Beyond Christendom* (New York: Orbis Books, 1982), p. 113; used with permission of Orbis Books, copyright 1982.

[5]Moore and Pachon, *Hispanics in the United States*, pp. 12-13.

[6]Pedro Sedillo, "The Forum of National Hispanic Organizations - First Steps Towards Unity," *Agenda (A Journal of Hispanic Issues)* 10 (January-February 1980): 6.

The "awakening of a sense of heritage" among Hispanics, notwithstanding the diversity of national origin and socio-cultural history, is a critical factor in the emerging status of Hispanics as a "national minority."[7]

Given the scope of this study, this section will focus on the rich and multi-faceted cultural heritage of Hispanics. It will do so by looking at three significant elements that have emerged in my research as critical for our understanding of Hispanics. The three elements of this cultural heritage are: (1) Culture Traits and Value Orientation; (2) Language; and (3) La Raza: Ethnicity and Race.[8]

Culture Traits and Value Orientation

The popular and material culture of Latin America has left an impressive and colorful heritage visible in play, food, dress, music, architecture, and the arts. Yet, it is mostly in the non-material culture, the depth of the Latin American "soul," that the most significant contribution, especially for this study, are to be seen. Beneath the surface are images, self-understandings, behavior patterns and values - cultural traits - that are far more important. The existence and pervasiveness of some, though not all, may be questioned. My study suggests that this particular profile is one consistent with the serious literature, and coherent with the reality of Hispanics.

As we look at the culture,[9] we note three distinct strands which converge to provide the cultural heritage of Hispanics: the Spanish, the Amerindian, and the African. Providing general cultural characterization is a very difficult task. This difficulty stems from the rather extensive historical, geographical, and social

---

[7]Moore and Pachon, *Hispanics in the United States*, pp. 2, 12-13, 169-199.

[8]Religion, which permeates all Hispanic life and culture, will be treated in the second chapter, "Hispanic American Religious Dimension."

[9]Utilizing Geertz's definition of culture, it "... is the framework of belief, expressive symbols and values in terms of which individuals define their world, express their feelings, and make their judgments ... culture is the fabric of meaning in terms of which human beings interpret their experience and guide their action." Glifford Geertz, "Ritual and Social Change: A Javanese Example," in William A. Lessa and E.Z. Vogt, ed., *Reader in Comparative Religion: An Anthropological Approach* (New York: Harper & Row, 3rd ed., 1972), p. 533; Geertz adds, "The concept of culture I espouse... is essentially a semiotic one. Believing, with Max Weber, that man is an animal suspended in webs of significance he himself has spun, I take culture to be those webs, and the analysis of it to be therefore not an experimental science in search of law but an interpretive one in search of meaning;" Clifford Geertz, *The Interpretation of Cultures* (New York: Basic Books, Inc., 1973), p. 5.

diversity within the general Latin American cultural tradition or heritage.[10]   My
research has identified from the three distinct "root streams" those particular
cultural traits and values that significantly contribute to Hispanic personality and
value orientations. This emergent profile will be summarized in a concluding brief
schema. From the heritage of these three distinct strands emerges a picture or
ideal type[11] of "homos Hispanicus."

The Spanish

First, the Spanish strand is the most influential in providing certain broad
features of culture traits and values. The noted Spanish writer Salvador de
Madariaga, former professor at Oxford University, wrote in 1928 *Englishmen,
Frenchmen and Spaniards*[12] in which he studied the dominant characteristics of
the three peoples mentioned in the title. Madariaga notes these as "characteristic
impulse manifesting itself in a complex psychological entity, an idea-sentiment-
force peculiar to each of the three peoples."[13]   The three impulses, or systems,
are: in the English, fair play; in the Frenchmen, *Le droit*; and in the Spanish, *el
honor*. The psychological center of the English people is action; of the French,
intellect; and of the Spanish, the soul or passion (by "passion" is meant fervor or
continuous emotional intensity). To "save his soul," not interpreted in the religious
sense, but rather psychological, is the most important concern of the Spaniard, for
it means to "maintain the spontaneity and integrality of the individual passion in
the face of social activity, of generally accepted ideas, and above all, of collective
passions."[14]

---

[10]See Jose Spielberg Benitez, "The 'little' Cultural Tradition of Hispanics," *Agenda* 10 (May-
June 1980); 30-36.

[11]Following the Weberian construct; The ideal type though a generalization it nevertheless yields
important insights about a particular person, people or socio-cultural reality; see, H.H. Gerth and
C. Wright Mills, *From Max Weber: Essays in Sociology* (New York: Oxford University Press,
1946).

[12]Salvador de Madariaga, *Englishmen, Frenchmen, and Spaniards* (London: Oxford University
Press, 1928).

[13]*Ibid.*, p. 4.

[14]*Ibid.*, p. 108.

The Spaniard is a person of passion, and it is "through passion that the Spaniard touches reality."[15]   In Spanish art, literature and religion the predominance of passion over the intellect and the will can be seen.   John A. MacKay, that great student of the Latin American soul, eloquently states:

> On account of the predominance of passion in all their efforts Spaniards have been gloriously indifferent to many of the comforts and amenities of so-called civilization.   They were born to express incandescent passion, and the moment another ideal sufficiently great burns in their souls they will again be found in their bygone potency and splendour on all the highways of the world.   For this race is everlastingly virgin.   It possess qualities which, if inadapted in many respects to the soulless civilization of today, may secure it a leading place in the more spiritual civilization of tomorrow.[16]

To the Spaniard the *heart* is central to life's vision -life lived heroically. Feeling and emotion are the "stuff" of life, to be integrated into a total life-and-world view.

"Personalism," along with passion, is another dominant and distinguishing trait.   John MacKay says, "unique, naked, primitive individuality has been the chief characteristic of the Iberian race."[17]   Yet, we must be clear as to the meaning of the word individuality as it refers to the Spanish character.   Joseph P. Fitzpatrick speaks of it as "a form of individualism which focuses on the inner importance of the person.   In contrast to the individualism of the United States, which values the individual in terms of his ability to compete for higher social and economic status"[18]   The intense individuality of the Spaniard

> does not necessarily mean egotism, or selfishness, but rather that the self provides the standard for determining the place of other social

---

[15]W.Stanley Rycroft, *Religion and Faith in Latin America* (Philadelphia: The Westminster Press, 1958), p. 45.

[16]See John A. MacKay, *The Other Spanish Christ: A Study in the Spiritual History of Spain and South America* (New York: The Macmillan Co., 1933), pp. 12-16.

[17]*Ibid.*, p. 4., see also, Miguel de Unamuno, *Ensayos* (Madrid: Aguilar, 1958) pp. 439-453.

[18]Joseph P. Fitzpatrick, *Puerto Rican Americans: The Meaning of Migration to the Mainland* (Englewood Cliffs, N.J.: Prentice-Hall, Inc., 1971), p. 90; used with permission of Prentice-Hall, copyright 1971.

entities.   Thus the self dominates the scale of values and relationships, and provides it with a subjective standard.[19]

This concept of the individual accounts for the highly sensitive quality of inner dignity (*dignidad*) and respect (*respeto*) that each person has and expects, irrespective of status in society.   It means that "all men have some sense of personal dignity and are sensitive about proper respect being shown them."[20]

It is important to note that this personalism is manifested in the lack of trust for systems or organizations, given a style of life based on a network of personal relationships.[21]   This characteristic accounts for the bringing to collective life and action a subjective and personal standard.   We may even see in Spanish personalism an "affinity" in the best tradition of Boston Personalism of the person "as the ontological ultimate and for which personality is the fundamental explanatory principle."[22]

Personalism, in the form of Spanish Individualism, impacts all areas of life. Personal relationships once established transcend abstract principles and values in all spheres of life, private and public.

Another trait to be noted is the "Paradox of the Spanish Soul" - Idealism and Realism intimately entwined.[23]   This is best depicted by the literary symbol of Don Quijote and Sancho Panza, the famous characters of Cervantes.[24]   Don Quijote forsakes all to follow his ideal.   At his side, on a donkey, rides Sancho

---

[19]W. Stanley Rycroft, *Religion and Faith in Latin America*, p. 45.

[20]Joseph P. Fitzpatrick, *Puerto Rican Americans*, p. 90; The author will seek to use inclusive language in his own writing, but will not revise quotations nor indicate "sic."

[21]It is significant to highlight that a study found that 40% of the Hispanics living in New York and Los Angeles did not own a telephone. This condition was found not to be a result of economic inability as much as cultural consistency.   "Hispanics prefer face-to-face interaction to the comparatively impersonal communication through the telephone."; quoted in, "A New Mission Field: The Hispanic Population of America," *Christian Marketing Perspective* (A Publication of the Barna Research Group), September - October 1986, p. 1.

[22]Paul Deats and Carol Robb, *The Boston Personalist Tradition in Philosophy, Social Ethics, and Theology* (Georgia: Mercer University Press, 1986), p. 2.

[23]Florinda Alzaga, *Raíces del Alma Cubana* (Miami: Editorial Universal, 1976); and John A. MacKay, *That Other America* (New York: Friendship Press, 1935), pp. 12-22.

[24]Miguel de Cervantes Saavedra, *El Ingenioso Hidalgo Don Quijote de la Mancha* (Madrid: Editorial Espasa - Calpe, S.A., 1981 ed.).

Panza, short, pragmatic - a realist. Through the Castilian steppe they ride, idealism and realism, in full harmony. "For Quixote was an idealist ... he would most certainly have perished of hunger but for the care of his loyal, inseparable companion, Sancho Panza, who supplied his master's material wants ... Sancho Panza represents the realistic side ... of the Spanish Soul."[25]

It is important to note that the realism and idealism entwined in the soul of the Spaniard is a strange paradox that defies neat classification and proves so difficult for other people to understand. "By the same law of polarity Don Quixote and Sancho Panza are ever found side by side on the road of life and not infrequently a Spanish wayfarer becomes both by turns." [26]

The realism of "Sancho Panza" has been seen in the welcome reception of Positivism in the late 19th and 20th century in Latin America, as expressed in the philosophy and literature of that period. The idealism of "Don Quijote" has been seen in the reception of the idealism and intuition of Bergson. This "Paradox of the Spanish Soul" is thus seen in no less a figure than in the thought of Jose Vasconcelos' linkage of culture to biology, of his dialectical idealism, that produced "La Raza Cósmica."[27]

While other culture traits and values imprinted through the ages on the Spanish "soul" may be enumerated,[28] we have underlined three basic and fundamental traits contributed by the Spanish and critical to the understanding of Hispanics: Passion, Personalism and the Paradox of the Soul.

The Amerindian

The Spaniards arrived in Latin America at the end of the fifteenth century. Already present on the continent were flourishing civilizations. There were the Aztecs of Mexico, the Mayas of Guatemala, Honduras, and Yucatan, the Incas of Peru, Bolivia and part of Ecuador, the Chibchas of Colombia, the Araucanians of

---

[25]John A. MacKay, *That Other America*, p. 17.

[26]*Ibid.*, p. 7.

[27]José Vasconcelos, *La Raza Cósmica: La Misión de la Raza Iberoamericana* (Barcelona: Espasa - Calpe, 1925); more will be said about "La Raza Cósmica" in the section on, "La Raza: Ethnicity and Race."

[28]See, Francisco Ugarte, *España y su Civilización* (New York: Odyssey Press, 1952); Virgilio P. Elizondo, *La Morenita: Evangelizer of the Americas* (San Antonio, Texas: Mexican-American Cultural Center, 1980).

Chile, the Caribs, Arawak and Taínos of the West Indies, and other smaller
tribes.[29]   Notwithstanding the oppression and destruction of the Amerindian
empires, the destruction of most of the Amerindian population (especially in Puerto
Rico and Cuba), given the marriage between the Spaniard and Amerindian and the
dynamic of cultural fusion, significant cultural traits left their impress upon Latin
American civilization and heritage.   This impress was greater in certain nations
(i.e., Peru, Bolivia, Mexico) and lesser in others (i.e., Cuba, Puerto Rico).   The
Amerindian contribution to the Hispanic heritage is greater than most would
acknowledge. Even in those Latin American nations where the Amerindian culture
is not visible or otherwise acknowledged, what Juan José Arrom says about the
Taínos of Cuba and Puerto Rico is true as well:

> Contrary to what has been traditionally repeated, there is ample
> evidence in existent documents from sixteenth and the seventeenth
> centuries to prove that the Indians were decimated but did not
> become extinct. And so it is possible that, during the initial process
> of transculturation, together with their tangible and visible customs,
> they may have left us some of their invisible and innermost
> feelings.[30]

Among the many cultural traits and values of the Amerindian two will be
highlighted: (1) Community; and (2) Romerías (pilgrimages).

The concept of community as lived out by many Amerindian tribes and
nations is most significant. Virgilio Elizondo reminds us that, "for our native
forefathers, it was not the individuals who by coming together made up the
community, but rather it was the community which ... actually brought the
individual person into existence."[31] The participation in the collectivity of the
group was the basis of human existence. The individuality of the person was
called forth by the community. The well-being and survival of the group was thus
the paramount responsibility of each member of the group.   A communal
consciousness permeated all of life. It was the basic unifying principle of social
organization which legitimated a family unity of immense extension and

---

[29]For detailed characterization of culture and history see Miguel Leon-Portilla, *El Reverso de
la Conquista* (Mexico: Editorial Joaquin Mortiz, 1970); Lewis Hanke, *The Spanish Struggle for
Justice in the Conquest of America* (Boston: Little, Brown, and Company, 1965); Virgilio P.
Elizondo, *La Morenita: Evangelizer of the Americas*, 1980; Juan José Arrom, *El Mundo Mítico de
los Taínos* (Bogotá: Instituto Caro y Cuervo, 1967); John A. MacKay, *That Other America*, 1935.

[30]Juan José Arrom, *El Mundo Mítico de los Taínos*, p. 3.

[31]Virgilio Elizondo, *La Morenita*, p. 8.

complexity. This communal system was further reinforced by the many communal religious symbols and rituals. All of life - family, economics, politics, education, religion - was communally oriented.

W. Stanley Rycroft, making reference to the Bolivian writer Adolfo Gustavo Otero's *Figura y Caracter del Indio*, states: "At the time of the Spanish Conquest, says Otero, there was a clash of two cultures, the individualistic culture of the Spaniards and the collectivist pattern of life of the Indian."[32] Mexican historian Victor Alba goes deeper into the issue:

> Perhaps it was that very quality of something guided and oriented, so remote from their own religious concepts and mental habits, which frightened the Spaniards, the absence of individual salvation, that submersion of the individual in the collective. Worse than simple superstition, worse than idolatry to them was the spectacle of an entire people dedicated to the salvation of a common, collective soul, instead of the individual effort by each man to save his own soul.[33]

The love of *romerías* (pilgrimages) is one of those Amerindian cultural traits which has left its impress upon Latin American civilization. The journey or travel to a holy shrine or holy place was one that all Amerindians, young and old, looked forward to. The expense and time was of no consideration in such pilgrimages. John A. MacKay speaking about *romerías* and its continued relevance says:

> The new Christians must cultivate the equivalent of the *romerías*. There is no greater need than periodical and prolonged spiritual retreats, preferably in some lovely spot in the woods or by the sea, where unhurried time will be taken to bring people face to face with the realities of the spiritual world ... to cultivate ... a sense of the timeless.[34]

---

[32]W. Stanley Rycroft, *Religion and Faith in Latin America*, p. 48.

[33]Victor Alba, *The Mexicans* (New York: Pegasus, 1967), p. 19; quoted in Virgilio Elizondo, *La Morenita*, p. 62.

[34]John A. MacKay, *The Other America*, p. 188.

The African

The African contribution to Hispanic heritage is significant; its influence is evident in music, dance, folklore, religion, and language. From different African regions, in the sixteenth century, black persons began to arrive in the New World, brought by the opprobrious slave trade: Congos, Mandingas, Dahomeyans, Minas, Carabalis, Lucurins.[35] The presence of black persons in Latin America was found principally in the countries with tropical climates. Among them Haiti, Dominican Republic, Cuba, Puerto Rico, and other countries in the West Indies and in the coastal regions of Venezuela, Brazil, Colombia and Peru.

In referring to the contribution of black persons to Latin American culture, particularly to Puerto Rico and the Antilles, Luis M. Diaz Soler in his *Historia de la Esclavitud Negra en Puerto Rico* states:

> La contribución del negro a la 'cultura puertorriqueña' data desde el momento de su aparicion en las playas antillanas. Con él arribaron a estas tierras los ritmos misteriosos y sensuales de su música, impregnada de espiritualismos propios del corazón de Africa, sus tradiciones y costumbres.[36]

This "mysterious and sensual rhythms of his music" is what in the black experience in America Bishop Joseph A. Johnson calls "native musical instincts."[37] Referring to the chants heard on the plantations he says:

> The deep groans of their oppressed souls were expressed by and through musical incantations. Their moans for the dead and the anguish experienced in living were rounded out in musical notes, thereby giving release to their own spirits.[38]

---

[35]Florinda Alzaga, "The Three Roots of Cuban Heritage," *Agenda (A Journal of Hispanic Issues* 10 (January-February 1980): 24.

[36]"The contribution of the black to Puerto Rican culture dates from the moment of his appearance on the Antillean shores. With him there were brought to these lands the mysterious and sensual rhythms of his music, filled (impregnated) with spiritual feelings right from the heart of Africa, its tradition and customs."; Luis M. Diaz Soler, *Historia de la Esclavitud Negra en Puerto Rico* (Puerto Rico: Editorial Universitaria, Universidad de Puerto Rico, 1970), p. 23.

[37]Joseph A. Johnson, *The Soul of the Black Preacher* (Philadelphia: A Pilgrim Press Book, 1971) p. 149.

[38]*Ibid.*, p. 149.

Florinda Alzaga speaks of the slave not wallowing in bitterness, but in overcoming the oppressive situation through "music and drum." Thus, triumphing over anguish and sorrow found hope and "... joy through music and his drum. His sadness was diluted in dancing, in the momentary happiness that gave meaning to his life."[39]

It is important to remember that music serves other functions than to provide joy and a sense of wellbeing. Among these other functions that music serves, Carlos Rosas in his article, "La Musica al Servicio del Reino," notes a five-fold function: (1) music unites people; (2) music transmits social values; (3) music denounces injustices; (4) music influences human behavior; and (5) music can tranquilize and put to sleep or it can awaken and be a challenge for the struggle.[40]

At every stage of the development of black persons in the Americas one or more of these functions served them well. And it is through music that the African cultural contributions have left their most significant mark in the Latin American "soul." Puerto Rico, Cuba, Dominican Republic or Brazil, those locations of African presence, were given not only a particular musical form, but more importantly, a cultural and communal medium of expression of life at its most emotional depth.

For it is that "mysterious and sensual rhythm of his music" which has "spilled-out" and touched deeply all areas of the Latin American personality and graced his/her value orientations with a particular "élan."[41]

---

[39]Florinda Alzaga, "The Three Roots of Cuban Heritage," p. 26.

[40]Carlos Rosas, "La Música al Servicio del Reino," *Apuntes: Reflexiones Teológicas desde el Margen Hispano* 6 (Spring 1986): 3-6.

[41]See also, Maria Teresa Babin, *The Puerto Rican's Spirit: Their History, Life and Culture* (New York: The Macmillan Company, 1971), pp. 43-51; W. Stanley Rycroft, *Religion and Faith in Latin America*, pp. 42-43; 48-49; also instructive is James H. Cone, *The Spirituals and the Blues: An Interpretation* (Minnesota: The Seabury Press); and José Luis González, *El País de Cuatro Pisos* (Puerto Rico: Ediciones Huracán, Inc. 1983).

"Fiesta" and Family

In the amalgamation of the distinct cultural elements of the Spanish, the Amerindian, and the African, there emerged two unique social or communal institutions of Latin Americans: (1) "fiesta" and (2) family.

"Fiesta"

The role of "fiesta" in Latin American culture and society is deeply meaningful. The "fiesta patronales" (patron saint festivals/celebrations) is typical throughout the Latin American world. Religious and non-religious events in the calendar year mark the occasions that are the basis of a marvelous sense of community that celebrates life through "fiesta." The ubiquity and propensity for fiesta is underscored by Rev. Rafael Aragon's statement, "The Hispanic will find any occasion for getting together and find a pretext to stop the flow of time and commemorate people and events with festivals and ceremonies."[42]

Octavio Paz speaks of the *"fiesta"* as "it marks a return to the beginning, to the primordial state in which each one is united with the great all. Every true fiesta is religious because every true festival is communion."[43] Virgilio Elizondo in his *Galilean Journey: The Mexican-American Promise* makes it a central theological category. Though he speaks about the Mexican-American, it can be equally said about all Latin Americans:

> The happiness and joy ... is immediately obvious to outsiders. The tragedies of their history have not obliterated laughter and joy ... fiesta is the mystical celebration of a complex identity, the mystical affirmation that life is a gift and is worth living ... In the fiesta the Mexican-American rises above the quest for the logical meaning of life and celebrates the very contradictions that are of the essence of the mystery of human life.[44]

---

[42]Quoted by, Ruben P. Armendariz, "Hispanic Heritage and Christian Education," *ALERT* (November 1981): 26.

[43]Octavio Paz, "Reflections", *The New Yorker*, November 17, 1979, quoted by Ruben P. Armendariz, "Hispanic Heritage and Christian Education," *ALERT* (November 1981): 26.

[44]Virgilio Elizondo, *Galilean Journey: The Mexican-American Promise* (Maryknoll, New York: Orbis Books, 1983), p. 43; used with permission of Orbis Books, copyright 1983.

Amidst the experience of oppression, domination and the struggle for mere survival, the "fiesta" - with games and rituals, music and dance, food and "familia" - speak eloquently of joy, hope and life.

Family

Commitment to family is one of the salient characteristics of Latin American culture. Notwithstanding the diverse historical, geographical and social experience of Latin America (including the impact of industrialization and urbanism) there are shared family values and cultural attributes among them.[45] The family structure and cultural-ethos, which informs it, have maintained a particular family pattern. Studies show common themes, two of which are: (1) familism and (2) patriarchalism.

Familism emphasizes family relations over individual ones. The value of family well-being overrides in importance individual well-being.[46]   Joseph P. Fitzpatrick, an expert in the field of intergroup relations and the social life of Hispanics (particularly Puerto Ricans), notes the great influence of the family in Latin American culture:

> ... the individual in Latin America has a deep consciousness of his membership in a family. He thinks of his importance in terms of his family membership ... it is as strong among the families of the very poor as it is among those of the very wealthy. The world to a Latin consists of a pattern of intimate personal relationships, and the basic relationships are those of his family. His confidence, his sense of security and identity are perceived in his relationship to others who are his family.[47]

---

[45]National Conference of Catholic Bishops, *The Hispanic Presence: Challenge and Commitment*, p. 21; Ramon Fernandez-Marina, Eduardo D. Maldonado-Sierra and Richard D. Trent, "Three Themes in Mexican and Puerto Rican Family Values," *Journal of Social Psychiatry* 48 (1958): 167-181.

[46]Frank D. Bean, Russell Curtis, Jr. and John P. Marcum, "Familism and Marital Satisfaction Among Mexican Americans: The Effects of Family Size, Wife's Labor Force Participation, and Conjugal Power," *Journal of Marriage and the Family* 39 (November 1977): 759-767; Joan Moore and Harry Pachon, *Hispanics in the United States*, p. 96.

[47]Joseph P. Fitzpatrick, *Puerto Rican Americans: The Meaning of Migration to the Mainland*, p. 78.

But family means not only the nuclear parent-child but the extended family of relatives on both sides. Familism, as a psycho-social and cultural value, is responsible for "Compadrazgo" (godparentage), a "method of knitting the community together and of formalizing informal ties of friendship."[48] While "compadrazgo" is a religious act committing the godparents to bring up in the faith the godchild should anything happen to the child's parent, it really is more important as a tie between the two age peers. The man and the godfather of his child become "compadres." The extended family, including "compadrazgo," is also a critical source of economic security and survival. According to Joan W. Moore, "It is the main focus of obligations and also a source of emotional and economic support."[49]

The theme of patriarchalism speaks about the family structure where authority is vested in the male head of the family. A corollary is that complex of values known as "machismo." "Machismo" "is a particular cultural definition of masculinity ... associated with a strong double standard of sexual morality, with masculinity to be demonstrated through display of physical and sexual prowess."[50]

Debate and controversy surround the concept of "machismo." The traits associated with it are seen as compensation for feeling of inferiority and have been condemned by researchers as close to pathological. Yet, other researchers claim that such a view of "machismo" is a caricature and put forward a more positive view. Nathan Murillo states that "an important part of ... machismo ... is that of using authority within the family in a just and fair manner."[51] Some see in "machismo" a desirable combination of virtues of courage and fearlessness in man - the head and protector of the family, responsible for their well being and defender of their "dignidad y honor." Only then, it is believed, will he receive the proper "respeto" from his community. Both sides of the debate do not deny that in the traditional Latin American family women hold a subordinate role and status.

---

[48]Joan W. Moore and Harry Pachon, *Hispanics in the United States*, p. 96.

[49]Joan W. Moore, *Mexican Americans* (Englewood Cliff, New Jersey: Prentice-Hall, Inc., 1970), p. 104.

[50]Joan W. Moore and Harry Pachon, *Hispanics in the United States*, p. 96; see also Marco A. Espinoza, "Pastoral Care of Hispanic Families in the United States: Socio-Cultural, Psychological, and Religious Considerations," (Unpublished D.Min. Project, Newton, Massachusetts: Andover Newton Theological School, May 1982), pp. 136-138.

[51]Nathan Murillo, "The Mexican Family," in N. Wagner and M. Haug, ed., *Chicanos: Social and Psychological Perspective* (St. Louis: C.V. Mosby, 1971), p. 103.

In concluding this section I present a brief schematic summary of the culture traits and value orientations noted, and that provide us with an ideal type or profile of:

"Homos Hispanicus"

Passion   -   Life is to be heroic; feelings/emotions are to be accepted in a wholistic response to life.

Personalism   -   Personal relations paramount, above abstract principles and institutions.

Paradox of the Soul   -   Realist and Idealist, one can be both without confusion or confinement.

Community   -   Communal consciousness permeates all of life.

Romerías   -   A sense of timelessness is to be cultivated.

Musical élan   -   Unity, liberation, transcendence and joy is to express and impress all of life.

"Fiesta"   -   Celebration affirming that life is a gift and worth living.

Family   -   Intimate group relations as sense of security, identity and recognition of accomplishments. The existence of that ambiguous cultural trait - "machismo."

Language

The Spanish language is the unmistakable contribution of Spanish culture to Hispanics. It is a "living language" which has been infused by the contributions and vitality of the Amerindian and African cultures. As such, it has given Hispanics not just a linguistic tool of communication but a particular *Weltanschauung*. The sciences of anthropology, linguistics and philosophy have documented well that language is indeed a mediating tool between human beings and their world.[52] Ruben Alves states it well:

> We do not contemplate reality face to face. From the moment we are born, things do not come before us in all their nakedness; they come dressed in the names that some community has given them. The community has already defined how the world is, and hence it knows what the world is. This knowledge of the world is crystallized in language ... Language is always interpretation. In interpretation objects fuse with emotions, the world and the human being embrace ... Talk about the world, then is always interpretation of the world.[53]

Given the intimate and profound nature of language[54] and the potential political power implicit in its unifying force, it is no surprise that the Spanish language is once again under attack in North American society.

Consistent with a self-understanding as a nation of immigrants, but equally consistent with a socio-history of oppression and racism in North American society, the public awareness that is emerging about Hispanics is shrouded in ambiguity. While openly celebrating the progress and development of a particular ethnic group - Hispanics - nevertheless in xenophobic style many individuals are attempting to pass legislation of "English only" as the official language of the U.S.A. and many are calling into question Bilingual Education.[55]

---

[52]David Bidney, *Theoretical Anthropology* (New York: Schocken Books, 1967), pp. 3, 4, 93-96.

[53]Ruben Alves, *Protestantism and Repression* (Maryknoll: Orbis Books, 1985), pp. 26-27.

[54]See, Pablo Polischuk, "Language Processing in Bilinguals," (Unpublished M.A. thesis, San Francisco State University, San Francisco, California, 1975).

[55]Lucy Keyser, "English-from Sea to Shining Sea," *Insight*, 20 October 1986, pp. 51-53; Lisa Rein, "Language Debate," *The Tab*, 22 October 1985, pp. 22-23; Thomas B. Moran, "The Latinization of America," *Esquire*, (May 1983), pp. 47-48, 50-56; Joan Moore and Harry Pachon, *Hispanics in the United States*, pp. 153-155; Orlando Costas, *Christ Outside the Gate: Mission Beyond Christendom*, p. 108.

Though granted that the legislation has in mind other ethnic groups as well, it nevertheless is perceived as targeted at Spanish-speaking Hispanics given their numbers and political aspirations.[56] Joan Moore's and Harry Pachon's response is important:

> The Hispanic community has quite generally reacted to these emotional and xenophobic ideas with bewilderment. Very few Hispanics would argue that English is not the language of this nation. Furthermore, New Mexico has been bilingual since its entry into the Union, and Puerto Rico has used Spanish as its first language since its annexation. The reemergence of this nativism, dormant at least since the 1920's, brings up may issues that do not bode well for the future of Hispanic minority.[57]

Yet, language is critical for Hispanics. Jose Garcia Mazas, professor of Romance Languages at the City College of the City University of New York, in his insightful article, "Reflecting on Language," underlines this by stating: "The millions of Hispanics who live in the United States must make a great effort to preserve and enrich their language, for language, and not race, gives us our Hispanic identity."[58]

While recognizing the importance of English as a "public language" in North American society, Spanish is the "intimate language" that has provided not only a sense of identity but behavior networks vital to Hispanic survival.[59] Paquita Vivo, while speaking of Puerto Ricans, underlines a truth applicable to all Hispanics in that they "understand the importance of English to their social and economic survival, the Puerto Ricans, nevertheless, think, sing, and pray in Spanish."[60]

---

[56]Joan Moore and Harry Pachon, *Hispanics in the United States*, p. 199.

[57]*Ibid.*, p. 122.

[58]José García Mazas, "Reflecting on Language," *Agenda* 10 (May-June 1980): 54.

[59]See Joshua Fishman, "Language Maintenance," in Stephen Thernstrom ed., *Harvard Encyclopedia of American Ethnic Groups* (Cambridge, Mass.: Belknap Press, 1980).

[60]Paquita Vivo, "The Puerto Ricans-Two Communities, One Culture," *Agenda* 10 (January-February 1980), p. 30; For the history of the imposition of English in the school system of Puerto Rico in the beginning of the twentieth century - and its failure, see, Aida Negron Montilla, *Americanization in Puerto Rico and the Public School System: 1900-1930* (Rio Piedras, Puerto Rico: Editorial Universitaria de Puerto Rico, 1975).

Irrespective of variations, accents, colloquialism, idiomatic expressions and regionalism, the Spanish language has served as a unifying and ever increasing political force for Hispanics. Elizondo reminds us that "every cohesive human group has a language, and, the specific language of a group is tied in with its identity and uniqueness."[61] Language has been for Hispanics in Anglo-American history a force for solidarity and survival in the face of a dominant and oppressive culture. Marta Sotomayor expresses it well when she says:

> For the bilinguals of color, such as Chicanos, language has played a most significant social and survival function ... in providing the group feeling of solidarity to deal with the oppressive majority culture. It is a common language that often coordinates the activities of the in-group, by making individuals conscious of the relationships between members and outsiders, thus promoting a sense of belonging. Language ... has enable this group to retain its distinctive characteristics over many generations, despite the rejection and hostility experienced from the majority community, permitting a sense of symbolic continuity and thus ethnic survival.[62]

The importance of Spanish as a cultural heritage cannot be overstated. Yet, it must be further noted that the English language is playing a significant role for Hispanics, particularly among the "new generation" (sons and daughters of immigrants, who are English-language dominant), thus the ever-increasing reality of biligualism/ biculturalism of Hispanics.[63]

The linguistic reality of Hispanic Americans, while predominantly Spanish, has in the second and third generations (the second mestizaje) increasingly become English dominant. Justo González in his study for the Fund for Theological Education entitled, *The Theological Education of Hispanics*, notes the following:

---

[61]Virgilio Elizondo, *Galilean Journey: The Mexican-American Promise*, p. 27.

[62]Marta Sotomayor, "Language, Culture, and Ethnicity in Developing Self-concept," *Social Casework* 58 (April 1977): 195.

[63]For an insightful perspective relative to the "new generation," the second mestizaje Hispanics, see Robert W. Pazmiño, "Double Dutch: Reflections of an Hispanic-North American on Multicultural Religious Education," Newton Centre, Massachusetts, 1987 (Typewritten); see also the provocative and sensitive work of Richard Rodríguez, *Hunger of Memory: The Education of Richard Rodriguez* (New York: Bantam Books, 1982).

Although ... a high percentage of Hispanics are born in the United States, a very large percentage also report that Spanish is the language spoken at home ... 75% of all Hispanics counted by the census, reported that Spanish is the language spoken at home ... roughly one fourth of those who speak Spanish at home, or 19% of the Hispanic population, also declared that they do not speak English well, or that they do not speak it at all. There is no statistic regarding the use of Spanish by the 25% of Hispanics who declared that English is the language most used at home. It is likely that roughly half of these are bilingual, or have at least some use of Spanish. Thus, it would appear that the usage of language among *Hispanics* in the U.S. breaks down as follows:

English only	12.5%
Bilingual with English preference	12.5%
Bilingual with Spanish preference	56.0%
Spanish only	19.0%[64]

When you add some of these figures together, you come up with an interesting and significant communication scenario: (1) 68.5% of Hispanics are Bilingual; (2) If you spoke in English, 81% of Hispanics will understand you; and (3) If you spoke in Spanish, 87.5% of Hispanics will understand you! Justo González concludes, and I concur, "Thus, *bilingualism* is likely to continue being a feature of the Hispanic community in the foreseeable future."[65]

While it is true that "the cultural focus of Hispanic American identity is obviously the Spanish language and the culture associated with it",[66] we must note carefully that those English-language dominant Hispanics (bilingual/bicultural second and third generation Hispanics) are bonafide and genuine Hispanic Americans. In our sons and daughters, language alone should not exclude from having an Hispanic identity.

I think we do well in listening to the warning noted by Justo González when he states,

---

[64]Justo González, *The Theological Education of Hispanics* (N.Y.C.: Fund for Theological Education, 1988), pp. 11-12; Although the data is not based on the 1990 Census Bureau report, it nevertheless is relevant and indicative of a trend among Hispanics.

[65]*Ibid.*, p. 12.

[66]*Ibid.*, p. 32.

Among Hispanics, and specially among those whose sense of unity
is most acute, there is heard a frequent warning: let us not so
idolize our culture that we oppress another Hispanic who does not
speak as we do, or even one who has never learned how to speak
Spanish because the pressures of society were too great.[67]

Clearly, linguistic dominance or preference are critical elements defining Hispanic
identity and the matrix of intergenerational dynamics.

La Raza: Ethnicity and Race

The shared feeling of "peoplehood" (ethnicity),[68] has emerged in Hispanics
under the name of *la raza* - a powerful cultural and political self-referent term.
This word can be narrowly translated as "the race," but its real definition and
implications are far more complex. Throughout Latin America Columbus Day is
called "El Dia de La Raza" - celebrating the original fusion of the Spanish and the
indigenous people of the New World.

The term *la raza*, while used mainly by the Mexican-American, is
nevertheless used by and to include non-Mexican Hispanics.[69] *La raza* as a
general concept is similar to the term *pueblo*. *Pueblo* refers to both the town and
the people living in it. *La raza* and *pueblo* in this general sense become rich
cultural and political symbols of togetherness, community, and way of life -
integrating language, family, custom, traditions, and other spiritual and cultural
traits.

As *La Raza Cósmica* (the Cosmic Race), it has in addition a more specific
meaning and usage. Dating back to 1925, José Vasconcelos' seminal work, *La
Raza Cósmica: La Misión de la raza Iberoamericana*,[70] the emphasis in this

---

[67]*Ibid.*, p. 33.

[68]For a more extensive definition and discussion of ethnicity, see: Sallie Teselle, ed. *The
Rediscovery of Ethnicity* (New York: Harper and Row, 1973); E.K. Francis, "The Nature of Ethnic
Group," *American Journal of Sociology* 52 (March 1947): 393-400; Milton M. Gordon, *Assimilation
in American Life: The Role of Race, Religion, and National Origin* (New York: Oxford University
Press, 1964).

[69]Joan Moore, *Mexican-Americans*, p. 134; Joan Moore and Harry Pachon, *Hispanics in the
United States*, p. 15.

[70]José Vasconcelos, *La Raza Cósmica: La Misión de la raza Iberoamericana* (Barcelona: Espasa
Calpe, 1925).

conceptualization has been under the term *mestizaje* (from *mestizo*, "mixed," "hybrid"). As such *mestizaje* speaks of the "new people" originating from the two or more ethnically disparate parent peoples.[71] Isidro Lucas notes, "the settlement patterns of the Spaniards, differing from that of the English, has produced in Hispanics a mixed, *mestizo* race, with considerable biological contributions from Native American, and later African populations."[72] This mixture, *mestizaje*, has been described as a new, *cosmic* race, in that it denies any racist pretence to "pure blood," and in integrating into one the existing races. While the biological factor is important, the cultural factor is of greater significance. Antonio Stevens Arroyo referring to Vasconcelos' vision states, "The mixture of races in Latin America would eventually produce synthesis of previous world civilizations ... the cosmic culture is destined to supersede all other civilization."[73]

The Hispanic American heritage of *mestizaje* is a double process that goes beyond the first encounter of Spaniard (European), Amerindian and African.[74] The second encounter involves the Anglo-American civilization and the Latin American; which can be dated to the treaty of Guadalupe-Hidalgo (1848) - a formalization of a prior and ongoing conquest by the United States of almost half the territory of Mexico.[75] Thus, there is a sense in which one can begin to date (1848) the emergence of a new ethnos, a new people - the Hispanic American.

The significance of *mestizaje* is excellently summarized by Orlando Costas:

This double mestizaje is the result of the military, cultural and religious invasions and conquest that have characterized the history of Hispanics in North America. Each has produced multiple variants. In the case of the first mestizaje, it produced the multiple national and regional cultures of the Latin American mosaic; in the case of the second, the emerging regional and subcultural varieties

---

[71]*Ibid.*; Virgilio Elizondo, *Mestizaje: The Dialectic of Cultural Birth and the Gospel* (San Antonio, Texas: MACC, 1978); Virgilio Elizondo, *Galilean Journey: The Mexican-American Promise* (Maryknoll, N.Y.: Orbis Books, 1983).

[72]Isidro Lucas, *The Browning of America: The Hispanic Revolution in the American Church* (Chicago, Illinois: Fides/Claretian, 1981), p. 7.

[73]Antonio Stevens Arroyo, *Prophets Denied Honor: An Anthology on the Hispanic Church in the United States* (Maryknoll, New York: Orbis Books, 1980), p. 32.

[74]See, Virgilio Elizondo, *Mestizaje: The Dialectic of Cultural Birth and the Gospel*; *Galilean Journey: The Mexican-American Promise.*

[75]Virgilio Elizondo, *The Mexican-American Promise*, p. 15-16.

to be found in Hispanic communities through the U.S. Consequently, Mexican-American and Central American groups have the imprint of the Spanish-Indian confrontation out of which emerged the Mexican and Mesoamerican people, whereas Puerto Ricans and other Hispanics from Eastern Caribbean reflect the Spanish-Amerindian-African confrontation.[76]

This double *mestizaje* or bi-culturalism is critically important for one's understanding of Hispanics.[77]

For Virgilio Elizondo *mestizaje* is also a central theological category for understanding the Mexican-American. He notes well the ambivalent status of the *mestizo* in present North American society.

> The *mestizo* does not fit conveniently into the analysis categories used by either parent group. The *mestizo* may understand them far better than they understand him or her. To be an insider-outsider, as is the *mestizo*, is to have closeness to and distance from both parent cultures.[78]

The cultural understanding of the *mestizo* is insightful in our understanding racially mixed societies - so true of Mexican-Americans and Puerto Ricans, the majority of Hispanics in the United States. American culture has sharp racial distinctions which immigrants find difficulty in adjusting to. Clara Rodriguez, while speaking of Puerto Ricans, underlines the predicament of all "mixed races," as well as implicitly affirming the mestizo's unique culture:

> There are only two options open in biracial New York - to be white or black. These options negate the cultural existence of Puerto Ricans and ignore their insistence on being treated, irrespective of race, as a culturally intact group. Thus, U.S. racial attitudes necessarily make Puerto Ricans either white or black, attitudes and culture make them neither white nor black, and our own resistance and struggle for survival places us between whites and blacks ...

---

[76]Orlando Costas, "Hispanic Theology in North America" (B.T.I., Liberation Theology Consultation, Andover-Newton Theological School), October 25, 1986 (Typewritten).

[77]This is becoming ever more complex and critical for our understanding of the *mestizaje* of the "new generation" Hispanics who are further defined by their English language dominance and North American culture ethos.

[78]Virgilio Elizondo, *Galilean Journey: The Mexican-American Promise*, p. 18.

Historically, Puerto Ricans arriving in New York have found themselves in a situation of perpetual incongruence - that is, they saw themselves differently than they were seen ... Puerto Ricans, a culturally-homogeneous, racially integrated group, find themselves opposed to the demand that they become racially divided and culturally 'cleansed' of being Puerto Rican.[79]

One must note carefully that the cultural phenomenon of *mestizaje* produces what I call a "triple-consciousness" in the "new generation" Hispanic or "second and third generation Hispanic". Let me explain: W.E.B. DuBois, the great African-American thinker and writer, spoke about the "double-consciousness" experienced by Black persons in the U.S.A.[80] They were part of the U.S.A.'s society (insider), yet were conscious that they were "outsiders" because of their color and existing racism. This psycho-social reality has had serious implication in the development of the African American experience. In a similar matter the "triple-consciousness" of the (second *mestizaje*), second and third generation or "new generation" Hispanic places them often in the role of being "insiders" and "outsiders" to the dominant Anglo-White group, *but also* "insider" and "outsider" to the first mestizaje group (first generation Hispanics) *as well*. They are "insiders" - *totally* accepted and affirmed - only among themselves (the second mestizaje group). The plight and psycho-social, not to say spiritual, condition of the second *mestizaje* in this "triple-consciousness" is precarious.

It is important to understand that this cultural phenomenon of *mestizaje* and its "double-consciousness" (for first generation) and "triple-consciousness" (second and third generation) defines the matrix of intergenerational dynamics - a significant dynamic that can both *unite* or *divide* Hispanics.

Notwithstanding sociologists Moore and Pachon's labeling of *La Raza Cósmica* a glorified ideology,[81] it might well be that from the unique cultural-racial make up of the Hispanic *mestizos* we will see "the emergence of a fifth race

---

[79]Clara Rodríguez, "Puerto Rican: Between Black and White," in Clara Rodríguez et al., eds., *The Puerto Rican Struggle* (New York: Puerto Rican Migration Research Consortium, 1980) pp. 25, 28; see also, Clara Rodriguez, "Another Way of Looking at Race: To Latinos in America, People are not viewed as 'Black' or 'White'", *The Boston Globe,* May 12, 1991.

[80]W.E.B. DuBois, *The Souls of Black Folk* (1903; reprint, New York: Fawcett Premier Book, 1968), pp. 16,17.

[81]Joan Moore and Harry Pachon, *Hispanics in the United States,* p. 15.

that will fill the planet with the triumphs of the first really universal culture, one that is truly cosmic;"[82] which I may add, could teach/model proper race relations.

Hispanic Community as a Socio-demographic Phenomenon

Portrait of a Population

The Hispanic mosaic, reflecting a diversity of national origins: Mexico, Puerto Rico, Cuba, Santo Domingo, Central and South America, and diversity of socio-history, including migration experiences, have made the United States the fifth largest Spanish-speaking country in the world. Only Mexico, Spain, Argentina, and Colombia have more Hispanics in the more than twenty Spanish-speaking nations of the world.[83]

While reliable figures are tenuous at best, the U.S. Census Bureau in 1990 numbered 22.4 million Hispanics, representing 9% of the mainland U.S. population. The 22.4 million persons of "Spanish origin" counted in 1990 indicate that the Hispanic population has grown by more than 50 percent since 1980. At this rate many estimate that by the year 2005 Hispanics will outnumber African-Americans, thus becoming the largest "ethnic minority" in the United States.[84] They are also younger than the rest of the nation; the median age of the Hispanic population is 23, compared to a median age of 31 for the total U.S. population.[85]

---

[82]José Vasconcelos, *La Raza Cósmica*, p. 49.

[83]Antonio M. Stevens Arroyo, *Prophets Denied Honor*, p. 240; Earl Parvin, "Hispanics in the United States," *Missions USA* (Chicago, Illinois: Moody Press, 1985), p. 107.

[84]Joan Moore and Harry Pachon, *Hispanics in the United States*, p. 52; estimates of actual population for Hispanic range from 25 to 30 million, noting undercounted and uncounted.

[85]"A New Mission Field: The Hispanic Population of America," *Christian Marketing Perspective* (A Publication of the Barna Research Group), September-October 1986, p. 1.

The national origin/descent of the Hispanics in mainland U.S. breaks down as follows:

Mexico	-	61%
Puerto Rico	-	15%
Cuba	-	6%
Central and South America	-	10%
Other Nations	-	8%[86]

Hispanics are geographically clustered. Nine out of ten Hispanic people are located within nine states. It is noteworthy that almost two out of three Hispanics live in one of three states: California (34% of the total), Texas (21%) and New York (10%).[87] Meanwhile, this traditional clustering is dispersing and according to Moore and Pachon this is "... a process that is abruptly bringing the Hispanics into new areas of the nation and into national consciousness."[88]

The Mexican-Americans are concentrated in the American Southwest and West Coast, extending into Detroit, meeting the Puerto Ricans in Chicago and "thinning out" as one moves eastward from Chicago. Puerto Ricans live mostly in or near New York City and are the majority of the Spanish-speaking in the "crescent" stretching from Boston to Camden, New Jersey. Alongside the Puerto Ricans in the Northeast there is a growing population from the Caribbean islands of Santo Domingo and Cuba, as well as Central America. The third largest group of Hispanics, Cubans, are heavily concentrated in Miami, Florida.[89]

Another significant factor that was brought to light as early as the 1980 census is that Hispanics are highly urbanized. While the total American population registered 74 percent urbanized, Hispanics came in at 87 percent. Puerto Ricans are the most urbanized while the Mexican Americans are the least.

It is interesting to note that 93 percent of California's Hispanics live in cities. Although Mexican-Americans are often thought to be agricultural laborers, only 7 percent lived in rural areas of California in 1980.[90]

---

[86]*Ibid.*, p. 1.

[87]Source: U.S. Bureau of the Census, March 1989.

[88]Joan Moore and Harry Pachon, *Hispanics in the United States*, p. IX.

[89]Antonio M. Stevens Arroyo, *Prophets Denied Honor*, p. 8.

[90]Joan Moore and Harry Pachon, *Hispanics in the United States*, p. 58.

Portrait of a "Pueblo" at the Periphery
of the American Metropolis

I am Joaquín, Lost in a world of confusion Caught up in a whirl of a gringo society, Confused by the rules, Scorned by attitudes, Suppressed by manipulation, And destroyed by modern society. My parents have lost the economic battle and won the struggle of cultural survival. And now! I must choose, Between the paradox of Victory of the spirit, despite physical hunger Or to exist in the grasp of American social neurosis, sterilization of the soul and a full stomach. Yes, I have come a long way to nowhere, Unwillingly dragged by that monstrous, technical industrial giant-called Progress and Anglo success... I look at myself. I watch my brothers. I shed tears of sorrow. I sow seeds of hate. I withdraw to the safety within the circle of life ... MY OWN PEOPLE.
    - I Am Joaquín[91]

While there might be "pockets" of success (i.e. the Cuban "Golden Exile"),[92] highlighted by the media and others laud by such books as *Benjy López*,[93] "... the overwhelming majority of Hispanics have been condemned, along with the majority of Blacks, to be the permanent underclass of North American society."[94]

The pain, rejection, poverty and oppression of Hispanics is poetically expressed by Rodolfo "Corky" González's - *I Am Joaquín*. The condition of the over 25 million Hispanics, "caught up in a whirl of a gringo society ... confused

---

[91]Rodolfo González, *I Am Joaquin* (New York: Bantam Books, 1972); quoted in Antonio M. Stevens Arroyo, *Prophets Denied Honor*, pp. 15-16.

[92]"Golden Exile" refers to the Cuban-American migration, especially the political exiles and upper bourgeoisie who received favorable immigration treatment by the federal government and found a solid framework of public aid and private sponsors upon arrival; see, Jose Llanes, *Cuban Americans: Masters of Survival* (Cambridge, Massachusetts: Abt Books, 1982); Isidro Lucas, *The Browning of America*, pp. 31-35.

[93]Barry B. Levine, *Benjy Lopez: A Picaresque Tale of Emigration and Return* (New York: Basic Books, Inc., 1980).

[94]Orlando Costas, *Christ Outside the Gate*, p. 113.

... scorned ... suppressed," yet proud of their cultural heritage, is graphically portrayed in their present status at the "periphery of the American metropolis."[95]

Four areas will be looked at in this portrait: (1) Poverty; (2) Education; (3) Immigration and Sanctuary Movement; and (4) Politics.

Poverty

In a nation where the concentration of wealth continues to be in the hands of a very few,[96] Hispanics are increasingly being pauperized. In what is considered the most comprehensive survey of the wealth of America to date, the Census Bureau reported that the net worth of the typical white (Anglo) American household in 1984 was 8 times greater than the typical net worth of Hispanics. Overall, the median net worth of the nation's 86.6 million households in 1984 was $32,667. A great disparity is noted when one compares Anglo and Hispanic households: Anglo, $39,125, Hispanics, $4,913.[97]

A new study of poverty and income data was released by the Census Bureau and analyzed by the Center on Budget and Policy Priority of Washington. The Center's study noted that while the African-American poverty rate has remained virtually unchanged since 1979 - near 31 percent mark - the Hispanic poverty rate had jumped more than 7 percentage points from 21.8 percent in 1979 to 29 percent in 1985. For Hispanic children the new census data are especially grim, the number of Hispanic children under 18 who live in poverty rose from 207,000 to 2.6 million - a record - and 39.9 percent of Hispanic children now live in poverty.[98]

---

[95]*Ibid.*, p. 101.

[96]A study by the Joint Economic Committee of Congress found that the superrich - the top one-half of 1 percent of the population - held 35.1 percent of the nation's wealth in 1983. The superrich also controlled most of the nation's business assets: they owned 58 percent of unincorporated businesses and 46.5 percent of corporate stocks owned by individuals. By contrast, in the last 20 years the share of the nation's wealth held by the vast majority of Americans - the bottom 90 percent - has fallen 6.7 percentage points, to just 28.2 percent of the total net wealth held by households; data cited by Paul Magnusson, "Rich getting Richer, taking bigger share of US wealth, Study says," *The Boston Globe* 26 July 1986, p. 1.

[97]Cited in Spencer Rich, "Divisions of Race Mark Gap in Wealth," *The Boston Globe* 19 July 1986, p. 1, 4.

[98]Cited by United Press International, "Poverty on rise for Hispanics, says Policy Group," *The Boston Globe* 3 September 1986, p. 58.

The unemployment rate for Hispanics fell from 16.5 percent in March 1983 to 8.2 percent in March 1990, while the non-Hispanic unemployment rate dropped to 5 percent. While the median income of Hispanic households increased about 12 percent from 1982 to 1989, from $19,500 to $21,900, the median income for non-Hispanic households was much higher at $29,500 in 1989. Robert Paral, research associate at the National Association of Latino Elected and Appointed Officials, responds to the noted gains: "We see Hispanics making gains, but the question is: Are the gains sufficient? And the answer is almost always no. We still see Hispanics overrepresented at the lower socioeconomic levels."[99]

Sociologists Joan Moore and Harry Pachon upon looking at the Hispanic condition ask themselves, "But will this poverty endure? And what are the consequences?" Their response is not too encouraging, "regrettably, the best evidence is that poverty will dominate the lives of many Hispanics for years to come."[100]

Education

In a highly sophisticated society where the ever-increasing demand is for more education the Hispanic educational status is depressing. Only 51% of Hispanics age 25 and over have completed four or more years of High School, as compared to 78% for non-Hispanics.

A breakdown of the percentage of Hispanic persons 25 years old and over completing four or more years of High School, by type of origin, as of March 1988:

Hispanic	51%
Non-Hispanic	78%
Mexican	45%
Puerto Rican	51%
Cuban	61%
Central & South American	64%
Other Hispanics	65%[101]

---

[99]"Census Says Good Life Still Eludes Most of US Hispanic Population," *The Boston Globe*, April 11, 1991.

[100]Joan Moore and Harry Pachon, *Hispanics in the United States*, p. 78.

[101]Source: U.S. Bureau of the Census, March 1988.

Another grim statistic is the High School dropout rate. Hispanic dropout rates are nearly double those of African-Americans and Anglos between the ages of 14 and 25 years. This school retention, a significant measure of educational success, stated differently would read as follows: "for every 100 Hispanic children who entered kindergarten, only 55 graduate from high school, 25 enter college, and 7 complete college. Only 4 will enter graduate school and 2 will finish."[102]

Many educators, especially Hispanic ones, have pinned their hope of lifting Hispanic educational achievements in bilingual education. They are finding though increasingly hostile reactions by the present federal administration as well as by school committees and legislators at the local level.[103]

As a former bilingual public school teacher (my wife is currently a bilingual school teacher), I am aware that the pedagogical effectiveness of bilingual education, as measured to date, is ambiguous.[104] Yet, as a bicultural-bilingual effort it has shown a measure of success in affirming other worthy values - cultural pride, solidarity and sense of identity - badly needed in an otherwise hopeless situation.[105] Bilingual education has become an Hispanic issue, and it is a major objective of Hispanic social and political organizations.[106]

---

[102]Joan Moore and Harry Pachon, *Hispanics in the United States*, p. 68.

[103]See, Woody West, "Bilingual Education in Plain English," *Insight* 23 June 1986, p. 72; Lisa Rein, "Language Debate," *The Tab*, 22 October 1985, pp. 22-23.

[104]See, Herman La Fontaine, Barry Persky, and Leonard Golubschick, eds. *Bilingual Education* (Wayne, N.J.: Avery Publishing Group, 1978); Lisa Rein, "Language Debate," p. 23.

[105]Lisa Rein, "Language Debate," p. 23; for a succinct and still relevant rationale for bilingual education, and for ethnic studies, see, Eduardo Seda, "Bilingual Education in A Pluralistic Context," *The Rican: Journal of Contemporary Puerto Rican Thought* I (May 1974): 19-26; see also, José A. Cárdenas, "The Role of Native-Language Instruction in Bilingual Education", *Phi Delta Kappan*, January 1986.

[106]Isidro Lucas, *The Browning of America*, pp. 115-126; Joseph P. Fitzpatrick, *Puerto Rican Americans*, pp. 142-151.

Immigration and Sanctuary Movement

The migration experience of Hispanics is as diverse as their national origin and socio-history. Yet, one finds that by and large it has been one of trauma and vicissitude with all the accompanying syndrome experienced by uprootedness - depression, disillusionment and anomie, not to mention exploitation and racism.[107]

As an institution, immigration has been most critical for those of Mexican origin. As a result of the Treaty of Guadalupe-Hidalgo (1848), Hispanics in the Southwest became American citizens without crossing the border. Isidro Lucas reminds us that,

> It took a long time before the U.S.-Mexican border became an effective cultural and political boundary ... for many years two-way passage of the border took place every day, and migration between the two countries was a way of life.[108]

Economic and political factors both in Mexico and the United States have produced several waves of migration through the years. It was not until 1917 that the nearly 1900 mile border began to be patrolled. According to Joan Moore and Harry Pachon:

> The border and its ambiguities have concerned Mexican immigrants most of all, but lately these problems have been extended to Dominicans, Colombians, Salvadorans, and Guatemalans ... Immigration policy in the Western hemisphere is an

---

[107]Marta Sotomayor-Chavez, "Latin American Migration," *Apuntes* 2 (Primavera 1982): 18-14; Oscar Handlin, *The Uprooted* (Boston, Massachusetts: Boston, Little, Brown and Co., 1952); Milton M. Gordon, *Assimilation in American Life*, especially, pp. 84-114; It is important to note that Hispanics can be grouped into four major categories according to their pattern of immigration: (1) the early settlers of the South West (pre-dating Anglo-Americans); (2) the established immigrants (mostly the early 20th century migration); (3) the new immigrants (the 1970 and 1980 influx from Dominican Republic and Central and South America); and (4) the new generation (children of established immigrants, usually bilingual-bicultural, although may be English dominant); see, Orlando Costas, "Evangelizing An Awakening Giant: Hispanics in the U.S.," in *Signs of the Kingdom in the Secular City*, comps. David J. Frenchak and Clinton E. Stockwell, ed. Helen Ujvarosy (Chicago: Covenant Press, 1984), pp. 56-57.

[108]Isidro Lucas, *The Browning of America*, p. 24.

endless struggle between racial and culture prejudice
- and economic opportunism.[109]

No one is certain of the exact number of undocumented workers coming
into the United States; estimates run from 1.9 to 4 million (a conservative figure)
and 3 to 6 million. Undocumented workers are growing at the rate of 250,000 to
500,000 per year, including increasing numbers from the Middle East, the Far East,
Central and South America and the Caribbean (especially Santo Domingo and
Haiti). Mexicans comprise one-half of these undocumented workers.[110]

While many poor undocumented Mexicans are entering the United States
daily, it is to be noted that because of the economic crisis, due chiefly to losses
from its foreign oil trade, Mexico is also experiencing an emigration of
professionals. Although the number is small, it is nevertheless significant, and
perhaps a sign of future waves of new immigrants from Mexico.[111]

The migration experience of Puerto Ricans is different from the Mexican-
American in that since the Jones Act of 1917 Puerto Ricans are U.S. citizens.
Notwithstanding, they too have experienced the attendant effects of uprootedness,
along with virulent discrimination and racism.[112]

The Cuban migration (refugees) is quite different from that of other
Hispanics. Of all Hispanic groups their arrival en masse, following the Cuban
Revolution of 1959, was warmly received by the federal government and many
other public and private organizations. The political and ideological lines between
"communism" and the "free world" were exploited by the "welcome wagon" given
the Cubans.

Other subsequent refugees in the late 1960's have done well, not so the
most recent - "Los Marielitos." The 125,000 Cuban refugees leaving the Port of
Mariel in 1980 represented a significant shift in the constituency - definitely not

---

[109]Joan Moore and Harry Pachon, *Hispanics in the United States*, p. 135.

[110]Marta Sotomayor-Chavez, "Latin American Migration," p. 8.

[111]Philip Bennett, "Mexico Losing Professionals: Economic Crisis Spurs Brain Drain," *The Boston Globe*, 28 July 1986, pp. 1, 16.

[112]More will be said concerning Puerto Ricans in the next section on "Hispanics in the North East."

a "Golden Exile." They were mostly black persons, poor and "many who were taken from jails and institutions for the mentally ill."[113]

The "Refugee Movement" or "Sanctuary Movement," particularly with reference to Central America, has been a growing concern for a number of years now. Literally hundreds of churches in defiance of the law, but in response to a "higher law," have provided sanctuary to thousands of refugees coming into this country.

In the wake of oppression and civil war the influx of refugees from Central America has increased significantly. There are no exact figures. A most interesting demographic note by Fernando Santillana, indicative of the escalating conflict in Central America, is that while in 1979 there were in the United States 50,000 "Salvadorenos," by 1985 in the Los Angeles area alone there were between 350,000 to 400,000. He also noted 100,000 to 125,000 "Guatemaltecos" present.[114]

After three attempts, the 99th Congress in the last hours of the 1986 session passed the Simpson-Mazzoli bill into a new Immigration law. While to many it seems too early to judge the effect of the new law on the plight of Hispanic immigrants, to others all indications are that there is confusion and chaos among employers resulting in serious discrimination.[115]

Politics

The socio-economic conditions of Hispanics places them at the "periphery of the American Metropolis." To a great extent, Hispanic progress towards the "center" will be tied to building an effective economical and political base.

When Raul Yzaguierre, director of the National Council of La Raza, was asked about the most urgent concern of Hispanic communities today, his response

---

[113]Marta Sotomayor-Chavez, "Latin American Migration," p. 10; see also Robert L. Bach, "The New Cuban Emigrants: Their Background and Prospects," *Monthly Labor Review* 103 (October, 1980): 39-46.

[114]Fernando Santillana, "Refugiados económicos, o víctimas?" *Apuntes* 5 (Winter 1985): 83; see also, Rafael J. Aragón, "El Movimiento de Refugio," *Apuntes* 5 (Fall 1985): 65-67.

[115]María Laurino, "La Insuficiencia de las Leyes de Inmigración", *MAS*, Vol. II., No. 2, Invierno 1990.

was - "empowerment."[116]   Hispanics are not adequately represented in the councils of power - be they educational, religious, social, economic or political. They are barred from the decision-making process in so many areas that touch their lives deeply.[117]

There are some positive signs indicative that "Hispanic political power has moved from a potential to an emerging reality."[118]   There are 4,004 Hispanic elected officials at all levels of government throughout the United States.[119] While there has been no Hispanic member of the Senate since the defeat of the late Joseph Montoya of New Mexico in 1976, there are currently 10 U.S. House seats won by Hispanics.[120]

Certain states account for the bulk of Hispanic office holders. By 1986 ninety-five percent of the Hispanic elected officials were in the seven states of Arizona, California, Colorado, Florida, New Mexico, New York, and Texas. These states account for over 80 percent of the nation's Hispanic population. New Jersey showed the largest percent increase of Hispanic elected officials in 1986, while Florida stayed the same and the number declined by one in California.[121]

While some of the above data is impressive, it is doubtful whether the Serranos, Ros-Lehtinen or "Kika" de la Garza will be enough to make that significant impact and change needed so desperately by the Hispanic community. In 1989 the Hispanic Elected Officials (HEO's) were asked to rank the important issues facing the Hispanic community.   The ten top issues that the HEO's considered to be the most important were:

---

[116]Isidro Lucas, *The Browning of America*, p. 69.

[117]See Roberto Anson, "Hispanics in the United States: Yesterday, Today, and Tomorrow," *The Futurist* (August 1980): 31; John Selby, *En La Brega: Economía política popular para trabajadores Latinos: el Caso de Massachusetts* (Boston, Massachusetts: Red Sun Press, 1985).

[118]"Press Statement of Dr. Harry Pachon, Executive Director of the National Association of Latino Elected and Appointed Officials (NALEO)," September 17, 1986, p. 1 (Typewritten).

[119]Source: NALEO Educational Fund, 1990 National Roster of Hispanic Elected Officials.

[120]NALEO, the current roster (1991) of Hispanics in the U.S. Congress (House of Representative): (1) José E. Serrano (D-N.Y.); (2) Edward R. Roybal (D-Cal.); (3) Esteban Torres (D-Cal.); (4) Matthew G. Martinez (D-Cal.); (5) Ileana Ros-Lehtinen (R-Florida); (6) Bill Richardson (D-New Mexico); (7) E. "Kika" de la Garza (D-Texas); (8) Henry B. González (D-Texas); (9) Solomon Ortiz (D-Texas); (10) Alberto Bustamante (D-Texas).

[121]"Press Statement of Dr. Harry Pachon, Executive Director of the National Association of Latino Elected and Appointed Officials (NALEO)," September 17, 1986, p. 2. (Typewritten).

(1)   High Drop-Out Rate
(2)   Access to Higher Education
(3)   Drug Abuse
(4)   Unemployment
(5)   Job Training
(6)   Voter Registration
(7)   Need for Latino Civic Leadership Development
(8)   Latino Children in Poverty
(9)   Housing
(10)   Indigent Health Care[122]

A ray of hope is to be found at the national level in coalition building in Congress. The Congressional Hispanic Caucus founded in 1977 to "reverse the national pattern of neglect, exclusion, and indifference"[123] of Hispanics is composed of 10 Congresspersons of Hispanic heritage and over 150 honorary members who represent Hispanic population centers.

Numerous Hispanic political and quasi-political organizations and community groups exist on the local level of the political arena. By comparison only few are represented at the national level. Solid contributions have come through the years by such organizations as: National Council of La Raza (NCLR); National Association of Latino Elected and Appointed Officials (NALEO); League of United Latin American Citizens (LULAC); Mexican American Legal Defense and Educational Fund (MALDEF); American GI Forum; National Puerto Rican Forum; Cuban National Planning Council (CNPC); and the Forum of National Hispanic Organizations.[124]

It is to be noted that other organizations that have captured the national attention, although not necessarily a national organization in structure/scope or political for that matter, have played a significant political consciousness-raising role. They have also contributed greatly to concrete political action and to a deep sense of pride and identity in the Hispanic community. Among them are: COPS (Community Organized for Public Service) in San Antonio; UNO (United Neighborhood Organization) in Los Angeles - both of these are church-organized;

---

[122]NALEO Educational Fund, 1989.

[123]Hugh Cullman, ed., *A Guide to Hispanic Organizations* (New York, N.Y.: Philip Morris, U.S.A., Public Affairs Department, 1983), p. 25.

[124]*Ibid.*, for a somewhat comprehensive listing.

Cesar Chavez's UFW (United Farm Workers of America); and Aspira of New York City.[125]

It is the opinion of many Hispanic leaders that Hispanic political power in the United States is contingent in mobilizing political participation and tapping the growing political force and tremendous potential in the Hispanic community.[126]

It is important to note several key factors that limit the political participation and electoral impact of the Hispanic community commensurate with its numbers.[127]   (1) Hispanics are younger than the American population as a whole; Hispanic median age is 23, as 31 for total U.S. population. In 1980, 40 percent of the Hispanic community was below voting age. Illustrative of this reality was the case of Massachusetts where the Hispanic population in 1986 was estimated at 222,000, yet, 94,000 were of voting age - over half of the total Hispanic population was under the voting age of 18;[128]   (2) Hispanic population growth is still regional and it's mostly limited to a few key states. One implication of this geographic concentration is in the area of national political visibility; (3) Many Hispanics are recent immigrants.   Thus, there is a large non-citizen population, often overlooked in studies on political participation of Hispanics. Joan Moore and Harry Pachon have noted well that Hispanic political participation is comparable to the African-American population if one controls for citizenship.[129] (4) Other institutional obstacles can be noted, such as: residency requirements, gerrymandering, economic sanctions and even violence. (5) One final factor, that is shared by all minorities and by the poor in general is the "class factor" - also overlooked by research on Hispanic political participation. The poor do not have the economic resources for political activity. They are also concerned with what Isidro Lucas calls, "survival issues." The everyday struggle for economic survival

---

[125]See, Debra Luciano, "Cesar Chavez - Bringing Boycotts to the 1980s," *Agenda* 9 (July-August 1979): 18-19; Antonio M. Stevens Arroyo, *Prophets Denied Honor*, pp. 229-231; Joseph P. Fitzpatrick, *Puerto Rican Americans*, pp. 66-67.

[126]Robert A. Jordan, "Latinos Seeking Political Clout," *The Boston Globe*, 3 August 1986, pp. A17-A18; Roberto Anson, "Hispanics in the United States: Yesterday, Today, and Tomorrow," *The Futurist* (August 1980): 31.

[127]I am indebted to the excellent political commentary and analysis of Joan Moore and Harry Pachon, *Hispanics in the United States*, pp. 169-176; Sociologist Dr. Harry Pachon is currently the executive director of the National Association of Latino Elected and Appointed Officials (NALEO), Washington, D.C.

[128]Robert A. Jordan, "Latinos Seeking Political Clout," p. A18.

[129]Joan Moore and Harry Pachon, *Hispanics in the United States*, p. 173.

- not to mention physical survival and mental health - does not leave much "time for the less immediate concerns of political participation."[130]   Also, class biases can be noted throughout our political system (e.g. residency requirements) which hold back political participation.

The need for political education, voter registration and mobilization is agreed to by all Hispanic political leaders. Solid political foundations are being put in place across the United States. The "seed is being planted" and there is the recognition that it will yield much fruit in the not too distant future.[131]

Hispanics in the North East

The Puerto Rican Diaspora

Sale, loco de contento con su cargamento para la ciudad, ay, para la ciudad. Lleva, en su pensamiento todo un mundo lleno de felicidad sí ... de felicidad. Piensa remediar la situación del hogar que es toda su ilusión sí ...

......

Y triste el jibarito va llorando así, pensando así, diciendo así por el camino. Qué será de Borinquen mi Dios querido, Qué será de mis hijos y de mi hogar.

......

- Lamento Borincano[132]

---

[130]Isidro Lucas, *The Browning of America*, p. 97.

[131]See Rosa Estades, *Patrones de Participación Política de los Puertorriqueños en la Ciudad de Nueva York* (Rio Piedras, Puerto Rico: Editorial de la Universidad de Puerto Rico, 1978); John Selby, *En la Brega: Economía política popular para trabajadores Latinos: el caso de Massachusetts*; Roberto Anson, "Hispanics in the United States: Yesterday, Today and Tomorrow," p. 31.

[132]A "free" translation of the lyrics of the song of Rafael Hernandez's *Lamento Borincano*: He

While there are significant numbers of Mexican-Americans, Cubans, Dominicans, South Americans, and an ever-increasing number from Central America, when we speak of Hispanics in the North East, we speak predominantly about the Puerto Rican diaspora.

Rafael Hernández's *Lamento Borincano* (Puerto Rican Lament), speaks eloquently of this experience - of shattered dreams and clashed hopes. Although it speaks of the Puerto Rican *jíbaros'* (peasant) misfortunes in the Island, it nevertheless has had a double context and focus through the years - the Island's jíbaro and the Puerto Rican poor in the U.S. mainland.[133] Virginia E. Sánchez Korrol reminds us that the *Lamento Borincano* "assumed the role of an informal national anthem in some circles" and "succinctly captured the peasant's love for his homeland and the economic misfortunes underlying his move from the island" and the "migrants ... identified with its message interpreting the *jibaro's* journey as the voyage from Puerto Rico to New York."[134]

The experience of the oldest and largest of Hispanics, the Mexican-American, is best understood by the impact of conquest and colonialism.[135] Added to this is the institutionalization of the migration experience to "El Norte." In a similar historical affinity one must also understand the second largest Hispanic group - the Puerto Ricans. Their experience reflects a conquest (1898) and a "sophisticated" neo-colonialism, all by and within the hegemony of the United States. It is equally important to place other Latin American migration within this same perimeter. The migration from the Caribbean (Santo Domingo and Cuba) as well as Central and South America must be understood by the impact (directly or

---

leaves, wildly content with his cargo for the city, for the city. He carries in his thoughts a world full of happiness yes ... of happiness. He thinks of remedying the situation of the home that is all his hope, yes ...
And sadly the peasant goes crying so, thinking so, saying so by the road. What will happen to Borinquen (Puerto Rico) my dear God, what will happen to my children and my home.

[133]On September 5, 1986 at a small Hispanic pentecostal church in Haverhill, Massachusetts this writer was pleasantly surprised as I heard the afternoon message. A humble and simple layperson creatively used the *Lamento Borincano* to describe his experience as well as the plight of other Puerto Ricans coming to the "city" (USA, metropolis) with great expectations, only to suffer bitter disappointments.

[134]Virginia E. Sanchez Korrol, *From Colonia to Community: The History of Puerto Ricans in New York City, 1917-1948* (Wesport, Connecticut: Greenwood Press, 1983), p. 78.

[135]See, Joan Moore and Harry Pachon, *Hispanics in the United States*, pp. 18-24; Virgilio Elizondo, *The Galilean Journey: The Mexican American Promise*; Antonio M. Stevens Arroyo, *Prophets Denied Honor*.

indirectly) of neo-colonial policies and strategies of the "Colossus of the North" - the United States.[136]

Puerto Rico is a Latin American country - geographically, culturally and historically.[137] It is a colonial territory of the U.S., a war booty from the Spanish-American War (1898); notwithstanding it being called a "free-associated state" or "commonwealth," it is yet, a "colony."[138] The editors of *The Rican: Journal of Contemporary Puerto Rican Thought* summarize the incontrovertible evidence:

> Puerto Rico is a colony, we repeat. If it were a self-governing territory, it would have power and authority over the following areas now under the supreme authority and control of the United States:

> 1. Wages
> 2. Labor Laws
> 3. Citizenship
> 4. Agriculture
> 5. Military Service
> 6. Roads
> 7. Postal service
> 8. Currency
> 9. Air Space
> 10. Coastal waters
> 11. Tariffs and customs
> 12. Minerals and mines
> 13. Foreign relations
> 14. Radio and Television
> 15. Ports and Airports
> 16. Emigration and immigration
> 17. Patents
> 18. External commerce
> 19. Federal court jurisdiction
> 20. Military bases (upwards of 13% all the tillable land).

Even "La Fortaleza," the official residence of the governor of Puerto Rico, is the property of the United States Park District.[139]

---

[136]See, Manuel Maldonado-Denis, *Puerto Rico: A Socio-Historic Interpretation* (New York: Vintage Books, 1972); *The Emigration Dialectic: Puerto Rico and the USA* (New York: International Publishers, 1976); for a different "liberal view," see Joseph P. Fitzpatrick, *Puerto Rican Americans: The Meaning of Migration to the Mainland*.

[137]Manuel Maldonado-Denis, *The Emigration Dialectic: Puerto Rico and the USA* (New York: International Publishers, 1976), p. 16; Orlando Costas, *Christ Outside the Gate*, p. 103.

[138]Roland I. Perusse, *The United States and Puerto Rico: Decolonization Options and Prospects* (Lanham, MD.: University Press of America, 1987).

[139]"Editorial", *The Rican: Journal of Contemporary Puerto Rican Thought* 2 (October 1974): 4.

The migration from Puerto Rico, better named emigration,[140] reflects a continuous population flow between Puerto Rico and the U.S. metropolis. While the emigration of Puerto Ricans (U.S. citizens since 1917) to the U.S. mainland can be dated to the early 1900's,[141] it is not until post war years of the 1940's that the flood gates were opened, eventually resulting in the emigration of one third of the Puerto Rican population.

Maldonado-Denis, referring to the findings of the *International Migration Review*, suggests five factors contributing to this exodus: (1) the labor shortage in the postwar U.S.A. acting as a magnet for Puerto Ricans; (2) a high rate of unemployment in Puerto Rico; (3) the postwar economic boom in the U.S.; (4) stiffer immigration laws passed by Congress; and (5) "the policy of the Puerto Rican government to foster widespread migration to the States as a kind of 'escape valve' for a supposed surplus population considered an endemic Puerto Rican problem."[142]

Migration is a complex phenomenon with many variables. While not "falling for" an economic deterministic analysis, yet the market factors have been the predominant indicators of the migration waves from the Island (Puerto Rico). Sanchez Korrol states:

> Migration fluctuated according to the requirements of the labor market, drawing those facing critical futures in the island along with the family followers. In the words of the migrants themselves, almost all came in search of opportunity, the chance to make something for themselves and their families. They came on steamship shuttles ... In time they came by air, becoming the first airborne migration in history.[143]

The experience of the overwhelming majority of Puerto Ricans in the U.S. mainland has been by and large one of social margination and economic oppression - "condemned ... to be the permanent underclass of North American society."[144]

---

[140]Manuel Maldonado-Denis, *The Emigration Dialectic*, p. 24.

[141]For the definitive socio-history of this period, see Virginia E. Sanchez Korrol, *From Colonia to Community: The History of Puerto Ricans in New York City, 1917-1948*.

[142]Manuel Maldonado-Denis, *Puerto Rico: A Socio-Historic Interpretation*, p. 312.

[143]Virginia E. Sánchez Korrol, *From Colonia to Community*, p. 46.

[144]Orlando Costas, *Christ Outside the Gate*, p. 113; see, U.S. Commission on Civil Rights,

It is important to note that most other Hispanics in the North East, Dominicans and Central Americans particularly, are to be included in this same dire predicament.[145]   Martin Espada, recipient of a 1984 Massachusetts Artist Fellowship in Poetry, sums up the status and hopes of Hispanics in the North East well in his "Heart of Hunger," from which I quote but a few lines:

> ......
> Obscured in the towering white clouds of cities in
> winter, thousands are bowing to assembly lines,
> frenzied in kitchens and sweatshops, mopping the
> vomit of blond children, leaning into the iron's steam
> and the steel mill glowing.
>
> Yet there is a pilgrimage, a history straining its arms
> and legs, an inexorable striving, shouting in Spanish
> ... mexicano, dominicano, cubano, puertorri-
> queño.[146]

Puerto Ricans in the Continental United States: An Uncertain Future (Washington, D.C.: U.S. Commission on Civil Rights, 1976); "Hispanics in Massachusetts: A Progress Report" (Massachusetts: The Commonwealth of Massachusetts, Commission on Hispanic Affairs, 1985).

[145]See, Glenn Hendricks, *The Dominican Diaspora: From the Dominican Republic to New York City - Villagers in Transition* (New York: Teachers College Press, 1974); John Selby, *En La Brega: Economía política popular para trabajadores latinos: el caso de Massachusetts* (Boston, Massachusetts: Red Sun Press, 1985).

[146]Martin Espada, "Heart of Hunger," *The Immigrants Iceboy's Bolero* (Natick, Massachusetts: Cordillera Press, 1982), p. 15; used with permission of Cordillera Press.

CHAPTER II

HISPANIC AMERICAN RELIGIOUS DIMENSION

> Trasmutar el de Caná que fue en efecto técnica de
> conquista del medio circundante, para servicio del
> prójimo...   Trasmutar que resulta ejemplo y
> paradigma y patrón de todos los actos de Jesús sobre
> la tierra...   Religión emprendedora y activa la de
> Jesús: Religión que se ocupa de las cosas triviales,
> como la de volver el agua en vino. Religión que en
> vez de opio resulta tónico vigorizante que le instila
> nuevas fuerzas al ente audaz que se dá a la tarea de
> transformar su ambiente.
>
> - Alberto Rembao, "Gloria A Lo Trivial"[1]

The Hispanic American is a "homo religiosus." There is no area of life, no matter how trivial, that is not "transmuted" by the religious sentiment. The depth of Hispanic religiosity cannot be fathomed by mere statistical quantification of church attendance, or for that matter, statistical surveys or religious profiles. The Hispanic culture and person cannot be understood apart from this religious dimension.

In this chapter I will address the Hispanic religious dimension under four sections: (1) The Roman Catholic Church; (2) The Hispanic Protestant Church; (3) The Pentecostal Movement; and (4) Hispanic Spirituality and Indigenous Pentecostal Theology. Given the focus of this study, the parameters (scope) of this chapter's first two sections will be set by a selective descriptive-analysis under two basic categories: (1) Socio-history; and (2) Socio-vision or Socio-role.

---

[1]Alberto Rembao, "Gloria a lo Trivial," *Meditaciones Neoyorkinas* (Buenos Aires: Librería "La Aurora," 1939), pp. 105-106. "Transmute the one from Cana which was in effect technique of conquest of the surrounding area, for service to the neighbor... Transmute that the result is an example and paradigm and pattern of all the acts of Jesus on the earth... Religion that is enterprising and active is the one of Jesus: Religion that occupies itself with trivial things, like that of turning water into wine. Religion that instead of opium results in a vigorous tonic that instills new strength to the brave one who is committed to transforming the surroundings."

A corollary emphasis will be given to "reading anew" from the Hispanic religious past and present those "symbols of resistance, survival and hope... the 'subversive' and 'liberating' memory of Hispanics in North America."[2] This latter thrust is in keeping with Justo L. González's excellent essay on Latin American Catholicism, "The Two Faces of Hispanic Christianity."[3] While not pretending to be exhaustive, nevertheless, I will highlight representative events, symbols, persons and ministries.

The Roman Catholic Church

> What do we want the Church to do? We don't ask
> for more cathedrals. We don't ask for bigger
> churches or fine gifts. We ask for its presence with
> us, beside us, as Christ among us. We ask the
> Church to sacrifice with the people for social change,
> for justice, and for love of brother. We don't ask for
> words. We ask for deeds. We don't ask for
> paternalism. We ask for Servanthood.
>
>   - Cesar E. Chavez[4]

---

[2]Orlando Costas, "Hispanic Theology in North America," p. 4.

[3]Justo L. González, "Two Faces of Hispanic Christianity," *The Judson Bulletin* Vol. VI, No. 1 (Andover Newton Theological School, 1987), pp. 17-26; In this mostly Latin American Catholic analysis, González notes the existence throughout the history of Latin American Catholicism of two churches - the "topside," official and oppressive serving the interest of conquest and colonization, and the "underside of the church" or the "other church" - one that "decried and opposed" the oppressive powers.

[4]Cesar E. Chavez, "The Mexican American and the Church," in Octavio I. Romano, ed. *Voices: Readings from El Grito* (Berkeley, Calif.: Quinto Sol Publications, 1971), p. 104.

Socio-history

Christendom: Cultural Domination
and "Spiritual Colonization"

In order to comprehend the enormous cultural, socio-political, and religious role played by the Roman Catholic Church among Hispanics one must do so within the framework of understanding the religio-cultural phenomenon of "Christendom." This complex phenomenon, which is so critical for understanding the role of the church in society, is succinctly defined by Orlando Costas:

> Christendom is not the sum total of Christians in the world. It is, rather, a "historical project" that has taken various shapes and forms from the time when it was introduced in the Edict of Milan (A.D. 313), when Constantine made Christianity the state religion. Whatever its form, however, Christendom is the vision of a society organized around Christian principles and values with the church as its manager or mentor.[5]

In another section of his book Costas adds, "The fundamental problem with Christendom projects is that they confuse the Kingdom of God with the institutional church, the gospel with culture, and the power of the cross with the power of the sword."[6]

The Spaniards arrived in the New World with "La Cruz y la Espada."[7]

---

[5]Orlando Costas, *Christ Outside the Gate: Mission Beyond Christendom*, p. 189; for an excellent historical development of Christendom in Latin America, see especially the chapter, "Colonial Christendom in Latin America" in Enrique Dussel's *History and the Theology of Liberation: A Latin American Perspective* (New York: Orbis Books, 1976), pp. 75-109; I may add here, which will be developed later, that Christendom projects mean the alignment of the Church with the "powers that be" that eventually leads not just to physical and psychological colonization but to "Spiritual Colonization" of the people and its leadership.

[6]Orlando Costas, *Christ Outside the Gate: Mission Beyond Christendom*, p. 181; the history of Christianity through the ages documents well the many and varied Christendom projects of the church, one should not overlook the fact or intent of Protestant Christendom projects, either (e.g., Calvin's Geneva, early U.S.A. colonial period, contemporary U. S.A. "Religious Right").

[7]"The Cross and the Sword"; I agree wholeheartedly with Edwin E. Sylvest, Jr. that "The stereotype of the conquest as a union of cross and sword is too simplistic and, in prejudiced hands, results in the perpetuation of the 'black legend,' but it has its value. It indicates two dimensions of the conquest of the newly found lands and peoples. These dimensions can be distinguished, but not separated. The conquest had material and spiritual dimension that together represent a cultural conquest, the result of which was the invention of the Americas and the creation of Americans of

They were imbued with zeal for "God, Gold and Glory," particularly after having just vanquished the Moors in their unifying of Spain in 1492. A partnership was formed by the Cross and the sword - a partnership that Mackay states was "... formed in the name of evangelism, in which the sword opened the way for the cross, and the cross sanctified the work of the sword, that constituted the originality of Spanish Christianity."[8]

One should note the power of *Patronato Real* ("Royal Patronage") which the crown had over the church. Alexander VI granted the Spanish crown not only political but also religious authority over all lands discovered. According to Justo González, "The result was that the church in Spanish America had very few direct dealings with Rome, and became practically a national church under the leadership of the Spanish kings and their appointees."[9] The conquest and eventual cultural domination of the Amerindians and later the Africans represented this "unholy alliance" of the Church and the State, which, according to Luis N. Rivera-Pagan, saw the "genesis" of the modern system of colonialism and slavery.[10]

Enrique Dussel notes three different periods to Latin American Christendom: (1) 1492-1808 (colonial expansion); (2) 1808-1962 (colonial crisis) and (3) 1962-present (signs of liberation, my term).[11] In each of these periods the Catholic Church's power relations vis-a-vis the State would be challenged. The colonial expansion (1492-1808) represented the Church's alignment with the State (meaning, the elite Spaniards that rule) as "hand and glove." In the colonial crisis (1808-1962) the Church faced the challenge of the independence movements and the anti-clericals (mostly due to the church's support of the Spaniards over the "freedom" aspirations of the developing "Latin American Creole"). Notwithstanding an exception here and there, the socio-political reality pictured the development of an elitist and oligarchical oppression of the masses with the blessing of the Church. 1962 marked a new spirit in the Catholic Church - Vatican

---

whatever description. If the material conquest was most obvious, the spiritual was more insidious and profound because it touched the essence of the human being and challenged its original expression;" "Rethinking the 'Discovery' of the Americas: A Provisional Historico-Theological Reflection," *Apuntes* 7 (Primavera 1987): 6.

[8]John A. Mackay, *The Other Spanish Christ*, p. 26.

[9]Justo L. González, *The Story of Christianity, Vol. 1: The Early Church to the Dawn of the Reformation* (New York: Harper & Row, 1984), p. 381.

[10]Luis N. Rivera-Pagan, "La Cristianizacion de America: Reflexion y Desafio," *Apuntes* 7 (Primavera 1987): 16-17.

[11]Enrique Dussel, *History and the Theology of Liberation*, pp. 80-81.

II. The "windows were opened" leading to the historic Medellin Conference (CELAM, 1968) and the Church's "preferential option for the poor," thus the beginning of the Liberation Movement. This movement injected a new spirit in the Catholic Church in siding with the poor and oppressed, and the recapturing of Christianity as a "Church" and not as "Christendom."[12] In the words of Dussel:

> Christendom - that vast cultural, religious, and socio-political reality of the past - is on its way out. That is the reason behind all the critical problems we as Christians are now facing in Latin America. Some want to hold on to Christendom, but time spent on seeking to preserve Christendom is so much time lost for Christianity.[13]

The historical development of the Catholic Church during these periods and its dominance of the culture of Latin America has been well documented.[14] One cannot fathom the Latin American "mind and heart," for that matter the Hispanic American (who shares equally this cultural heritage), without noting the extent of this dominance:

> The Church was everywhere and with every individual all of his life and filled all of his days. The day began with early morning mass and ended with an Ave Maria, and every occasion, every sorrow, every joy, every holiday had its own special religious symbolism to be acted out in church. During the colonial period the Church was also the school, the university, the hospital, the home of the aged, the sick and the abandoned. It served the individual and the community in many ways. In the absence of newspapers, libraries, museums, theaters, the religious exercise and ritualism in the churches, the orders, the monasteries and the convents filled the role of giving the individual his place in an enchanted and meaningful world. And everything that happened from a bull fight to the arrival of a new Viceroy, an earthquake, or the King's birthday always required public manifestations, processions, prayers, masses

---

[12]See, *Ibid.*, p. 80.

[13]*Ibid.*, p. 109.

[14]See, Robert Ricard, *The Spiritual Conquest of Mexico* (Berkeley: University of California Press, 1966). Americo Castro, *Iberoamérica: Su Historia y su Cultura*, 4ta. ed. (New York: Holt, Rinehart and Winston, 1971); Pedro Henriquez Ureña, *Historia de la Cultura en la América Hispana* (Mexico-Buenos Aires: Fondo de Cultura Economica, 1947); Lewis Hanke, *The Spanish Struggle for Justice in the Conquest of America*; Carlos A. Loprete and Dorothy McMahon, *Iberoamérica: Síntesis de su Civilización*, 2da. ed. (New York: Charles Scribner's Sons, 1974).

and sermons in which the Church was active, perhaps the chief actor in the drama, or better, the chief embodiment of the symbolism that endowed every activity with meanings.   It surrounded life at all turns and all times. The church or cathedral bell dominated the community, and daily life was disciplined and ordered to its sound.[15]

It is within the framework of Christendom and its cultural dominance that we picture the conquistadores, friars and the early mission settlement in Florida, the Southwest and California. Juan Ponce de Leon landed on April 2, 1513 in Florida, which according to Ricardo Santos dates the history of the Latin American Church in the U.S.A.[16] In 1539 Franciscan Marcos de Niza and the black slave Estevan begin exploration in what is now New Mexico in search for the Seven Cities of Cibola and its stories of great riches. The zeal for "God, Gold and Glory" follows the settling of New Mexico in 1595 by Juan de Onate, the ill fated expedition into the territory of Florida by Panfilo de Narvaez and Juan Rodriguez Cabrillo's original exploration of California and the pathway, "El Camino Real" (The King's Highway).[17]

The ceding by Spain of Florida to the U.S.A. in 1819, Texas Independence in 1836, and the treaty of Guadalupe-Hidalgo (1848), giving half of all territory of Mexico to the U.S.A., all led to the transfer of political power to U.S.A. in these conquered territories, leaving subsequently several thousand Spanish and Mexicans "captive strangers in their own land."[18]

To complicate matters for these Hispanics the existing Catholic Church in the USA ousted the native Mexican clergy and bishops and replaced them with

---

[15]Frank Tennenbaum, "Toward an Appreciation of Latin America," in Herbert L. Mathews, ed. *The United States and Latin America* (New York: Columbia University, The American Assembly, 1959) p. 26.

[16]Ricardo Santos, "Missionary Beginnings in Spanish Florida, the Southwest, and California," in Moises Sandoval, ed., *Fronteras: A History of the Latin American Church in the USA Since 1513* (San Antonio, Texas: Mexican American Cultural Center, 1983), p. 3; Used with permission of Mexican American Cultural Center, copyright 1983. Of course, if one notes the present political status of Puerto Rico as being a colony of the USA, then one would have to date the "discovery" of Puerto Rico by Cristobal Colon in November 19, 1493 as the beginning of Roman Catholicism in USA territory.

[17]*Ibid.*, pp. 3-54.

[18]Andrés Guerrero, *A Chicano Theology* (New York: Orbis Books, 1987) p. 11; used with permission of Orbis Books, copyright 1987.

French and Spaniards. These were replaced in turn, in the twentieth century, by Irish and German Americans. This trend has continued to exist to this date, with attempts at redress beginning to appear in the late 1960's and early 1970's.[19]

Andrés Guerrero, while writing about the physical and psychological colonization of the Chicano by the Anglos, also speaks strongly about their "spiritual colonization," which has been perpetuated by the USA Catholic Church since the conquest and colonization.

> The systematic denial of spiritual leadership to Chicanos constitutes a form of spiritual colonization. The leaders of the institutional church insured the occupation of the Southwest by denying Chicanos responsible representative leadership in our Catholic Church. Just as we are treated as strangers in our land, so we are also treated as strangers in our own church, which has existed in the Southwest since the 1500s.[20]

One can speak of "spiritual colonization" at various levels, the "spiritual colonization" of the Amerindian and Africans being the most obvious. But most fruitful in this conceptualization is the "spiritual colonization" of likeminded religious confessions (i.e., Catholics vs. Catholics) as the case of the Puerto Rican and Mexican American.

In my conceptualization of the socio-religious idea of "spiritual colonization" the religious "powers that be" (those aligned with the conquering forces - coming with them or already present in the society) exercise "spiritual colonization" when at least these three criteria are present:

1.   Disenfranchisement of "native" clergy - The denial and lack of development and empowerment of indigenous leadership.

---

[19]According to Isidro Lucas (1981), approximately 25% of all Catholics in the USA are Hispanics. Citing Father Rutilio del Riego of the Hispanic Pastoral Center for the Northeast, Lucas indicated that only 2.4 percent of the priests in the USA are Hispanics. Adding, "But the fact that there are only 400 native-born Hispanic priests - so few in proportion to the Hispanic population - seriously affects the relationship of the Hispanics with the Church in America." In Isidro Lucas, *The Browning of America*, p. 40.

[20]Andrés Guerrero, *A Chicano Theology*, p. 25.

2.   Real or attempted religious and cultural domination of a people -
        a domination over the linguistic and symbolic culture and religious
        expression, so critical for the identity and liberation of a people.

3.   Sacramentalizing the ruling economic-political system -which
        ultimately means siding with the oppressors.

As a socio-religious concept, "spiritual colonization" can be a useful
analytic tool, yielding valuable insight on the power relations of a church and a
people, particularly of the same religious confession.[21]

One early and "representative" Hispanic American who resisted "spiritual
colonization" is Padre Antonio José Martínez of Taos, New Mexico. Padre
Martínez resisted the policies of both civil and ecclesiastical authorities that were
unjust to the poor. A publisher, lawyer, educator, political leader and a priest,
Padre Martínez struggled for the liberation of his people from the oppressive
structures outside and inside the Roman Catholic Church.[22]

Moises Sandoval notes well Padre Martínez's refusal to capitulate to the
cultural domination of his "Superiors":

He refused to surrender his culture to the demands of the
authoritative French bishop, Jean Baptiste Lamy, who came to New
Mexico determined to implant a Christianity in a cultural mold
foreign to its inhabitants... Padre Martínez was excommunicated,
but defiantly continued to minister to his parish until his death.[23]

The conquest and colonization of Puerto Rico (1898) by the USA also led
to a trend of importing of American and foreign priests and religious personnel on
the Island. This was in keeping with a history, first by the Spanish Catholic

---

[21]I have been influenced by many and varied books on colonization, but two works stand out,
namely: Frantz Fanon, *The Wretched of the Earth* (New York: Ballantine, Inc. 1963); and Albert
Memmi, *The Colonizer and the Colonized* (Boston: Beacon Press, 1967).

[22]Thus he followed the long tradition of Latin American's "other church" Champions of
Liberation: Antonio de Montesinos, Bartolomé de las Casas, St-Luis Beltrán, Gil González de San
Nicolás, Pedro Claver, José Gabriel Tupac Amaru and Father Miguel Hidalgo y Castilla, among
others; see, Justo L. González, "The Two Faces of Hispanic Christianity," *The Judson Bulletin*, vol.
VI, no 1.

[23]Moisés Sandoval, "The Church and El Movimiento," in *Fronteras: A History of the Latin
American Church in the USA Since 1513*, p. 377; see also, Juan Romero, with Moisés Sandoval,
Reluctant Dawn: Historia del Padre A.J. Martínez, Cura de Taos (San Antonio: Mexican Cultural
Center, 1975); Andrés G. Guerrero, *A Chicano Theology*, pp. 11-16.

Church and then by the USA Catholic Church, of not developing and empowering "native" clergy. "Spiritual colonization" was thus perpetuated in Puerto Rico by the U.S. Catholic hierarchy.[24]

According to Antonio M. Stevens-Arroyo, "... this practice of importing clergy and the inability to imbue Puerto Rican Catholicism with a nationalistic flavor carried over to the pastoral practice of the Church towards Puerto Ricans in the mainland of the United States."[25]

It is one of the tragic notes of the Puerto Rican migration to the U.S.A. that "they came without their priest" and no "national parishes" received them. They were thus "received" in "integrated parishes"[26] - again experiencing "spiritual colonization." The Hispanic Roman Catholic Church in the USA has indeed been "a people without clergy" and "invisible to the American Church."

"Power corrupts and absolute power corrupts absolutely," so said Lord Acton. The penchant of the Roman Catholic Church throughout its history in Latin America, including Puerto Rico and mainland USA, has been to align itself with the economic-political "powers that be." In the interest of "Evangelization" and

---

[24]See, Jerry Fenton, *Understanding the Religious Background of the Puerto Rican* (Cuernavaca, Mexico: Centro Intercultural de Documentación, Sondeos, No. 52, 1969); Joseph P. Fitzpatrick, *Puerto Rican Americans*, pp. 118-119; Justo L. González, *The Development of Christianity in the Latin Caribbean* (Grand Rapids, Michigan: Wm. Eerdmans Publishing Co. 1969), pp. 100-101.

[25]Antonio M. Stevens-Arroyo, "Puerto Rican Migration to the United States," in *Fronteras: A History of the Latin American Church in the USA Since 1513*, p. 271.

[26]See, *Ibid.*, pp. 271-275; Joseph P. Fitzpatrick, *Puerto Rican American*, pp. 123-127; While there have been Spanish speaking chapels in New York: Our Lady of Guadalupe (1902); Our Lady of Esperanza (1912); and specifically opened for Puerto Ricans, La Milagrosa (1926) and Holy Agony (1930), "The Spanish chapels were deliberately kept small. However, the Puerto Ricans did not bring clergy with them, so that the priests of the National Chapels were Spaniards, separated from Puerto Ricans by many cultural differences," Antonio M. Stevens-Arroyo, "Puerto Rican Migration to the United States" in *Fronteras*, p. 274; Also, under the integration (read, Americanization) policies of Cardinal Spellman in 1939 the "National parish" approach deviated to one "integrated parish," thus critically affecting the "airborne migration" of Puerto Ricans of the postwar years of the 1940's. According to Fitzpatrick the integrated parish
> tends to perpetuate among the Puerto Ricans the feeling that they are newcomers who are inheriting something established rather than creating something of their own. They have not had the confidence of knowing that this parish, church, or school is "theirs" in the sense in which Italians, for example, knew the Italian parish was "theirs." As a result, the parish has not been able to serve as the basis of a strong, stable Puerto Rican community the way it had served for earlier immigrant groups, in *Puerto Rican Americans*, p. 124.

institutional development and survival (read, Triumphalism) it has thrown its fate with the conquering forces of oppression. It has desired to be not just respected or tolerated but to be the "manager or mentor" - eventually sacralizing the "status quo" and becoming a "spiritual colonizer."[27]

It has been only since the late 1960's and early 1970's that the Hispanic Roman Catholic Church has begun to make significant impact on the American Roman Catholic Church and to really begin to seriously challenge "spiritual colonization."

This challenge has been most noticeable in the movement to train more "native" clergy and in the appointment by August 1985 of seventeen (17) Hispanic Bishops in mainland United States (the earliest, Patricio F. Flores, May 5, 1970). Virgilio Elizondo notes this emerging "native" leadership:

> We are also beginning to see the first stages of a native leadership within the Hispanic church. By "native" I mean born in the United States. Often in the past native-born American Hispanics have been oppressed and dictated to by U.S. taskmasters and by Latin Americans, who also took it for granted that we could not do our own thing. Today leadership is beginning to grow out of the Hispanic communities. We have learned much from Latin America but we have also learned much from our own U.S. experience. Today we are blending aspects of both to put together new models of thought and action.[28]

Noteworthy in the emerging indigenous leadership is the development of the organization of PADRES (Priest Associated for Religious, Educational, and Social Rights); Las Hermanas; the Northeast Catholic Pastoral Center for Hispanics, in New York City; the Mexican American Cultural Center, in San Antonio; the establishment of the Office of the Secretariat for Hispanic Affairs, U.S. Catholic Conference; the issuing on December 12, 1983 of "A Pastoral Letter on Hispanic Ministry: The Hispanic Presence: Challenge and Commitment" by the National Conference of Catholic Bishops; and the growth of "Cursillo" and "Comunidades

---

[27]We should always remember Justo L. González's indication, namely, that all along there has existed the "Other Church," one that stood for linguistic and cultural affirmation and liberation of the poor and the oppressed; "Two Faces of Hispanic Christianity," *The Judson Bulletin*, Vol. VI, no. 1.

[28]Virgilio Elizondo, "Toward an American-Hispanic Theology of Liberation in the U.S.A." in Virginia Fabella and Sergio Torres, eds. *Irruption of the Third World: Challenge to Theology* (New York: Orbis Books, 1983), p. 51.

de Bases" throughout hundreds of Hispanic communities. These developments are some of the positive signs of hope and liberation among the Hispanic Roman Catholic Church in the U.S.A.[29]

---

[29]See especially, Isidro Lucas, *The Browning of America: The Hispanic Revolution in the American Church*; Moises Sandoval, ed., *Fronteras: A History of the Latin American Church in the U.S.A. Since 1513*; Antonio M. Stevens-Arroyo, ed., *Prophets Denied Honor: An Anthology on the Hispanic Church of the United States*. During the "III Encuentro Nacional Hispano Pastoral," on August 15-18, 1985 at the Catholic University, Washington D.C., Archbishop Roberto Sanchez of Santa Fe noted five (5) areas in which significant change had occurred during the past 13 years (since the 1971, "Primer Encuentro"):

Administration:

a.   The Office of the Secretariat for Hispanic Affairs was established within the Episcopal Conference of the United States.
b.   7 regional offices for hispanic affairs were established.
c.   More than 100 diocesan offices for hispanic affairs were established.
d.   The Ad Hoc Committee for Hispanic Affairs in the Episcopal Conference was established.

Education:

a.   6 pastoral centers on a regional level for cultural formation were established.
b.   The study of the language and hispanic culture was integrated in various seminaries and centers of formation for the priesthood and religious life.
c.   Bilingual education has been initiated in many Catholic schools and religious education programs.
d.   Various publications have appeared in Spanish or in bilingual editions.
e.   Many areas have bilingual or Spanish television and radio programs.

Leadership:

a.   The hispanic bishops and archbishops have reached to 17.
b.   More hispanics have been named to positions within the offices of the diocese and to other responsible positions.
c.   Mobil teams were formed and have been sent to *evangelize*.
d.   The candidates for permanent deacons have grown dramatically.
e.   Many leaders have been trained in "Las Comunidades de Bases" and in apostolic programs.
f.   The Episcopal Conference has drawn up a pastoral letter about the Hispanic Apostleship.

Liturgy:

a.   The bilingual and Spanish liturgies have multiplied.
b.   An Institute of Hispanic Liturgy has been established.
c.   Many Hispanic musicians and composers have been identified.
d.   The Hispanic and bilingual choirs have grown in quantity and quality.

Social Justice:

a.   The cooperation and support of the church to Cesar Chavez and towards the UFW have been strengthen.

Socio-Vision
Descriptive and Guiding Myths and Symbols

La Morenita: La Virgen de Guadalupe

The religious symbols and images of a people in a given community, given an internalization development through their history, combine in the complex narrative known as myths.[30] We are reminded by Barbour that as "religious symbols become part of the language of a religious community..." and "are expressive of man's emotions and feelings...;" they "are powerful in calling forth his response and commitment."[31]

In the "evangelization" of the Americas no other myth or symbol has played such a dominant role as "the religious symbol of Guadalupe," such is the opinion of Guerrero and Elizondo.[32] La Morenita's ("the brown lady") appearance to Juan Diego, an Aztec in December 9, 1531 on the hill of Tepeyac, became such a strong religious symbol that eight million native Americans were baptized into the Catholic Church during the seven years after her apparition.[33] Virgilio Elizondo states that:

---

b.   The involvement of the church in the needs and the ministry of the migrant workers has grown.

c.   The church was the largest agency that relocated the Cuban refugees.

d.   The church is extensively involved in the reform of the immigration laws.

e.   The church has taken an active role in the Central American situation.

(Translated by Naomi Wilshire from the Newsletter, *En Marcha!* (Office of the Secretariat for Hispanic Affairs), Ano V, Vol. 4, Septiembre 1985, pp. 2-3).

[30]The historicity or ontological status of myth is not in question, the greater value or significance lies rather in its function in human life. According to Ian G. Barbour, myths provide critical psychological, social, and cognitive functions. In their psychological functions, "they are a source of security and a symbolic resolution of conflicts." In their social functions, "they are a cohesive force binding a community together and contributing to social solidarity, group identity and communal harmony." In their cognitive functions when summarized in models, "they lead to conceptually formulated, systematic, coherent, religious beliefs...;" Ian G. Barbour, *Myths, Models, and Paradigms: A Comparative Study in Science and Religion* (New York: Harper and Row, 1974), pp. 23-28.

[31]*Ibid.*, p. 15.

[32]Andrés G. Guerrero, *A Chicano Theology*, pp. 96-117; see especially, Virgilio Elizondo, *La Morenita: Evangelizer of the Americas* (Texas: Mexican American Culture Center, 1980).

[33]Andrés G. Guerrero, *A Chicano Theology*, p. 97.

The symbolism of *la Morenita* opened up a new possibility for racio-cultural dialogue and exchange. The synthesis of the religious iconography of the Spanish with that of the indigenous Mexican people into a single, coherent symbol-image ushered in a new, shared experience. The missioners and the people now had an authentic basis for dialogue. What the missioners had been praying for had now come in an unexpected (and for some, unwanted) way. The cultural clash of sixteenth-century Spain and Mexico was resolved and reconciled in the brown Lady of Guadalupe. In her the new *mestizo* people finds its meaning, its uniqueness, its unity. Guadalupe is the key to understanding the Christianity of the New World, the self-image of Mexicans, of Mexican-Americans, and of all Latin Americans.[34]

Symbol systems are critical tools for religious affirmation and theological reflection. Andrés Guerrero explored the Chicano oral tradition by interviewing nine leaders (seven men and two women) using selective "share themes" vital to the Chicano community.[35] It is important to note that in analyzing the theme "Nuestra Señora de Guadalupe" from the oral tradition in the chapter, "The Religious Symbol of Guadalupe" he summarizes the significance of Guadalupe under five symbols: "Guadalupe as a symbol of faith, as a symbol of identity, as a symbol of hope, as a symbol of women against *machismo*, and as a symbol of liberation."[36]

Guadalupe as a symbol of faith speaks to the Chicano Catholic in terms of God's motherly love for them, the oppressed - after all the mother of Jesus has taken on their color, their clothes, their cause. She is the symbol of trust and of the impossible.

Guadalupe as a symbol of identity provides a sense of meaning, a cultural sense of belonging and ultimately a reference point and glue, "that keeps the structures together: the politics, the kinship system, the mutual aid societies,

---

[34]Virgilio Elizondo, *Galilean Journey: The Mexican American Promise* p. 12; while some would not express the important role of *La Morenita* in such glowing terms, others (personal conversation with church historian Dr. Justo L. González at the Center for Urban Ministerial Education in Boston on April 9, 1987) would equally posit the apparition of other "Vírgenes" in the Caribbean and Latin America as playing similar symbolic religious and cultural affirming roles and evangelistic impact.

[35]Andrés Guerrero, *A Chicano Theology*, pp. 33-95.

[36]*Ibid.*, pp. 105-117.

modern-day association groups, and the church as an institution."[37]   It is noteworthy that the two protestants of the nine leaders interviewed are the ones who emphasize more strongly the identity factor.   Guerrero cites Ruben Armendariz, former Director of Latino Studies Program and Professor of Ministry at the McCormick Theological Seminary in Chicago, as relating his experience in the Navy and the unity among Chicanos based on the Virgin of Guadalupe: "In the service, when it came to the nitty-gritty, it was for *La Virgen y mi madre.*"[38]

Guadalupe as a symbol of hope is a symbol that is rooted deep in the consciousness of the Chicano, appealing to positive Amerindian and Spanish heritage and influence. According to Elizondo, "The power of hope offered by the drama of Guadalupe came from the fact that the unexpected good news of God's presence was offered to all by someone from whom nothing special was expected: the conquered Indian, the lowest of the low."[39]

Guadalupe as symbol of woman against *machismo* "is important because she guarantees a place for womanhood..." and challenges the worst elements of machismo by reminding the *macho* that the "Chicana is not his scapegoat and that Our Lady of Guadalupe, a symbol of our mother, is against *machismo.*"[40]

Guadalupe is also a symbol of liberation.   Her inspirational role was graphically displayed in the banner and flags leading the Mexican Independence under Father Hidalgo and most recently Cesar Chavez's struggles with the exploitation of farm workers.

Guerrero asks, "What is Guadalupe saying to Chicanos about their church, which has no Chicano leadership? What is Guadalupe saying in terms of the educational deficiencies of Chicano children... in terms of Texas Chicano children having a health record worse than any other children in the other forty-nine states?... in terms of human rights issues? In terms of world solidarity?" His resounding response is loud and clear: "Guadalupe as a symbol of liberation is the

---

[37]Guerrero quotes Tomás Atencio, a protestant sociologist, *Ibid.*, p. 108.

[38]*Ibid.*, p. 110.

[39]Virgilio Elizondo, *Galilean Journey: The Mexican-American Promise*, p. 12.

[40]Andrés Guerrero, *A Chicano Theology*, p. 113, 115; It should be noted that notwithstanding this powerful symbol of *La Morenita*, Guerrero thinks that "the church has much homework ahead to overcome *machismo*. It was stressed that much of the *machismo* in Chicano culture can be traced to the church's attitudes toward the inferiority of women," p. 158.

Mother of the Oppressed. Like any mother, she does not abandon her children nor does she fail to respond to their cries."[41]

La Raza Cósmica: Mestizaje
As Paradigm and "Locus Theologicus"

In Chapter I - "Hispanic American Reality," we looked at "La Raza: Ethnicity and Race," as one of three basic elements of Hispanic heritage. In this section *La Raza Cósmica* will be looked at more as a paradigm or symbol of Hispanic-religious self-understanding and communal vision. As such, it is suggestively rich for theological reflection, for it is one of those "deep symbols" that has emerged in the experience of an oppressed people and that Hispanics, particularly Mexican-American Catholic theologians, have and are developing into insightful theological constructs.[42]

For Virgilio Elizondo the essence of *La Raza Cósmica* is to be seen in the conceptualization of *Mestizaje* as the "dialectic of cultural birth and the Gospel." The double mestizaje: the first encounter of Spaniard (European) and Amerindian is followed by the second encounter of the Anglo-American and Mexican, producing a new ethnos, a new people - critically significant not so much on the basis of race as of *culture*. In the Mexican-American as a *mestizo* there emerges a culture synthesis of the positive values of its parent stock and the infusion of the Gospel values of its Catholic religiosity.

The *Mestizo Norte-Americano* is marginated and rejected by both parent cultures. Total assimilation into either culture is seen as forfeiting ones true identity and mission, "the path of living out the radical meaning and potential of a *mestizo* regeneration," and thus to "lead the way to a new creation."[43]

---

[41]*Ibid.*, pp. 116-117; There is a resurgence in the importance of the symbol of the Virgin in Catholic religiosity as noted by Pope John Paul II issuing an 114 page encyclical entitled "The Mother of the Redeemer." In it he outlined the church's goal for a special Marian year, starting June 7, 1987 ending August 15, 1988, in Samuel Koo, "Pope Reaffirms Church Teachings on Mary," *The Boston Globe* 26 March 1987, p. 19; see also, Charlotte Low, "The Madonna's Decline and Revival," *Insight* 19 March 1987, pp. 61-63.

[42]Virgilio Elizondo, *Mestizaje: The Dialectic of Cultural Birth and the Gospel*; *Galilean Journey: The Mexican-American Promise*; Andrés G. Guerrero, *A Chicano Theology*.

[43]Virgilio Elizondo, *Galilean Journey: The Mexican-American Promise*, p. 18.

Elizondo offers a re-reading of the Gospel from the perspective of *Mestizaje*. Three themes or principles emerge, incarnated in the life and mission of Jesus of Nazareth; the Galilee principle, the Jerusalem principle and the Resurrection principle. Galilee is the "symbol of multiple rejection," suffering and margination, of *mestizaje*. Jerusalem in turn was the center of belonging - political, intellectual, religious - of power. Jesus is the Galilean, rejected by his own - but elected by the Father. He confronts the "powers that be" of Jerusalem, whose power apparently destroys Him, only to be shown by the Resurrection that the love of the Galilean is triumphant.

In an analogous or paradigmatic manner Elizondo sees in the Mexican-American *mestizo* the "worldly rejection - divine election." Because of their mestizaje and consequent rejection, they have been chosen by God. Their election is not necessarily for their own good, but for the greater prophetic mission of taking the message of the liberating love to Jerusalem - to the center of power. In the process they too will have to live out the "theology of the cross" - a struggle until death - a redemptive death, though. For the defeat is likened to Jesus on the cross, and the "resurrection principle" is also present and certain for them; "one love can triumph over evil, and no human power can prevail against the power of unlimited love. Out of suffering and death, God will bring health and life."[44]

Andrés Guerrero posits the theme of *La Raza Cósmica* as a secular-religious symbol.[45] He develops the theme by an analysis of the oral tradition among nine Chicano leaders. His findings are summarized under seven symbols: (1) *La Raza* as a Symbol of Cosmicity; (2) *La Raza* as a Symbol of "Auto-Identificarse" (Identifying Oneself); (3) *La Raza* as a Symbol of *Mestizaje*; (4) *La Raza* as a Symbol of Hope; (5) *La Raza* as a Symbol of Unity; (6) *La Raza* as a Symbol of New Creation; and (7) *La Raza* as a Symbol of Liberation.

La Raza as a symbol of cosmicity "is a concept that makes one inclusive with the universe."[46] But this universal aspect can be *so* in that it affirms the particular identity of the Chicano.

La Raza as a symbol of "auto-identificarse" (identifying oneself) addresses the socio-cultural and psychological, and theological as well, issue of "naming

---

[44]*Ibid.*, p. 115.

[45]See, "The Secular-Religious Symbol of *La Raza Cósmica*" in Andrés Guerrero, *A Chicano Theology*, pp. 118-137.

[46]*Ibid.*, p. 125.

themselves." This is a theological as well as political self-understanding as *mestizos*, as *la raza*.

   La Raza as a symbol of *mestizaje* speaks to the fact that "we are a mixture of the two, the Hispanic and the gringo. This is the Chicano experience today."[47]

   The "corazón latino" (the Hispanic heart) combines with the "gringo" impulse in this conceptualization; "in other words the *Latinoamericano mestizo* is different from the Chicano *mestizo* in that the Chicano lives in a gringo society."[48] *Mestizaje* is seen as a synthesis, "an inclusivity of human relationships."[49]

   La Raza as a symbol of Hope is seen as a symbol that helps fight against despair. The Chicanos themselves provide the bridge between the *latino* world and the gringo world. They can bring these two cultures together since in their experience and reality they relate to both.

   La Raza as a symbol of unity speaks about its implicit power as a unifying principle for all Hispanics.

> All the Hispanos - Cubans, Puerto Ricans, Chicanos, Mexicans, Central Americans, South Americans, Spanish-speaking Caribbeans - are all *La Raza*. Not only Hispanos can unite under this symbolic concept; all of Latin America can unite under this concept. It is a powerful concept because of the unifying strength it carries.[50]

   La Raza as a symbol of new creation is seen by Ruben Armendariz theologically, in contrast to Jose Vasconcelos' more secular notion. Armendariz notes the eschatological dimension of *La Raza* in bringing together the theme of New Creation and the Kingdom of God. The Chicano can model and transcend the many differences in contemporary society and thus be a sign of the Kingdom of God.[51]

----

[47]*Ibid.*, p. 128.

[48]*Ibid.*, p. 129.

[49]*Ibid.*

[50]*Ibid.*, p. 132.

[51]*Ibid.*, pp. 113-134.

La Raza as a symbol of liberation underlines the reality of a people who though "poor" have learned to survive, no, live with dignity! - a liberating model or demonstration of the blending of two cultures and two races. "The phenomenon of *la Raza*, of the mixture of peoples, needs to be developed to encourage inclusivity and equality among people."[52]

There is great symbolic and paradigmatic value in *La Raza: Mestizaje* concept. It is indeed very rich and suggestive as a locus of theological reflection, definitely not exhausted by the above summary of Elizondo and Guerrero. Justo L. González, in reviewing Virgilio Elizondo's *Galilean Journey: The Mexican-American Promise*, raises the question: "What does it mean to be a protestant and Hispanic at the same time? Could this be a third *mestizaje*, beyond the two discussed by Elizondo?"[53]

I will suggest that, of all Hispanics, the Puerto Rican American is perhaps most representative of *mestizaje* in the U.S.A. The *mestizaje* of Puerto Ricans is threefold: Spaniard, Amerindian, and African, while of the Chicano is Spaniard and Amerindian. This is highlighted by Don Pedro Albizu Campos in his "Discurso del 'Día de La Raza'" of October 12, 1933:

> Que hay sangre africana? Yo también la llevo en las venas y la
> llevo con el supremo orgullo de la dignidad humana. Aquí tenemos
> sangre india ... Yo también tengo sangre india y por eso me siento
> perfectamente americano, americano autóctono ... Que hay sangre
> blanca en nosotros? Yo también la llevo en las venas ... Nosotros
> somos un pueblo predestinado en la historia, porque Puerto Rico es
> la primera nación del mundo donde se forma la unidad del espíritu
> con la unidad biológica del cuerpo.[54]

Puerto Rico experienced a conquest and a colonialization (1898), that, with the emigration to the U.S. metropolis, resulted in the emigration of one third of the

---

[52]*Ibid.*, p. 135.

[53]My own translation, Justo L. González, "Receña Bibliográfica," *Apuntes* 3 (Invierno, 1983): 95.

[54]Pedro Albizu Campos, *La Conciencia Nacional Puertorriqueña* (Mexico: Siglo Veintiuno Editores, SA, 1974) pp. 195-196; "That there is African blood, I too carry it in my veins and I carry it with the supreme pride of human dignity. We have here Indian blood ... I too have Indian blood and because of that I feel perfectly American, indigenous American... That there is white blood in us? I too carry it in my veins... We are an historically predestined people, because Puerto Rico is the first nation in the world where the unity of the spirit with the biological unity of the body takes form."

Puerto Rican population. Puerto Ricans have been U.S.A. citizens since 1917. It has also experienced the double *mestizaje* encounter with the Anglo-American civilization.

In the political status of Puerto Rico is that of a "commonwealth" - neither a state of the Union nor Independent. A status which has created no little havoc in the identity of Puerto Ricans.

In mainland U.S.A. the Puerto Rican is marginalized and rejected; compared to the Chicano in such areas as schooling, politics and poverty the Puerto Rican is at the bottom of the totem pole.[55]

It would be fair to say that Elizondo and Guerrero have used a symbol - *La Raza* - which has much currency in their Chicano culture. While Puerto Ricans have not developed or utilized this rich symbol as a self-referent term, nevertheless, it would be more true to reality and politically of greater significance if "Hispanics" in general, and not just Mexican-Americans (Chicanos), are used as the *Mestizo Norte-Americano*. The bilingual and bicultural reality, coupled with the critical need for socio-political solidarity, demands it.

The Hispanic Protestant Church

The Reformation has appeared in Hispanic dress;
there has been a new birth of religious consciousness
affecting the daily life of millions of people.

Alberto Rembao[56]

Indeed the "Reformation has appeared in Hispanic dress" both in Latin America and in the Hispanic American context. Yet, it is a "reformation" shrouded in ambiguity, given the nature of the many vicissitudes attending, to continue the metaphor, the would-be "wearer of the dress," given the attitude/spirit of those whose generosity facilitated, as well as dictated, the proper "design of the dress."

---

[55]Joan Moore and Harry Pachon, *Hispanics in the USA*. pp. 79-80.

[56]Alberto Rembao, "Foreword" in W. Stanley Rycroft, *Religion and Faith in Latin America*, p. 8.

Edwin Sylvest underscores the ambiguous nature of Hispanic American Protestantism in no uncertain terms:

> Hispanic American Protestantism is an exceedingly complex and comparatively recent phenomenon. It is a concomitant of the processes that have led to the internal colonization and marginalization of Hispanic Americans. As Hispanic Americans became U.S. citizens, either through conquest or out of economic or political necessity, some also became Protestant. Protestants have immigrated to the United States from Latin America... Even these people owe their Protestant heritage to the growth of Anglo-American hegemony in the western hemisphere.[57]

To understand the genesis and development of the Hispanic Protestant church one must come to terms with the ideology of "Manifest Destiny," so prevalent in the nineteenth and early twentieth century.[58] Manifest Destiny was a critical factor in defining the milieu of those early contacts between United States Protestants and Mexicans, Cubans and Puerto Ricans.[59] Sylvest reminds us that "Manifest Destiny was indeed a critical element in the cultural ethos of the first Protestant efforts to minister among Hispanic Americans... In the religious sense it became the task of Protestant churches to undertake the mission of regeneration that had become the national obligation."[60]

The "White Man's burden" was thus to regenerate backward people and the colonial conquest by the United States was thus justified on religious and humanitarian grounds. Sylvest goes on to add that, "It was,of course, only coincidental that economic opportunity should attend the task of uplifting benighted people. As in midcentury, imperial expansion rested upon the foundation of racist paternalism and economic advantage."[61]

---

[57]Edwin Sylvest, Jr., "Hispanic American Protestantism in the United States," Moises Sandoval, ed., *Fronteras: A History of the Latin American Church in the USA Since 1513*, p. 279.

[58]See Frederick Merk, *Manifest Destiny and Mission in American History: A Reinterpretation* (New York: Vintage, 1963); Albert K. Weinberg, *Manifest Destiny: A Study of National Expansion in American History* (Chicago: Quadrangle Books, 1963).

[59]Edwin Sylvest, Jr., "Hispanic American protestantism in the United States", Moises Sandoval, ed. *Fronteras*, p. 281; see also, Daniel R. Rodríguez. *La Primera Evangelización Norteamericana en Puerto Rico 1898-1930* (Mexico, D.F.: Ediciones Borinquen, 1986).

[60]*Ibid.*, p. 286.

[61]*Ibid.*, p. 286.

While Sylvest's words may seem harsh and certainly not the "conscious conspiracy" of the early Protestant missionaries, it nevertheless reflects the ideological mileu during which those early contacts were made. The paternalism and structures of dependence established by the Anglo Protestant churches in their relations with Hispanics owed not a little to this "reigning" ideology. As we have learned from the Sociology of Knowledge, the social and cultural ethos of a given context informs and forms the cognitive, psychical, social, emotive and valuative matrix of an individual and of a group.[62] The early missionaries, products of their times, offered a "benign paternalism" - but paternalism nonetheless. Its impact is still felt by the Hispanic Church, which in recent history has demonstrated powerful signs of liberation.

Socio-history: The Mainline Protestant Church

From Paternalism and Structures of Dependence
to Liberation and Self-determination

The westward movement of Anglo settlers provided the initial contact with the Hispanics in the early 1800's. Texas became "the locus of this initial contact between Protestant Christianity and Hispanic culture within the present limits of the United States."[63] While the principal interest of the Anglo Protestant missionary was for the care and nurture of the Anglo "colonist," it was not long before they became aware of the needs of the "spiritually" neglected Hispanics. The Anglo Protestant missionaries' endeavors to serve the needs of the Mexicans of Texas was met with great intolerance, prejudice and "downright" racism by the Anglo colonist. Brackenridge and Garcia-Treto state that:

> Anglo prejudice against the Mexicans of Texas made it difficult for
> potential missionaries to drum up any enthusiasm for their cause.
> Most white settlers considered Mexicans to be lazy, apathetic people

---

[62]See, Karl Mannheim, *Ideology and Utopia: An Introduction to the Sociology of Knowledge* (New York: Harvest Book, 1936); Peter Berger and Thomas Luckmann, *The Social Construction of Reality* (New York: Doubleday, 1966).

[63]Edwin Sylvest, Jr., "Hispanic American Protestantism in the United States," Moises Sandoval, ed. *Fronteras*, p. 290.

whose motto was "aguarde un poco" (wait a little). by nature, therefore, they were deemed poor prospects for conversion to Protestant Christianity.[64]

Notwithstanding the resistance and lack of support by the Anglo colonist, and given the paternalism and incipient racism of the Anglo missionaries themselves, most of the missionary endeavors to reach out and minister to Hispanics were of true Christian commitment that often reached heroic proportions.

The major missionary thrust among Hispanics in California and the Southwest by the mainline Protestant churches was by the Presbyterian, Methodist and Baptist churches. In the late 1820's, 1830's, and early 1840's the name of Summer Bacon, Cumberland Presbyterian minister and Bible colporteur, David Ayers, Methodist layperson and Bible colporteur, William C. Blair, Presbyterian minister, and the New England woman Melinda Rankin are to be noted among the few early "seedlers" in the Southwest. The creation in 1897 of the ecumenical California Spanish Missionary Society is noteworthy as "one of the earliest known Protestant efforts to establish an organized ministry among the Spanish-speaking people in Southern California."[65] Noteworthy among the Hispanic Protestant indigenous leadership that emerged at this time are the names of Ambrosio González; former priest Benigno Cardenas; Alejo Hernandez and José Maria Botello to name only a few.

By the close of the nineteenth century in California, Texas, and the Southwest a significant number of Hispanic churches had been planted. They were ministered by mostly Hispanics, though under the "tutelage" of Anglo missioners.[66] Although there has been significant progress in the Hispanic mainline Protestant churches in the Southwest through the years, even with regard to the question of "control" and empowerment, Sylvest's indictment is still relevant:

---

[64]R. Douglas Brackenridge and Francisco O. Garcia-Treto, *Iglesia Presbiteriana: A History of Presbyterians and Mexican Americans in the Southwest* (San Antonio, Texas: Trinity University Press, 1974), p. 13; for documentation of similar attitudes in Southern California see, Clifton L. Holland, *The Religious Dimension in Hispanic Los Angeles: A Protestant Case Study* (Pasadena, California: William Carey Library, 1974), pp. 190-191.

[65]Clifton L. Holland, *The Religious Dimension in Hispanic Los Angeles*, p. 191.

[66]See especially, Edwin Sylvest, Jr. "Hispanic American Protestantism in the United States," in Moises Sandoval, ed., *Fronteras*, pp. 290-323; see also, Leo Gebler, Joan W. Moore, and Ralph C. Guzman, *The Mexican-American People* (New York: The Free Press, 1970), pp. 489-493.

The essential patterns and structures of Hispanic American Protestantism in the Southwest were set in the years 1859-90. Texas and New Mexico were the principal geographic foci of Protestant missionary effort during the period. Methodists and Presbyterians were the principal missionary agents. Allowing for differences in polity, their efforts and results were remarkably similar. Within both groups significant indigenous leadership, lay and clerical, emerged, but in neither group was there any serious inclination to allow the churches to develop without paternalistic, however benevolent and enlightened, control by Anglos. Even though the Methodists established Spanish-speaking annual conferences, control of those conferences was placed in the hands of Anglo superintendents and bishops.[67]

It is at this early missionary stage that the paternalism of the Anglo missionary resulted in the establishment of structures of dependence that have had a long and serious impact among Hispanic mainline Protestant churches.

In many ways the experience of the Hispanics in the Northeast (meaning, the Puerto Ricans) parallels that of the Mexicans in the Southwest. It is important, however, to note some historical antecedents on the Island of Puerto Rico.

With the "take over" of Puerto Rico in 1898, as a "war booty" of the Spanish-American War, Anglo Protestant missionaries began their presence on the Island. By 1904 a "comity agreement" was reached by the mainline Protestant churches that originally included the Presbyterians, American Baptist, Congregationalist, Episcopalian Methodist, and which later other denominations joined in it. This "comity agreement" divided the island into sectors or territories of missionary outreach, thus avoiding competition.[68]

---

[67]Edwin Sylvest, Jr., "Hispanic American Protestantism in the United States," in Moises Sandoval, ed. *Fronteras*, pp. 314-315.

[68]See, Enrique Rodríguez-Bravo, *Origen y Desarrollo del Movimiento Protestante en Puerto Rico* (Ph.D. Dissertation, The George Washington University 1972), pp. 33; Jerry Fenton, *Understanding The Religious Background of the Puerto Rican*, pp. 1/6-1/7; See especially the section "Las juntas misioneras se dividen el territorio" in Daniel R. Rodríguez, *La Primera Evangelización Norteamericana en Puerto Rico, 1898-1930*, pp. 184-207. It is interesting to note that this "turf carving" was experienced by Hispanics in Los Angeles that by 1914 it included the Baptist, Congregational, Methodist, Episcopal and Presbyterian denominations, see, Clifton L. Holland, *The Religious Dimension in Hispanic Los Angeles*, p. 198.

It is to be seriously noted that at the coming of the USA to Puerto Rico in 1898 the struggle for independence was once again frustrated in the Island. The Protestant missionaries gave implicit support to an unjust and oppressive USA government invasion, much in keeping with the "manifest destiny" ideology, and certainly indicative of a "truncated" Gospel. Professor Samuel Solivan's assessment rings true:

> The American Evangelical Church through its mission programs served to quiet the cry for Independence. Its focus on personal sin and salvation weakened the natural desire to overthrow the bonds of colonialism. The churches brought with them their schools, hospitals, and seminaries, which served to prepare and assimilate Puerto Ricans into the American culture.

> Because the Church at that time was insensitive to its prophetic role, it was unable to see and feel the cry against the injustices perpetuated upon the Puerto Rican people... The Church could have played a significant role in relation to Puerto Rico's Independence, yet it did not because it failed to understand the prophetic ministry of the Church. It had dichotomized the spiritual from the social-political.[69]

Although indigenous leadership quickly emerged in the mainline Puerto Rican Protestant churches, the polity and nature of denominational structures, economic poverty of the island and the prevalent paternalistic spirit all contributed at this time to structures of dependence within many denominations. This was the case particularly in the financial dependence on missionary departments on the mainland.

Traverzo Galarza, citing Benjamin Alicea's study, "Religion and Missions in Puerto Rico," notes by 1905 there was at least one Protestant church in most towns of Puerto Rico and that by 1949 about 300 churches had been established (including Pentecostals) throughout the Island.[70]

---

[69]Samuel Solivan, "Puerto Rico, A History of Struggle for Liberation" (paper delivered at the Symposium on the Self-determination of Puerto Rico, the Inter Church Center, New York City, March 26, 1981), p. 5.

[70]David Traverzo Galarza, "A New Dimension in Religious Education for the Hispanic Evangelical Church in New York City" (M.A. Thesis, New Brunswick Theological Seminary, New Brunswick, New Jersey, 1979), pp. 5-6; The 1949 date is most significant since it parallels the large-scale migration to mainline USA by Puerto Ricans during the post-war years of 1940's and early 1950's.

January 14, 1912 is set by many as the beginning of Hispanic Protestantism in the North East, more specifically New York. This date corresponds to the official organization of the first Spanish-speaking congregation - "La Primera Iglesia Evangélica Española" (later renamed, "Iglesia El Buen Vecino").[71] It is to the credit of the "para-church" (to use a modern idiom), the New York City Mission Society, that under its auspices this Hispanic work developed. As Frederick L. Whitam noted, "The Society has been a point of focus and a guiding hand throughout the history of Protestant work with Spanish-speaking persons."[72]

Following World War I, Hispanic congregations began to be established throughout New York City where the Hispanic "colonias" existed. Most of these churches operated under Spanish-speaking leadership and were identified with the many denominations that existed in Puerto Rico. By 1937 Whitman tells us that 55 Hispanic Protestant congregations were established in New York City. Of these, 6 were affiliated with the New York City Mission Society, 18 with Pentecostal groups, others represented were Baptist, Lutherans, Methodist, Adventist, Christian and Missionary Alliance, and Presbyterian churches.[73]

The "first airborne migration" from Puerto Rico during the post-war years of 1940's and 1950's brought thousands to New York City. By 1960 there were approximately 430 Protestant churches in New York City ministering to Hispanics.[74] It is important to note that it is about this time that Hispanic churches begin to extend beyond the original port of entry, New York City; and one can note church planting efforts in the neighboring states of New Jersey,

---

[71]There is a minor debate as to the formation in 1898 of the "Iglesia-Hispana-Americana" of Brooklyn, that ministered to mostly Cubans, as the first Hispanic church in the metropolitan New York area, see, David Traverzo Galarza, *Ibid.*, pp. 16-20; for further historical details on the founding of "Iglesia El Buen Vecino" by Hispanic Baptists see S. Soto Fontanez, *Mission At the Door (A History of Hispanic Baptist Work in New York)* (Santo Domingo, Republica Dominicana: Editora Educativa Dominicana, 1982), pp. 18-24.

[72]Frederick L. Whitam, "New York's Spanish Protestants," *Christian Century*, February 7, 1962, p. 162.

[73]*Ibid.*, p. 162.

[74]*Ibid.*, p. 162; Special note should be made at this time of two ecumenical Protestant ministries with Hispanics: (1) East Harlem Protestant Parish, founded 1948 and supported by six denominations (American Baptist, Evangelical United Brethren, Methodist, United Presbyterian, Reformed, and United Church); and (2) the Migrant Ministry of the National Council of Churches, a ministry originated by missionary-minded women in 1920 to meet the needs of Black migrants in New Jersey and which played a significant role in the 1960's with Cesar Chavez and the Farm Workers Movement; see, Kyle Haselden, *Death of a Myth: New Locus for Spanish American Faith* (New York: Friendship Press, 1964), pp. 112-118.

Connecticut, Pennsylvania, Rhode Island and Massachusetts in the late 1950's and early 1960's.[75]

It is significant that the Anglo mainline Protestant denominations once again exhibited the same characteristic traits that they showed in their contact with the Hispanics in the Southwest, namely, prejudice, discrimination and racism. This was expressed in inadequate planning or strategies to respond to this "Mission at the Door." The Protestant Council of the City of New York reached the following conclusions:

> ... few Protestant churches established in communities into which Puerto Ricans are moving have made an attempt to welcome the Protestant Puerto Ricans. Few churches have reached out to help the new comers in their adjustment process. Even fewer have attempted to evangelize the Puerto Ricans. There is no evidence of any strategy on the part of Protestantism...[76]

Federico Ribes Tovar, looking over the inadequate outreach in service and ministry to the Hispanic community by the Anglo Protestant churches, states: "... whether due to vision or because of more or less conscious prejudice, Protestantism failed on this occasion to live up to its mission."[77]

Presently this historical "insensitivity" and lack of vision and mission have been somewhat remedied, attested by the fact that most Anglo Protestant denominations have some ministry outreach among Hispanics and have some written strategy statements. Yet, David Traverzo Galarza's statement is pertinent not just for New York City but for the whole Northeast, and I would venture to say for many other parts of the nation:

------

[75]Adam Morales, *American Baptist with a Spanish Accent* (Valley Forge, PA: The Judson Press, 1964), p. 48.

[76]Protestant Council of the City of New York, Mid-Century Pioneers and Protestants: *A Study of the Protestant Expression Among Puerto Ricans of New York City* (New York: Department of Church Planning and Research of the Protestant Council, 1954), p. 14, quoted in David Traverzo Galarza, "A New Dimension in Religious Education for the Hispanic Evangelical Church in New York City," p. 12; for similar conclusions in ministry to Hispanics in the Southwest, see Edwin Sylvest, Jr., "Hispanic American Protestantism in the United States", in Moises Sandoval, ed. *Fronteras*, pp. 294-295.

[77]Federico Ribes Tovar, *Handbook of the Puerto Rican Community* (New York: Plus Ultra Educational Publishers, 1970), p. 120; see also Adam Morales, *American Baptist With a Spanish Accent*, p. 48.

Interestingly, the realization of the visibility and permanence of the Hispanic Evangelical community did not emerge until Hispanic indigenous movements and leaders began to establish their own churches in New York City. Thus, in comparison to the well-to-do established churches in the city, it was the economically disadvantaged indigenous church that attempted to minister to the needs and conditions of the Hispanic community in New York City. Presently, there are many Hispanic churches that are reaching out to the community by way of a number of programs and services...

If there is any growth and vitality within the Hispanic Evangelical church in New York City, it certainly is not due to the historical response of the mainline Protestant churches of the city. Rather it has been the emergence of a Hispanic clergy and church that has impacted the development of the Hispanic Evangelical church in this city. The initiative and follow-up has come from indigenous movements spurred under the guidance and power of the Holy Spirit.[78]

One must further note Orlando Costas' biting indictment in his essay, "Evangelizing an Awakening Giant: Hispanics in the U.S.," where he states that the Anglo churches and Christian organizations themselves have become obstacles to Hispanic evangelism and that they "often undermine struggling Hispanic congregations." I quote him at length:

... one of the key obstacles to Hispanic evangelism is the Anglo church itself. In the past, most Anglo churches and Christian organizations simply ignored the whole question of mission to Hispanics and concentrated instead on Latin America. More recently, many Anglo congregations and denominations in the inner city have been too preoccupied with their own survival to consider the needs of their Hispanic neighbors. Attempts at joint ministry to the Hispanic community have been frustrated by social tensions between North American and Hispanic congregations. Hispanic churches that might otherwise grow are often limited by a lack of funds and inadequate meeting space. Anglo congregations leaving the inner city often compound this problem by listing church properties on the open market, rather than negotiating with Hispanic

---

[78]David Traverzo Galarza, "A New Dimension in Religious Education for the Hispanic Evangelical Church in New York City," p. 14.

churches to ensure a continuity of Christian witness in urban
neighborhoods.

Thus, the majority of mainline and evangelical denominations not
only fail in direct support to Hispanic evangelism, but they also
often undermine struggling Hispanic congregations. The investment
of evangelical outreach ministries in the Hispanic community has
been so recent and so tentative as to be almost negligible.[79]

The "polity" and "nature" of mainline Protestant denominational structures
have historically proven to be "mixed" blessings to Hispanics. From an early spirit
of paternalism, structures of dependence were established that at first seemed to
respond to the needed personnel, finances and resources. Yet, the emerging
Hispanic leadership and its empowerment was often restrained by these well-
meaning gestures and "institutionalized giving." The resources offered were never
enough and the sharing in the decision-making process (i.e., power), affecting the
very life of the Hispanics, was often more rhetoric than substance.

In the Southwest the "representative" cases of Benigno Cárdenas, Ambrosio
González and Alejo Hernández and their Hispanic churches are historical "bench-
marks" that still speak loud and clear to paternalism and structures of dependence.
This was to be repeated in many similar ways in the Northeast, in this case with
the emerging Puerto Rican leadership. It was then, as it often is still prevalent
today, that:

> Institutional structures had come into being and capable persons had
> emerged as leaders, but no effort or thought seems to have been
> given to the possibility of enabling Mexican Americans to control
> policy making or administrative processes.[80]

The marginalization, paternalism and the oppression experienced by the
Hispanic Protestant churches and its community at the hands of "mainline
Protestants, conservative Fundamentalist and established Evangelicals" was
significantly highlighted at what has been historically labeled, "El Grito de
Riverside" - for all intents and purposes a still unmet cry!

---

[79]Orlando Costas, "Evangelizing An Awakening Giant: Hispanics in the U.S.," p. 63.

[80]Edwin Sylvest, "Hispanic American Protestantism in the United States," Moisés Sandoval, ed.,
Fronteras, p. 309; this struggle for leadership empowerment can be noted implicitly (not made
explicit, I suppose because of the kindness of the author) in the development of the Hispanic Baptist
churches in New York City; see J. Soto Fontanez, *Mission at the Door.*

In the cover letter I personally received, dated April 1, 1981, which included a list of five major complaints, by the Coalition of Hispanic Christian Leadership, it noted that:

> On March 13, 1981, at the Riverside Church Conference on the Church and the City, the Coalition of Hispanic Leadership disrupted a panel on "Liberation Theology" to protest the exclusion of Hispanics from the conference program. The chant of protest (Basta ya! No nos pueden ignorar!) echoed the sentiments of millions of Hispanics living in American urban centers whose cry is not being heard by the religious establishment.[81]

It is of historical significance that the "Riverside Manifesto" (the Coalition's name for their Complaints and Demands) against the "White Protestant Establishment" took place at the same altar that in 1969 James Forman and other Black leaders presented their "Black Manifesto." The Coalition was chaired by Rev. Benjamin Alicea, then of New Brunswick Theological Seminary and now with the Fund for Theological Education; other original members included: Rev. Alejandro La Fontaine and his wife, Ms. Edith La Fontaine, of the United Methodist Church; Rev. Ramon Rivera then with the Reformed Church of America and Rev. Samuel Solivan of the Reformed Church of America (now, of the Assemblies of God, Spanish Eastern district).[82]

The continued relevance of "El Grito de Riverside" is such that I cite it in full (see Figure 2-1):

---

[81]From photo-copy "cover letter" dated April 1, 1981 mailed personally to me by Benjamin Alicea, including "Riverside Manifesto."

[82]It is noteworthy that of the five original members listed in the "Riverside Manifesto" three were "Pentecostals;" its chairperson Rev. Benjamin Alicea is the grandson of Rev. Juan L. Lugo, the Pentecostal pioneer to Puerto Rico and New York City.

The Liberating Spirit

Figure 2-1

Riverside Manifesto

COMPLAINTS AND DEMANDS PRESENTED TO MAINLINE PROTESTANTS, CONSERVATIVE FUNDAMENTALISTS AND ESTABLISHMENT EVANGELICALS AT THE RIVERSIDE CHURCH CONFERENCE ON THE CITY, MARCH 13, 1981.

THE COALITION OF HISPANIC CHRISTIAN LEADERSHIP as a prophetic act of conscience charge the American religious establishment with the following complaints:

1. THE SOCIAL ISSUES RELEVANT TO THE HISPANIC COMMUNITY ARE NOT SERIOUSLY ADDRESSED in the conferences, radio and television programs funded and staffed by the Mainline Protestants, Conservative Fundamentalists and Establishment Evangelicals. Social issues of particular interest to Hispanics are: undocumented workers, U.S. foreign policy in Latin America, the impact of multinational corporations in Latin America, bi-lingual education in America and the adverse impact of Reagan's economic policy on Hispanics.

2. THE CONTRIBUTIONS OF HISPANIC PEOPLE IN THE LIFE AND MINISTRY OF THE CHURCH IN THE CITY ARE SYSTEMATICALLY AND CATEGORICALLY IGNORED. National and regional conferences (such as the Riverside Church Conference on the City, Washington '80 and the American Festival on Evangelism) exclude significant participation of indigenous Hispanics in the planning and implementation stages. The absence of Hispanic speakers in regional and national events deprive the Christian community of an Hispanic perspective.

3. THE AMERICAN RELIGIOUS ESTABLISHMENT MUST ASSUME ITS SHARE OF THE RESPONSIBILITY for (1) the decay of urban areas and the deplorable conditions under which Hispanics must live in American cities, and (2) the Church's policy to neglect, desert or undermine the resources of the Hispanic people. The only churches that have remained to service the spiritual needs of the Hispanic people residing in the inner cities of our country are the indigenous and independent Hispanic churches.

4. HISPANIC LITURGY AND THEOLOGY HAVE BEEN DENIED THEIR RIGHTFUL PLACE IN THE AMERICAN RELIGIOUS COMMUNITY. Our music, theology, literature and language have been rejected. The Church has served as an instrument of assimilation instead of human liberation and fulfillment. The Church has perpetuated paternalism, division and oppression which have aggravated and deprived the American religious establishment of the contributions of the Hispanic religious experience.

5. THEOLOGICAL SEMINARIES AND GRADUATE SCHOOLS OF RELIGION HAVE DISCRIMINATED AGAINST HISPANICS by refusing to hire indigenous Hispanic faculty, provide supportive services and allocate financial resources. The educational establishment has rejected the legitimacy of bi-lingual theological education as a viable and indispensable ingredient for men and women in the ministry. There has always been plenty of rhetoric, but very little action or financial and academic support.[83]

---

[83]Coalition of Hispanic Christian Leadership, "Complaints against Mainline Protestant, Conservative Fundamentalist, and Establishment Evangelicals," presented to the participants at the Conference on the City, Riverside Church, New York, N.Y., March 12-14, 1981 (personal photocopy); also listed in Orlando Costas, *Christ Outside the Gate: Mission Beyond Christendom*, pp. 115-116.

The early pioneering foundations set in their respective denominations by such Hispanic Protestant leaders as: Rev. Samuel F. Giordano, the Mexican-American Christian who organized and pastored the first Hispanic Protestant Church in New York City; José and Esperanza Toro Santiago, layleaders who founded the First Spanish Baptist Church; Rev. Hipólito Cotto Reyes; Rev. Santiago Soto Fontanez; Rev. Edicer N. Rodríguez; Ignacia y Manuel León, layleaders and founders of the first Hispanic Mennonite Church in North America; Rev. David Castillo, former Pentecostal preacher and later the first Hispanic pastor in the Hispanic Mennonite Church of North America; and other such leaders as Rev. Rogelio Archilla and Rev. Cecilio Arrastía, to name but a few, have produced an ever-growing and vibrant mainline Hispanic Protestant Church.

The growth and development of the mainline Hispanic Protestant Church has been significant, particularly after the 1890-1920 Mexican migration in the Southwest, the "airborne migration" of the 40's and 50's in the Northeast, the Cuban migration in the 1960's in Florida, and in the 1980's the "exodus" from Central America and the Dominican Republic. Although speaking for all Spanish-speaking churches, but no less true of mainline Hispanic Protestant churches, Orlando Costas states:

> Another favorable sign is the presence of vigorous Spanish-speaking
> churches in every major Hispanic neighborhood. These churches
> have generally gone unnoticed by mainstream Christianity, perhaps
> because many of them meet in storefronts or in other settings as
> unlikely as old theaters, former synagogues and temples, and
> assorted commercial buildings. Inside, however, one finds
> enthusiastic communities of faith, bearing vibrant witness for Jesus
> Christ and nurturing those who come to faith.[84]

Along with the pioneering efforts of the aforementioned, and others, who have served with distinction the early and late migration movements of Hispanics into the U.S.A., there has developed a cadre of Hispanic leaders whose conceptualization of the Gospel goes beyond Paternalism and structures of dependence to self-determination and "wholistic" Liberation. Among this latter rank in mainline Hispanic Protestantism are: Benjamin Alicea, Ruben Armendariz, Cecilio Arrastía, Jorge Lara-Braud, Edwardo Font, Manuel Ortiz, Robert Pazmiño, Edwin Sylvest, Jr., Justo L. González, Michael G. Rivas-Druck, Ismael García, and many others.

---

[84]Orlando Costas, "Evangelizing An Awakening Giant: Hispanics in the U.S.," p. 63.

The progressive thinking and challenges of these mainline Hispanic Protestants are making an impact, especially, the "new generation" Hispanics in seminaries and theological forums, with the fruits of their labor beginning to show in newer and renewed definitions of Hispanic service and ministry.

To date all major mainline Protestant denominations, and some smaller ones too (i.e., the Hispanic Mennonite Church of North America, with 50 congregations and about 2,000 members by 1982),[85] have planted churches among Hispanics. While, "further research needs to be done about Hispanic churches in the United States, since until now there is not enough statistical data...,"[86] there is sufficient data to document a steady and significant growth.

Nationally, among the mainline Hispanic Protestant Churches the Southern Baptist Convention is the largest. In 1960 they registered 559 churches[87] that by 1980 had increased to 1,400 churches.[88] The United Methodist numbered 221 churches[89] in 1980 and by June 1987 they had 300 churches;[90] American Baptist churches which had 106 churches[91] in 1960 and by 1982 increased to 195.[92] The Presbyterian Church in the U.S. registered 38 churches[93] in 1960 and by 1987 they had approximately 70 churches;[94] while the Lutheran Church - Missouri

---

[85]Rafael Falcon, *The Hispanic Mennonite Church of North America, 1932 - 1982*, (Scottdale, Pennsylvania: Herald Press, 1986), p. 71.

[86]Marco Espinoza, "Pastoral Care of Hispanic Families in the United States: Socio-cultural, Psychological, and Religious Concerns," pp. 187-188.

[87]Leo Gebler, Joan Moore and Ralph Guzman, *The Mexican-American People*, p. 488.

[88]John Maust, "The Exploding Hispanic Minority: A Field in our Back Yard," *Christianity Today* (August 1980), p. 14.

[89]Gebler, Moore and Guzman, *The Mexican-American People*, p. 488.

[90]This figure includes 68 churches in Puerto Rico; As per telephone conversation of June 22, 1987 with Rev. Eli Rivera, Executive Secretary for Ethnic Minority Local Church National program, General Board of Global Ministries, The United Methodist Church.

[91]Gebler, Moore and Guzman, *The Mexican-American People*, p. 488.

[92]Marco Espinoza, "Pastoral Care of Hispanic Families in the United States," p. 187.

[93]Gebler, Moore and Guzman, *The Mexican-American People*, p. 488.

[94]Estimate given by Dr. Jose Caraballo, Presbyterian Pastor in N.Y.C. and Professor at New York Theological Seminary, in personal telephone conversation, June 12, 1987.

Synod had 39 churches[95] in 1980. The Church of the Nazarene noted in 1980 a total of 89 churches,[96] while in the same year the Christian and Missionary Alliance had 73 congregations[97] nationally.

In a special study (prepared for this work by Rudy Mitchell of the Boston's Emmanuel Gospel Center's Research Department) to identify mainline Hispanic protestant churches in the Northeast, the following results were found (see Figure 2-2):

---

[95]John Maust, "The Exploding Hispanic Minority: A Field in our Back Yard," p. 14.

[96]*Ibid.*

[97]*Ibid.*, p. 39.

Figure 2:2

Hispanic Churches in the Northeast:
Enumeration of Mainline Congregations
(March 1987)

1)   Methodist Churches: approximately 60
      (United Methodist)   congregations - source: Multi-
                                      Ethnic Center for Ministry; (of
                                      these, 3 are in the S. New
                                      England Conference)

2)   American Baptist: 58 Hispanic churches
                                              7 ... Conn.
                                              6 ... Mass.
                                              1 ... R.I.
                                              2 ... N.H.
                                              6 ... PA.
                                             18 ... N.J.
                                             18 ... N.Y.

3)   United Presbyterian   35 Hispanic Churches
      (PCUSA):   Northeast; with 17 churches in
                                      N.Y.C.
                                      2 in New England
                                      (1 in R.I.; 1 in Hyde
                                      Park/Boston)

4)   Southern Baptist: Conn. - 6
                                      Mass. - 2

5)   Conservative Baptist: Mass.   ...1
                                      (CBA)(Cambridge)
                                      New York ...6-9 churches in
                                      NYC (cf. Ralph Kee)

6)   United Church of Christ: 9 Hispanic churches in the
                                      Northeast; a couple more are
                                      planned.

Types of Hispanic Protestant Church
Structures - Culture Liberation

It can be documented throughout the historical development of the Hispanic Protestant church that certain structures tend to create and/or perpetuate dependence rather than liberate and provide for self-determination; while it can also be documented that there exist structures that provide for cultural affirmation and liberation. It is not too difficult to locate the Hispanic Protestant churches within a multi-variable paradigm. I suggest that my construction of a typology - "Types of Hispanic Protestant Church Structures - Culture Liberation" - will prove fruitful.[98]

The basic comparison is between the Hispanic Protestant church's cultural liberation and self-determination vis-a-vis the dominant "parent" denominational structure in the USA. It can be further added that the construct can be interpreted to contrast the Hispanic community's cultural-religious liberation vis-a-vis the dominant Anglo culture-religious ethos. This typology seeks to reflect the existence of Christian unity within the reality of an Anglo dominant church and culture; one that provides for self-determination of a "minority church" and reflects authentic criteria of liberation for Hispanics.

While the basic or traditional church government polity structure might be useful (i.e., Episcopalian, Presbyterian, and Congregational), our construct cuts across such classification by suggesting certain specific criteria of liberation and self-determination.

We first need to explain in our paradigm the three variables that constitute its sorting criteria. They constitute the variables that differentiate the types of Hispanic Protestant church structures.

---

[98]Hispanic Protestantism is a complex phenomenon, in no way exhausted by my construct. It must be noted that as a type it represents an "Ideal type construction." Though a generalization, it nevertheless can yield important insights into the "cultural liberation" of the Hispanic church in the USA; we have decided to forego the utilization in this section of other typologies (i.e., Church-Sect) that will be used in our next chapter, "Socio-Theological Interpretation of the Hispanic Urban Pentecostal Reality." We must note further that the concept of "spiritual colonization" can be equally applied to the Hispanic Protestant churches one at a time. It is more suggestive and insightful when applied to just one denomination or church (i.e., Roman Catholicism, Presbyterians) than to the multiple denominations that are the focus of this section.

*Criteria: Variables of Cultural Liberation
and Self-determination*

I.   **Linguistic Affirmation and Culture Freedom** - The Spanish language, as explained in the section dealing with cultural heritage, is the critical self-referent tool of a particular *Weltanschauung* - so vital for Hispanic identity. For the "new generation," the children of the established immigrants, bilingualism is the order of the day. Culture freedom is understood as the freedom in utilizing and permitting the Hispanic cultural traits and values (see Chapter I "Hispanic American Reality," section on Culture Traits and Value Orientation) above to inform and transform liturgy, education, and ministry - the total life and mission of the church (i.e., worship style, hymnals, religious symbols, theology, literature and materials, programs, structures, emphases, etc.).

II. **Socio-Cultural Assimilation** - Reflects the degree to which church structures and life "pull" towards amalgamating with dominant Anglo culture. It is inversely correlated with class "aspiration/tendency" of major constituency served by churches. This is in keeping with the perception of many scholars that Protestantism is an acculturation agent for Hispanics.[99] Socio-cultural Assimilation is thus a negative variable.

III. **Leadership and Community Empowerment** - Leadership empowerment notes the degree of contextual leadership training and the Hispanic constituencies' input in selection of its leaders. Leadership (ministers) credentials are determined by Hispanic criteria and values. Hispanics have decicion-making powers at the local church level and at all levels relevant to the Hispanic community; as well as access to denominational structures. Community empowerment is interpreted to include the pursuit of an agenda or program for the socio-political liberation of the Hispanic community, as part and parcel of the "Good News of the Gospel of the Reign of God" vis-a-vis the dominant Anglo denominational/church agenda.

---

[99]See Lee Gibson, "Protestantism in Latin American Acculturation" (unpublished Ph.D. dissertation, University of Texas, 1959); and Fernando Peñalosa, "Class Consciousness and Social Mobility in a Mexican-American Community" (unpublished Ph.D. dissertation, University of Southern California, 1963).

Figure 2-3

Types of Hispanic Protestant Church Structures -
Culture Liberation

I. Linguistic Affirmation and Cultural Freedom

High   A. Independent Church   Low

C. Autonomous			
	D. Connectional- Autonomous		
	E. Connectional- Inclusive		
		F. Integrated- Autonomous	G. Integrated Inclusive

III. Leadership and Community Empower-ment

Low   B. Assimilated Church   High

II. Socio-cultural Assimilation

Types of Hispanic Protestant Church
Structures - Culture Liberation

A.   Independent Church - completely
B.   Assimilated Church - completely
C.   Autonomous
D.   Connectional - Autonomous
E.   Connectional - Inclusive
F.   Integrated - Autonomous
G.   Integrated - Inclusive

The above types are ones that emerge from the paradigm and are explained below. It must be remembered that these are "Ideal types" which can be "regarded as measuring points against which empirical religious organizations can be placed for comparison and contrast."[100]

The typology is specifically looking at the Hispanic "local church" in relationship to its parent denomination or "concilio," which is often, but not always, mediated by an Hispanic district or conference - a significant factor in the definition of the classification.

A.   **Independent Church** - This church structure falls outside our quadrant and by all variables or criteria is free to be completely indigenous to its ethnic minority status - in our case Hispanics. Churches can be placed here that "answer to no one but themselves." They are free to affirm their language and culture and by and large in the Hispanic Protestant community is a first generation church that is low in the socio-cultural assimilation scale. Leadership is autochthonous and the agenda for the health of their church and community is set by their own priorities. This church is not connected to any denomination, district or conference and whatever relationship it has to other churches is on a voluntary and fellowship basis. While it is free to be indigenous, it can suffer the fate of many "unconnected" churches - short lived, theological and missional parochialism, dogmaticism, and leadership demagoguery and manipulation - not to mention isolation, thus foregoing the needed solidarity to confront oppressive socio-cultural realities impacting Hispanics in the greater society. There is by definition no mainline Hispanic Protestant church to be placed in this category, except for the occasional independent Baptist church pioneered in our "barrios," that eventually

---

[100]J. Milton Yinger, *The Scientific Study of Religion* (New York: The Macmillan Company, 1970), p. 262; it should be further noted that it is a "historico-socio-ecclesiastical" approach that is dynamic and that often expresses differences as a matter of degree.

affiliates with a mainline denomination or is short lived. A case in point would be the history of the first Hispanic Protestant church in New York City ("Primera Iglesia Evangélica Española," later renamed, "Iglesia El Buen Vecino") not affiliated with any particular denomination at its founding, eventually coming under the aegis of the non-denominational New York City Mission Society and finally affiliating with the Presbyterian church. Hispanic Pentecostal churches abound in this category. Given the fluid calling and leadership self-authentication found in many Pentecostal churches, coupled with a particular conception of church and ministry, our "barrios" are literally dotted by independent indigenous Pentecostal churches. Illustrative of this in Boston is the "Iglesia Pentecostal Cristo El Rey," founded by Rev. Luis Aponte as an independent Pentecostal church that subsequently affiliated with the Hispanic Pentecostal "concilio" (denomination) "Asambleas de Iglesias Cristianas."

B.   **Assimilated Church** - This classification responds to the end of the continuum - from Independence to Assimilation - of our construct, thus at the bottom, outside the quadrant. Hispanic churches *cannot* be placed here, for by definition they would cease to be Hispanic. This is the complete amalgamation or assimilation classification. Historically many immigrant churches have ended here. I am not familiar with any Hispanic churches to date which can be so designated, although there are several churches that minister mostly to "new generation" Hispanics, where English is the dominant language (i.e., "Templo de la Cruz," pastored by Dr. Richard Tañon, Jr. in Hayward, California) and in which one hopes the cultural values of Hispanics are alive. "Love Gospel Assembly" in the Bronx, pastored by Rev. Jerry Kaufman, a converted Jew and married to a Puerto Rican, represents a congregation founded in an Hispanic church ("Iglesia Cristiana Juan 3:16") to minister to the English speaking, that drew "new generation" Hispanics, which were English dominant (many bilingual), and that by all indications is assimilated to the dominant ethos and culture. The assimilated church is thus an Anglo church.

C.   **Autonomous** - The Hispanic Protestant churches of this type are culturally affirming and self-determining. Structurally they represent indigenous churches that respond to their own "concilio" or denomination. As such they are free to affirm their linguistic and cultural heritage, which is quite obvious in their cultic/liturgical expressions; witness their guitars, "maracas" and many autochthonous "coritos," preaching and worship style. Theirs is a crescive leadership, trained in their nocturnal Bible institutes (though a significant number of the "new generation" youth are entering mainline Protestant theological seminaries); these institutes are contextual in form and substance. The churches of this type do not answer to nor are connected to any anglo denomination, except for voluntary fraternal fellowship. The churches in the indigenous Pentecostal "concilios" can be placed here: "Asambleas de Iglesia Cristiana," whose government polity is congregational; Damascus Christian Church, whose government polity is similar to Episcopalian (the church has Bishops); and the "Iglesia Universal Pentecostal," whose government polity tends towards Presbyterian. This last is historically the first and only Hispanic denomination or "concilio" founded in New England (church planter/founder Rev. Alfredo Pérez). These are just three representative Hispanic Pentecostal "concilios." As can be noted, of all types found inside the quadrant, type C is the lowest in socio-cultural assimilation, and highest in linguistic and culture freedom. They are also the highest in leadership empowerment and credentialing of ministers, and placement is within their authority. They are also free to seek their own peoples' agenda, without concern for other Anglo church/denomination standards/priorities/ ideologies. Churches of this type generally seek fellowship and solidarity, for common agenda issues or ministry, among other type C churches and type D (connectional-autonomous) Hispanic churches. Financially they are self-sufficient (they sink or swim by themselves), overcoming the paternalism usually attached to the financial "string." There is no mainline Hispanic Protestant church of this type in mainland U.S.A.

D.   **Connectional-Autonomous** - Churches that are connected to an Anglo denominational structure can be placed in type D if they exhibit to a great extent the autonomous characteristics found in type C churches. In other words, type D churches must answer to and must respond in the final analysis to a parent denomination in matters such as: government polity, administrative accountability, leadership (ministerial) credentialing, theological formulations and missional priorities, etc. They have, though, potential access to financial and other expertise and services of the parent denomination. It is in this type that we see a significant number of mainline Hispanic Protestant churches, as well as other Hispanic Pentecostal churches - "Asambleas de Dios," to name the largest. Examples of this type D church in the Boston area are: "Iglesia Bautista Central de Cambridge," connected to the Conservative Baptist Church; "Iglesia Bautista Hispano-Americana," connected to the American Baptist Church; and "La Iglesia el Buen Pastor," connected to the Assemblies of God. The distinction between type D (Connected-Autonomous) and type C (Autonomous) at first may seem minor, yet substantively we are dealing with a church (type D) that, particularly its leadership, must bear the weight (i.e., pressure, or power) of the Anglo parent denomination looking (when it chooses to do so) over its shoulders. Paternalism and structures of dependence tend to be fostered in this type D church, although type D churches are often buffered by Hispanic districts or conferences that provide a significant leverage in negotiating with parent denominations. Great freedom is found in some of these churches; in many cases are for all intents and purposes completely autonomous (i.e., "Iglesia Cristiana Juan 3:16 in the Bronx under Rev. Ricardo Tañon).

E.   **Connectional - Inclusive** - One step removed from type D are the type E churches, that are connected to an Anglo denominational structure but exhibit less self-determination in the life and mission of the church. They exhibit, as can be noted in the paradigm, less control of leadership/ ministerial empowerment and placement, understood in many cases as determined by conference superintendents (of course, in "council" with the local church concerned) and bishops. Many of the churches that exhibit an Episcopalian form of church government tend to fall here, given the enormous power outside the local church. While many churches are in districts or conferences that are Hispanic controlled, many are not, and thus the degree that distinguishes this type from type D. It is often the case that type E churches must pursue programs and agendas mandated from Anglo denominational headquarters that, when analyzed critically, do not provide for community empowerment, but for appeasement and dependence. The inclusive nomenclature is indicative of the centripetal thrust of the denominations which are trying to make all churches participants in their common good, but in the process tightens the strings of dependence, thus minimizing self-determination. Among the mainline Protestant churches many local churches of the United Methodist Church, can be placed here. There are several critical reasons to place in this type E the Pentecostal churches of the "Iglesia de Dios, Mission Board." The highly developed form of centralized government and control exerted by the parent denomination (Church of God) over finances, freedom of the Superintendent of districts and "modeling role"[101] is significant.

F.   **Integrated - Autonomous** - "Integrated" churches are the type that exhibit, at a particular junction of their history, a consistent and overriding thrust for amalgamation or assimilation of their ethnic constituency. It is a church that is *ambivalent* regarding the freedom it wishes to give to its ethnic minority (Hispanic constituency), believing the need to have but one church serving all. Historically and socio-politically, I suggest this is a misplaced emphasis and reification of one noble value-goal.

        Type F (Integrated-Autonomous) represents that historical stage of local Hispanic church bodies, that by and large meet in an Anglo church and have sufficient autonomy to have their own language (Spanish) service and leadership (though often not credentialed sufficiently to perform all ministries of the church). As can be noted in the paradigm, these local churches (oftentimes not even called churches - but departments or missions) are at the bottom of leadership and

---

[101]By "modeling role" I refer to that not too subtle influence on local churches to emulate the parent denomination's church liturgy, programs and agenda and in social ethical and "patriotic" issues and values. Type E, Connectional - Inclusive churches are prone to exhibit these characteristics.

community empowerment as defined in our criteria. They also have a pull towards social-cultural assimilation.

In an historical sense, many of the mainline Hispanic Protestant churches can be placed here as they began their ministry. A great number of them have moved on to type E and type D throughout the years. Yet, some denominations are presently either beginning their ministries with Hispanics or by nature of church structure and policy (not necessarily by explicit design) are locked into this type - type F, awaiting a full liberation!

This type resonates with the early experience of the Hispanic Presbyterian church in New England, particularly in Boston.

G. **Integrated - Inclusive** - Type G is that church one step removed from assimilation. As an integrated church exhibiting all the characteristics aforementioned in type F (Integrated - Autonomous), it further adds the "inclusive centripetal thrust" mentioned in type E (Connectional - Inclusive). Here there is no *ambivalence* regarding the status of ethnic or the Hispanic constituency vis-a-vis parent denomination or in many cases, districts, conference or sponsoring church. The Hispanics are to be integrated totally; while language and other cultural factors are to be accepted (i.e., tolerated), they (the parent denomination) has "read the future" and it is to be an *Anglo* one for all Hispanics. In this type G, there are a significant number of Hispanic congregations housed in Anglo churches whose (the Anglo church, that is) motivation and planning is often for one big Anglo church in the near future. In mainline Hispanic Protestant churches and in Pentecostal churches (i.e., "Assemblies of God") one finds local expression of the body of Christ of this type. It was not too long ago when many of the Hispanic local congregations in the Episcopal Church could have been placed here.

In concluding this segment one must underline the dynamic nature of this "historico-socio-ecclesiological" typology. In the history of a church body there are always possibilities of "moving" towards structures of dependence or of liberation. Further, it should be kept in mind as we utilize this "Typology of Hispanic Protestant Church Structure - Culture Liberation," J. Milton Yinger's admonition:

> It may be well to stress again that in describing types we are not creating a set of categories into which groups can readily be placed. Although we have selected a limited number of nouns and adjectives, and have drawn lines ... as if there were clear marking points, we are in fact dealing with matters of degree. Actual religious organizations seldom correspond precisely to the types we

are defining, but the type pictures should make comparison more
accurate.[102]

The Pentecostal Movement

The beginning of the 20th century heralded the arrival of the Pentecostal
Movement into the religious scene. Its rapid growth and worldwide scope - a true
modern missionary phenomenon[103] - has challenged both friend and foe to take
note of this "ragged" (and not so "ragged" in many places today) group of
"disinherited."[104]   The significance of the Pentecostal Movement as a new

---

[102]J. Milton Yinger, *The Scientific Study of Religion*, p. 271.

[103]See especially, Paul A. Pomerville, *The Third Force in Missions: A Pentecostal Contribution
to Contemporary Mission Theology* (Peabody, Mass: Hendrickson Publishers, 1985); Gary B.
McGee, *This Gospel Shall Be Preached: A History and Theology of Assemblies of God Foreign
Missions to 1959* (Springfield, Missouri: Gospel Publishing House, 1986); L. Grant McClung, Jr.
(ed.), *Azusa Street and Beyond: Pentecostal Missions and Church Growth in the Twentieth Century*
(South Plainfield, N.J.: Bridge Publishing, Inc. 1986); The phenomenal growth of Pentecostalism
is noted in *MARC Newsletter*, Number 91-1, March 1991, "Pentecostal and Charismatic Churches",
which I quote at length:

> The MOST SIGNIFICANT missiological fact of the last part of this century is the
> enormous   upsurge   of   the   Pentecostal/charismatic   movement.
> Pentecostal/charismatic churches worldwide:
>
> -   have 382 million members, or one of every five Christians;
> -   gain 19 million members each year; and
> -   donate $34 billion to Christian causes every year.
>
> People involed in this movement are, on average, more likely to be urban than
> rural; female than male; impoverished than affluent; family-oriented than
> individualistic; and younger than 18. Two of every three church members live
> in the Two-Thirds World.
>
> The movement includes over 11,000 Pentecostal denominations and more than
> 3,000 independent charismatic denominations.   Using 7,000 languages and
> spanning 8,000 ethno-linguistic cultures, the movement is a dominant force in
> world evangelization.

[104]See especially, Robert Mapes Anderson, *Vision of the Disinherited: The Making of American
Pentecostalism* (New York: Oxford University Press, 1979); see also, Walter J. Hollenweger, *The*

reformation, emerging alongside Roman Catholicism and mainline Protestantism as the third major type and branch of Christendom, has been called *"The Third Force."*[105]

What is not so well known, and not justly acknowledged by many, is that Pentecostalism as a *Movement* had its genesis at the "Azusa Street" (los Angeles, California) revival in 1906 under the leadership of a Black American minister, William J. Seymour. "Unheralded by those who are contemptuous of his race, William J. Seymour is nevertheless the 'father of modern-day Pentecostalism'."[106]

It must be noted early that when we speak of Pentecostalism we are dealing with a complex and multi-faceted religious movement. While in the minds of many it is usually and, narrowly in my opinion, defined just as a "tongues movement." It is much more than that. Kilian McDonnell's broader definition of Pentecostals, I think, is helpful: "Those Christians who stress the power and presence of the Holy Spirit and the Gifts of the Spirit directed toward the proclamation that Jesus Christ is Lord to the glory of God the Father."[107]

The important distinction thus between Pentecostals and other Christians "is the unique Pentecostal emphasis on the person, work, and gifts of the Spirit."[108]

Pentecostals: The Charismatic Movement in the Churches; John T. Nichols, *The Pentecostals*; Vinson Synan, *The Holiness - Pentecostal Movement in the United States* (Grand Rapids, Michigan: William B. Eerdmans Publishing Company, 1971).

[105]Henry P. Van Dusen, "The Third Force in Christendom," *Life* June 9, 1958, pp. 113-124; "The Third Force" concept is implicit in Bishop Lesslie Newbigin's positive evaluation and his classification of the ecclesiological contribution of the Pentecostal Movement alongside the Catholic and the Protestant understanding of the church, see Lesslie Newbigin, *The Household of God* (New York: Friendship Press, 1954).

[106]James S. Tinney, "Who Was William J. Seymour?" James S. Tinney and Stephen N. Short, eds., *In The Tradition of William J. Seymour* (Washington, D.C.: Spirit Press, 1978), p. 11; see also p. 19 footnote No. 1 for commentary relevant to the more than 26 Pentecostal church bodies that trace their charismatic experience and doctrine to Azusa.

[107]Quoted by Vinson Synan, "Pentecostalism: Varieties and Contributions" presented at the consultation on Confessing the Apostolic Faith from the Perspective of the Pentecostal Churches, Fuller Theological Seminary, Pasadena, CA., October 22-24, 1986, p. 2 (unpublished lecture).

[108]*Ibid.*, p. 2.

One must note further the major streams of Pentecostalism; here I am indebted to Vinson Synan's excellent classification and summary.[109]

1. **The Classical Pentecostal Movements** - These are the churches who trace their origins to the teachings of Charles F. Parham (Topeka, 1901) and William J. Seymour (Los Angeles, 1906). While there are differences in groups in this classification around the Godhead (i.e., Unitarian Pentecostals or "Jesus Only"), divine healing and sanctification, the common denominator is their acceptance of "glossolalia" (speaking in tongues) as the necessary initial physical evidence of "baptism in the Spirit."

2. **Mainline Protestant Charismatics (Neo-Pentecostals)** - This group represents the Charismatic Movement in mainline Protestantism beginning about 1960. The distinguishing factors from classical Pentecostals are: (a) not necessarily subscribing to "initial evidence" theory; (b) a more subdued form of worship; and (c) the higher socio-economic class and educational and theological training of participants. One should note the tremendous role played in the genesis of Neo-Pentecostalism and Catholic Charismatics by David Wilkerson's *The Cross and the Switchblade.*[110]

3. **The Catholic Charismatics** - 1967 marked the beginning of the Catholic Charismatic Renewal at DuQuesne University in Pittsburgh. It is important to cite Synan regarding the Catholic Charismatics:

    > Yet, beyond many similarities with both classical and Protestant Pentecostal movements, the Catholic Charismatic Renewal developed a unique style and structure which made it an indigenous Catholic movement with little of the theology and "cultural baggage" of protestant pentecostalism.[111]

4. **The Independent Groups** - This classification is a "fluid" one, centering on charismatic leaders (understood in a Weberian sense) who draw a significant following. They are independent churches not connected with the aforementioned historical expressions of this movement. In many cases

---

[109]*Ibid.*, pp. 2-5.

[110]David Wilkerson, *The Cross and the Switchblade* (Westwood, N.J.: Fleming H. Revell Company, 1963).

[111]Vinson Synan, "Pentecostalism: Varieties and Contributions," p. 3.

they represent, both here in the USA and abroad, the genesis of what may eventually become a denomination.

5.   **Third World Indigenous Groups** - The churches classified in this category are "the fastest-growing pentecostal movements in the world."[112] They are not connected with western mission boards, and some exercise unorthodox Pentecostal worship and theological forms. An example given by Synan is the Zionist Apostolic movement in South Africa which has over 3,000,000 members.

Socio-history

The Oppressed of the "spirit"
and
The "spirit" of the Oppressed

Given the rapid industrialization and urbanization at the turn of the century, coupled with alarming corruption and crime in the socio-political and economic world, it is no surprise to see the negative moral and spiritual impact experienced by American Protestantism at this time.[113] It is also to be noted that there was a strong sense of alienation from churches, especially among industrial workers.[114]   The socio-political, moral and spiritual climate then prevalent challenged many among the working class and poor to seek in their religious experience a "purifying" element. There was a sense of "escapism" and indeed a sense of "protest" in this quest.

Two particular religious movements had emerged and developed in response to the oppressed of the "spirit" - the Holiness camp (representing a Wesleyan theological perspective) and the Keswick camp (representing a Reformed theological perspective). The common denominator of both these influential and

---

[112]*Ibid.*, p. 4.

[113]See Aaron Ignatius Abell, *The Urban Impact on American Protestantism, 1865-1900* (Cambridge, Mass.: Harvard University Press, 1943); A.M. Schlesinger, *The Rise of the City, 1878-1898* (New York: Macmillan Company, 1933).

[114]Charles Howard Hopkins, *The Rise of the Social Gospel in American Protestantism, 1865-1915* (New Haven: Yale University Press, 1940).

antecedent streams of Pentecostalism were their acute sense of oppression of the "spirit."

American Protestantism seemed cold, formal and unresponsive to their social, economic, political, moral and spiritual needs. There was a real sense of "deprivation" and oppression at the hands of the "powers-that-be," be they economical, political or religious.[115]

The breakthrough of the Pentecostal revival at Topeka (1900-1901) and the Azusa Street revival (1906-1909) can be seen as millenarian and ecstatic responses to this "deprivation" and oppression of the "spirit" of the working class and poor. Anderson's statement is pertinent:

> Millenarianism proclaimed the existing world to be wicked and beyond redemption by any human efforts... Millenarianism also predicted the imminent destruction of this world and the creation of a new one. This answered perfectly to the psychological needs and aspirations of those whose social world was indeed collapsing and, from their standpoint, worthy of destruction... Pentecostalism was indeed an oblique expression of social protest.

> Ecstasy was combined with millenarianism in the Pentecostal movement. Since ecstasy and millenarianism have, more often than not, been combined in lower-class religious movements in societies undergoing severe crisis, it was Pentecostalism, ... which conformed to the norm. For the Pentecostals, the problems arising from a social milieu ... could only be resolved by a millenarianism of emotional power and ecstatic dimensions.[116]

Thus, the significant socio-reality in the genesis and development of Pentecostalism was its attraction and ministry among the "disinherited." It was among the socially marginalized, "ragged," disenfranchised, "ethnically

---

[115]See especially Robert Mapes Anderson's chapter, "The Sources and Functions of Pentecostalism" in his *Vision of the Disinherited*, pp. 223-240.

[116]*Ibid.*, pp. 229-230; See also, Sylvia L. Thrupp (ed.), *Millennial Dreams in Action: Studies in Revolutionary Religious Movements* (New York: Schocken Books, 1970). It must be noted that the above "psycho-social" causal explanations are necessary but not sufficient; In my next chapter, "Socio-theological Interpretation of the Hispanic Urban Pentecostal Reality," I will be looking at other factors in the genesis and development of Pentecostalism, especially Hispanic Pentecostalism (i.e., social anomie, Otto Maduro's conflict analysis, Gerlach and Hine's functional-structural analysis, etc.).

heterogenous, struggling working classes and impoverished unemployed that the Pentecostal movement drew its following in the urban area of the nation."[117] While it is true that as Pentecostalism has been institutionalized it has drawn recruits from higher levels of the class structure, it has nevertheless remained the "haven of the masses."[118]

The Hispanics shared the same aforementioned social milieu, although their social and economic condition was more oppressive, but for many the resolution in a religious response was the same.

Hispanics have been part and parcel of the Pentecostal Movement since its inception. The Azusa Street revival drew a significant number of Hispanics living in the Los Angeles area. Victor De León tells us that

> ... no one was surprised to see Mexicans around the Azusa street meeting even though the number was not large. Many of them were well-to-do ranchers and very devout Catholics. Nonetheless there were some who had recently arrived from Mexico, and by the turn of the century they found themselves displaced in an environment controlled by the Gringo culture and language.[119]

The names of Luis López and Juan Navarro are noted as early participants of the Azusa Street revival, thus among the first Hispanic Pentecostals. Juan Navarro was the first preacher.[120]

---

[117]Robert Mapes Anderson, *Vision of the Disinherited: The Making of American Pentecostalism*, p. 122.

[118]Robert M. Anderson underscores this constituency at the turn of the century in America, one that is still a relevant description of the Hispanic and Third World influx into the urban scene: "the working poor from whose ranks the Pentecostal movement drew the overwhelming bulk of its recruits...They were mostly semi-skilled and unskilled workers who made up the urban and rural proletariat of industrial capitalism. They constituted the lowest base of the work force of the nation, and also a free-floating labor reserve. As a class, they were brought into being by the movement of rural Americans to the city and by the influx of masses of immigrants during the period of transition from competitive to monopoly capitalism." *Ibid.*, p. 225.

[119]Victor De León, "Growth of Hispanic Pentecostals," *Paraclete* (A Journal Concerning the Person and Work of the Holy Spirit) 15 (Winter 1981): 18.

[120]*Ibid.*, pp. 18-19; Clifton L. Holland, *The Religious Dimension in Hispanic Los Angeles: A Protestant Case Study*, p. 356.

The Azusa Street revival resulted in a literal world dissemination of the Pentecostal message. In transit from California to the Orient a group of Pentecostal missionaries stopped on the Hawaiian island of Oahu. In 1912, already in the island there was a significant number of Puerto Rican immigrants working on a government experimental station.[121] It was there that the young Juan L. Lugo was converted and received the baptism in the Holy Spirit under the ministry of Francisco Ortiz, Sr. He thus began a long and fruitful ministry as the "Pentecostal Apostle to Puerto Rico," to which we need to add New York City and, in a small way, California.

In the Southwest and California, H.C. Ball and Alice Luce, among Anglo Pentecostal missionaries to Hispanics, manifested that quality of dedication and sacrificial ministry that was to have a deep and lasting impact in the Hispanic Pentecostal church. Among the giants of Hispanic Pentecostalism, a man whose influence was not limited to the Southwest and California, was "The Great Aztec" - Francisco Olazabal. De León reminds us that "Right along with H.C. Ball, Alice E. Luce, and Juan L. Lugo, Francisco Olazabal played an important role in the early beginning of Pentecostalism among Spanish-speaking people in the United States."[122]

By the use of the term, "'spirit' of the oppressed" we want to underscore or "read anew" from the Hispanic Pentecostal past those symbols of resistance, survival and hope. We recall the "subversive" and "liberating" memory of Hispanics as they were, fleshed-out in five representative persons: Francisco Olazabal, Juan L. Lugo, Leoncia Rosado Rousseau, Reis López Tijerina and Ricardo Tañon.

Francisco Olazabal's struggle with the Anglo Pentecostal officialdom of the Assemblies of God, of which he was a minister, is both instructive and significant. By the 1910's and 1920's, the Assemblies of God had a significant outreach to Hispanics in the Southwest. Henry C. Ball was the key Anglo missionary, who while deeply committed to the Hispanics, was also responsible and responsive to Anglo headquarters, the General Council of the Assemblies of God. In what De

---

[121]The Puerto Rican migration to Hawaii can be seen as part of that "escape valve" economic response by United States policy in Puerto Rico to deal with "supposed surplus population;" see Manuel Maldonado-Denis, *Puerto Rico: A Socio-Historic Interpretation.*

[122]Victor De León, *The Silent Pentecostals: A Biographical History of the Pentecostal Movement Among Hispanics in the Twentieth Century*, p. 23; see also, Juan L. Lugo, *Pentecostés en Puerto Rico: La Vida de un Misionero*; Roberto Domínguez, *Pioneros de Pentecostés: En el Mundo de Habla Hispana.*

León calls the "Pentecostal Revolution"[123] a serious "split" developed between H.C. Ball and Olazabal that resulted in Olazabal leaving the Assemblies of God (January 13, 1923), along with other ministers.

It appears that H.C. Ball received instruction from the Mission Department (under whose aegis the Hispanic work operated) not to organize into a separate Spanish-speaking district, but to wait another year. This development, at the Mexican convention of the Texas-New Mexico District held in Victoria, Texas in 1922, alarmed many who expected the formation of their own Spanish-speaking district.

It is believed by many that Olazabal's election as Superintendent was a sure thing. De Leon's assessment of the situation is as follows:

> ... many thought it was a personal problem with Ball, that he was actually afraid that Francisco Olazabal would be elected superintendent if they would organize as a district. This was not true; Henry C. Ball never thought such a thing! Rumors had quickly spread that the Anglos (gringos) did not trust a Mexican in the position of leadership in spite of the fact that Francisco Olazabal was better educated than Henry C. Ball and had better ministerial training than Ball at that time. This same feeling remained for many years, even with some of the ministers that did not leave.[124]

Francisco Olazabal founded in 1923 the Latin American Council of Christian Churches. His ministry flourished as he left the Assemblies of God. In the opinion of Roberto Dominguez and many others, his evangelistic revivals in the summer of 1931 in New York City (when there were but few Spanish-speaking congregations) was the equivalent for Hispanic Pentecostal church growth in the Northeast to the "Azusa Street" revival of 1906. Ironically it was also in a Black church that he began his campaign in New York City. By the time of his early death in 1937 (he was only 50 years old), the Latin American Council of Christian Churches, which he founded and presided over, had established 150 churches throughout the United States, Mexico and Puerto Rico.[125]

The loss to the Assemblies of God of Olazabal and many others that followed him is significant. Notwithstanding how one reads the situation, at

---

[123]Victor De León, *The Silent Pentecostals*, p. 29.

[124]*Ibid.*, p. 100.

[125]Roberto Domínguez, *Pioneros de Pentecostés*, pp. 22-23.

bottom, Olazabal's stated reason for leaving - "because the 'gringos' had control"[126] -is still relevant wherever the "spirit" for self-determination and liberation of the oppressed lives.

Juan L. Lugo, then an ordained minister of the Assemblies of God, reached the Island of Puerto Rico August 30, 1916. A few months later Lugo made his way from San Juan to the southern city of Ponce. With the support of Salomon and Dionicia Feliciano, who were to be the pioneers of Pentecostalism in the Dominican Republic, they began their Pentecostal service on a street corner in Ponce ("Calles Acueducto e Intendente Ramírez de la Cantera," near the "Plaza del Mercado"). It is in Ponce where Puerto Rican Pentecostalism has its roots, beginning November 3, 1916.[127]

Lugo notes in the section of his book "Empieza la Persecucion" (the Persecution Begins) the opposition received at the hands of both civic and ecclesiastical bodies. With great tenacity he labored under the most hostile circumstances - persecutions by Catholics and Protestants alike. The "new" Pentecostal message and worship service scandalized the "southern" and "sophisticated" Ponce ecclesiastical hierarchy. While persecution from the Catholics was to be expected, Lugo was taken aback by the response of the Protestant church. The existing "comity agreement," the turf carving in Puerto Rico by mainline Protestantism, aggravated this situation.

Lugo tells of a meeting that the Felicianos and he attended. It was called by the Protestant ministers of Ponce who were disturbed by Lugo and the Pentecostals. He was informed that they were not helping the evangelical work in Ponce with their work and that it was bringing about confusion. Lugo notes that in their attempt to persuade him to leave, they reminded him that he lacked adequate training and financial support to produce an enduring work. He was accused of "poniendo el evangelio en un nivel demasiado de humilde..."[128] They went so far as to offer financial help for the Felicianos to continue on their trip to the Dominican Republic and even offered Lugo a pastorate at another church in the Island, on the condition that he preach "el evangelio 'evangélico'."[129]

---

[126]Victor De León, *The Silent Pentecostals*, p. 99; Olazabal's "spirit" was indeed ahead of his time and time still remembers this man, "considered by many who knew him and his ministry as the greatest Latin American Pentecostal evangelist the Spanish-speaking church has produced," *Ibid.*, p. 28.

[127]Juan L. Lugo, *Pentecostés en Puerto Rico*, p. 40.

[128]"Placing the gospel at a too humble (low) a level;" here one begins to see the class factor coming into play, for the appeal of Pentecostalism was among the poorest of the poor.

[129]"the evangelical 'gospel'."

Needless to say, Lugo and the early Pentecostals of Ponce continued to preach an "evangelio completo" (a full gospel). From that beachhead in Ponce the Pentecostal message and experience was to overtake all of Puerto Rico, although much misunderstanding and suffering followed their every step. By the year 1930, a year before Juan L. Lugo began his Pentecostal work in New York City, there were forty-nine Pentecostal preaching points in Puerto Rico, most of them organized into churches.[130]

Among the early pioneers in Puerto Rico, the following names are also noteworthy: Francisco Ortiz, father and son; Lorenzo Lucena; Frank O. Finkenbinder (father of Paul, known as "El Hermano Pablo" throughout Latin America); John Roberts, and Felix Rivera Cardona, to name but a few.

Hispanic Pentecostalism in the Northeast dates to the late 1920's and early 1930's. Like many of the other Protestant church beginnings in the Northeast, it was the result of immigrants coming from Puerto Rico to New York City.

In 1928 Thomas Alvarez was sent by Juan L. Lugo from Puerto Rico to organize and pastor one of the first Pentecostal churches in New York City - "La Iglesia Misionera Pentecostal," in Brooklyn. It is to this church that Lugo in 1931 came to pastor and to begin church planting among Puerto Ricans.

1931 was a momentous year for Hispanic Pentecostalism in the Northeast. Not only did the "Pentecostal Apostle to Puerto Rico" come to New York City but, as noted before, the summer of 1931 was to see the Hispanic Northeast's "Azusa Street" Pentecostal revival under the anointed preaching of Francisco Olazabal. This was at a time that according to Roberto Domínguez there existed only "un par the iglesias pequeñas establecidas, de las llamadas del Evangelio Completo."[131]

The impact of Olazabal and the pioneering efforts of Lugo and others resulted in a new spirit of evangelism and church planting that by 1937, out of a total of 55 Hispanic Protestant congregations in New York City, 25 were Pentecostals.[132]

---

[130]Luis Otero, *El Evangelista Pentecostal*, VIII (February, 1930), p. 4, cited in José A. Caraballo, "A Certificate Program for Hispanic Clergy and Lay Persons in an Accredited Theological Seminary: A Case Study with Projections," p. 42.

[131]"a few (literally a pair) small established churches, of the so-called Full Gospel.", Roberto Domínguez, *Pioneros de Pentecostés*, p. 22.

[132]Frederick L. Whitman, "New York's Spanish protestants," *Christian Century*, February 7, 1962, p. 162, 163.

Juan L. Lugo confronted in the city an increasing structural racism that was being put in place by the powers-that-be against the also increasing numbers of Puerto Ricans coming from the Island. Notwithstanding the limited resources at hand, and the Anglo Protestant church's lack of response to the new immigrants, he nevertheless struggled and succeeded to build an indigenous base of support and leadership.

Juan L. Lugo's pastorate of "La Sinagoga" Church in Harlem "... served as a center for the development of the Pentecostal movement in the city. It was there that the first Bible School was started in the year 1935, and missionaries were sent to different Spanish countries including Cuba and the Dominican Republic."[133]

Among the early Pentecostal leadership in the Northeast, besides Lugo and Olazabal, were Thomas Alvarez, Antonio Caquías, Edmundo and Manuel Jordan, Frank Finkenbinder, Eleuterio Paz, Manuel T. Sánchez, Meliton Donato, Felipe Sabater, Francisco Hernández, Carlos Sepúlveda, Leoncia y Francisco Rosado, to name a few.

The name of Juan L. Lugo would eventually be associated with the pioneering and/or development of several Hispanic Pentecostal denominations, both in Puerto Rico and in mainland USA. Among these "concilios" are "La Iglesia de Dios Pentecostal;" "Las Asambleas de Dios;" "Las Asambleas de Iglesias Cristianas; "and "La Iglesia de Dios Pentecostal, Mission Board."

The spirit of Juan L. Lugo speaks to us of total commitment and sacrificial service in church planting. He met head-on every opposition whether by other Hispanics of different religious persuasion or of Anglo racism and insensitivity in the cold metropolis.

"Mama Leo," is what all the hundreds of ex-addicts, prostitutes, alcoholics and street people call Rev. Leoncia Rosado. These are the social "outcasts" no one cared for, sad to say, even the church. But "Mama Leo" was called, along with her husband, Rev. Francisco Rosado, to minister God's grace to these so-called outcasts. She cared. They both cared enough to begin in 1957 the "Damascus Youth Crusade," while they were pastoring "La Iglesia Cristiana Damasco" in the Bronx. The "Damascus Youth Crusade" was to become the "seedbed," leader and inspiration for hundreds of Christian Drug Programs throughout the United States, Puerto Rico and Latin America.

---

[133]José Caraballo, "A Certificate Program for Hispanic Clergy and Lay Persons in an Accredited Theological Seminary: A Case Study with Projections," p. 63.

"Mama Leo" was born April 11, 1912 in Puerto Rico. She was converted and baptized in the Spirit in 1932 during the religious revival sweeping the Disciples of Christ Church in the Island. It wasn't long before, under the watchful eyes of her pastor, Rev. Vicente Ortiz, that she responded to the Lord's calling to preach the Gospel. As a woman, she had to battle sexism early on in her ministry. As she said, "Nosotras las mujeres nos trataban como soldado de 3ra clase."[134] With the support and encouragement of such leaders as Herminio Narvaez, Leonardo Castro, and Juan Rosa Alvarez, who noted the spiritual gifts of this extraordinary woman, she traveled all over the Island preaching and ministering the Word.

In September 22, 1935 she came to New York City as an Evangelist-Missionary working with Rev. Francisco Hernández, pastor of "la Iglesia Cristiana Del Valle" in the Bronx. As noted by Roberto Domínguez in *Pioneros de Pentecostés*, she was among the early Pentecostal leaders in the Northeast who were associated with Francisco Olazabal and the Latin American Council of Christian Churches.[135] With the death of Olazabal in 1937 there came about a split within the Latin American Council of Christian Churches. Several "concilios" emerged out of the split. Mama Leo and her husband, along with other early Pentecostal leaders, were instrumental in founding the "Iglesia Cristiana Damascus," "concilio". Her husband, Rev. Rosado, eventually became its bishop years later.

Mama Leo's conception of the Gospel always included a social dimension. She speaks of her concern for social work, community involvement and helping the needy - "the outcasts," as she calls them. Her vision to work with the addicts in 1957, when no one cared, was to be realized in the "Damascus Youth Crusade."

John Gimenez, ex-addict and alumnus of "Damascus," who now pastors the large and influential "Rock Church" in Virginia Beach, Virginia, states:

> But all of us - directly or indirectly -trace our "delivery" to that
> little Spanish church at 861 East 162nd street. It was God's house
> all right. He was there. You go inside Damasco, and boy!
> something happens to you! It's like the excitement and the gripping
> power of a new love affair ... In the little parlor you see Mom
> Rosado sitting with the Bible in her lap and she's got two or three

---

[134]"We women were treated as 3rd class soldiers," Personal interview, via telephone conversation on July 19, 1987; much of the data that follows was confirmed by my conversation with "Mama Leo."

[135]Roberto Domínguez, *Pioneros de Pentecostés*, p. 22.

boys sitting around, listening to her explain the message of God...
And people come in - broken people, rotten people, no goods,
unwanteds. The misfits of society walk through those open doors
to new life ... Damasco was like the center of a new life for
addicts, and out from the temple there stretched life lines into the
gutters of the great city of New York, and then further out into the
towns and cities across America.[136]

Many of the "graduates" of Damascus Youth Crusade have gone on to
develop outstanding drug programs and outreach ministries. Evangelists,
missionary workers, and pastors are among the alumni of Damascus, nurtured
under the loving and dedicated ministry of Rev. Francisco Rosado and "Mama
Leo."

Among these are Rev. Jerry Kauffman, ex-addict Jew married to a Puerto
Rican and pastoring one of the largest Pentecostal churches in the Northeast, "Love
Gospel Assembly;" Rev. John Gimenez of Rock Church, Virginia Beach, Virginia;
Rev. and Mrs. Eddie and Ana Villafañe, founders and directors of "Way-Out
Ministries" in South Bronx, presently the largest Christian Drug Outreach Program
in the State of New York; Rev. William Cintrón, founder of "Silo" in Puerto Rico,
a Drug Outreach program; Rev. Leroy Ricksy (Black-American) pastor and psycho-
therapist; Rev. Joe Gagos Jr., psycho-therapist; Rev. Pedro Juan Falu, a Senior
Chaplain, in the Correction Department of the State of New York; Rev. Cedric
Rousseau, evangelist, who later was to become the second husband of "Mama
Leo."

It would be amiss not to note a gift for which "Mama Leo" has been known
for 54 years - besides other ministerial gifts noted previously or alluded to - her
preaching! She is considered by many one of the outstanding Pentecostal
preachers - men or women!

"Mama Leo" and "Papa Rosado" speak to us of costly discipleship - so
much so, that Rev. Francisco Rosado was struck with a heart attack while
ministering to an addict that resulted in his death several months after. Mama Leo
still speaks to us of commitment to the outcasts, to the poor and oppressed in our
inner cities.

Reis López Tijerina, who is still considered a Pentecostal minister,
represents that militant factor in the Hispanic community that during the 1960's
emerged as the Movimiento (movement). What surprises many is not that he is

---

[136]John Gimenez, *Up Tight!* (Waco, Texas: World Books, 1967), pp. 72-73.

a minister, but that he is a *Pentecostal* minister. Tijerina, a former Bible Institute student and evangelist, chose to exert his ministry for social justice, specifically around the issue of land.

"La Alianza Federal de Pueblos Libres," presided over by Tijerina, had in its possession land grants giving them rights as owner of large sections of the Santa Fe National Forest and other valuable land in the Southwest. This land after the 1848 Treaty of Guadalupe-Hidalgo was skillfully and manipulatively extorted by the "gringos."

Tijerina, who models himself after the "Prophets" of the Old Testament, with his supporters, occupied the Kit Carson National Forest in New Mexico to publicize and seek solidarity among other Hispanics for the land claims of the "Alianza," in 1966. The next year Tijerina led a sensational raid on the courthouse of Tierra Amarilla. This led the lieutenant governor of New Mexico to call out the National Guard and the State Police - with tanks and helicopters, an action that "grasped the imagination of a new generation of younger Hispanics."[137]

As noted by Andrés Guerrero, "for Tijerina, the struggle for land is not only a political quest; it is also a spiritual mission of justice against the oppression of Chicanos in the Southwest by the United States government."[138]

Reis López Tijerina, a controversial person - many Pentecostals do not claim him - nevertheless represents that "spirit" of the oppressed among Hispanic Pentecostals that sees the Gospel's concern for social justice and wholistic liberation.

Rev. Ricardo Tañon - Pentecostal Pastor "Extraordinarie." To all familiar with the Hispanic Pentecostal movement the names of Ricardo Tañon and the "Iglesia Cristiana Juan 3:16" conjure the image of a "Citadel in the City." The man and the church have been truly a "fortress" - a stronghold of Hispanic Pentecostalism in the Northeast.

During the 34 year pastorate of Rev. Tañon at "Juan 3:16", 17 new churches were planted throughout the Northeast, Puerto Rico and the Dominican Republic; 54 ministers nurtured at "Juan 3:16" and sent out all over the Spanish-speaking world; hundreds trained at the Bible Institutes; one year alone 12 full-time Bible School students were sent and fully supported by the church. The church

---

[137]Joan Moore and Harry Pachon, *Hispanics in the United States*, p. 181; see also, Peter Nabokov, *Tijerina and the Courthouse Raid* (Berkeley, Calif.: Ramparts Press, 1970).

[138]Andrés Guerrero, *A Chicano Theology*, pp. 36-37.

grew and developed a Sunday School with an average attendance of over 1,500 (with a staff of 120); over 1,000 attending every Sunday night worship service, and at baptismal and evangelistic services 2,000 would "jam" the church. At one time it had the largest Hispanic Christian Bookstore in the Northeast, whose profit at one point helped support 20 missionaries in foreign fields; a church library for its members and a print shop (which also produced thousands of Gospel tracts a year for distribution). It had several evangelistic teams and prison ministry teams, several standing Benevolent Programs, and provided the inspiration and leadership for a social service agency in the church's premises serving the church and community at large. At his official retirement on June 28, 1977, the "Iglesia Cristiana Juan 3:16" was the largest Hispanic church in the U.S.A.[139]

"Juan 3:16" was a church that because of its location, in one of the most blighted areas in the South Bronx, became an Evangelistic Center. Thousands upon thousands were converted and baptized at the old "Empire Theater" (former movie house), the site of "Juan 3:16." Because of the volatile complexity of the Hispanic "barrios," its constituency ever changing and unable to set rootage in the community, many members would stay for a short time. Because of this "turn-over" pattern, "Juan 3:16" had literally thousands of persons scattered among the hundreds of churches across the Northeast. It became a beachhead - evangelizing, maturing, equipping, and sending out Christians to other churches.

Rev. Tañon was born in Comerio, Puerto Rico on January 10, 1904. He came to New York City in 1929 and was converted in a street service in Harlem in 1934, under the preaching of the Mexican pastor, Rev. Eleuterio Paz. With the untiring support of his wife Filomena, he responded to God's call to ministry. He served as an assistant pastor for several years and then in 1943 accepted the pastorate of a "store front" mission with 12 members - "Iglesia Cristiana Juan 3:16." The struggles and triumphs of Rev. Tañon in developing this "store front" church in the Bronx amidst poverty, prejudice, institutional racism, and Anglo Protestant apathy is documented well in his biography.[140]

---

[139]See Rev. Ricardo Tañon's biography, Ramón Sánchez, *Ricardo Tañon: "El Poder y la Gloria de Dios"* (San Juan, Puerto Rico: Romualdo Real, 1980); my knowledge of Rev. Ricardo Tañon and "Iglesia Cristiana Juan 3:16" is somewhat "colored" by the fact that I consider Rev. Tañon my spiritual father and mentor. I also served "Juan 3:16" in various leadership roles since 1961, including Minister of Education, 1970-1973.

[140]It is noteworthy that it was at a Black minority-owned bank, Carver Federal Savings and Loans of Harlem that Rev. Tañon was able to get the needed loans for purchasing of church site. Rev. Tañon and Rev. Pedro Rios, his co-pastor, early in their ministry attended Black churches frequently and apparently had good contacts in the Black community. The words of solidarity by the Black president of Carver Federal are telling: "I know the predicament that you are in. I also know the value of your organization to the community and we who are in front of this banking

The achievement of this man of God is remarkable when one considers not only the hostile context of his ministry, but the fact that his formal education was limited to the fourth grade in Puerto Rico. He later was to attend the Spanish-American Bible Institute in New York City, graduating in 1938; and was to receive the Doctor of Divinity degree, *honoris causa* from Gordon-Conwell Theological Seminary on May 28, 1977.

Rev. Tañon never forgot his roots among the poor and disinherited. While other pastors and churches sought "greener" pastures, he stood firm. On many occasions as the church grew in numbers and economic resources, many wanted to move out of the "ghetto" - only to be reminded and challenged by Rev. Tañon that there in the dirty and dark streets of Prospect and Westchester Avenues in the Bronx God wanted them to shine like a lighthouse to offer a beacon to the shipwrecked.

Through Rev. Ricardo Tañon's aggressive and sacrificial leadership model many were inspired to enter the ministry. "Iglesia Cristiana Juan 3:16" became a true "liberation Citadel" under his anointed preaching and pastoring. With Rev. Pedro Rios, his co-pastor for 26 years at his side, he saw thousands upon thousands of lives transformed - finding faith, hope and love.

Francisco Olazabal, Juan L. Lugo, "Mama Leo" (Leoncia Rosado), Reis López Tijerina, and Ricardo Tañon are representative Hispanic Pentecostal leaders whose lives and ministry speak of that "spirit" of the oppressed that is willing to struggle against all odds for the liberation of their people.

The Hispanic Pentecostal Church has grown phenomenally through the years. As noted previously, in 1937 there were about 25 Hispanic Pentecostal churches in New York City. Sixteen years later (1953), according to Renato Poblete, out of 204 non-Catholic Spanish-speaking churches in New York City, seventy percent (approximately 143) could be classified as Pentecostals.[141] By 1960, according to Frederick L. Whitman, there were 240 churches.[142] This growth was also in keeping with the "airborne migration" of the late 1940's and

---

institution are interested in the welfare of the poor and abandoned communities by the large banks;" *Ibid.*, pp. 190-191.

[141]Renato Poblete and Thomas F. O'Dea "Anomie and the 'Quest for Community': The Formation of Sects Among the Puerto Ricans of New York," *American Catholic Sociological Review*, 21: 18-36, Spring 1960.

[142]Frederick L. Whitman, "New York Spanish Protestants," *The Christian Century*, p. 163.

1950's. By 1983, according to José Caraballo, in New York City alone there were 560 Hispanic Pentecostal congregations.[143]

David Traverzo Galarza notes:

Today in the city of New York it is considered to be quite rare indeed to enter virtually *any* Hispanic neighborhood without encountering at least two or three Pentecostal churches. Such growth is in deep contradiction to some sources that wish to undermine the positive widespread impact that this movement has within the Hispanic community.[144]

Whitman identifies the six major Hispanic Pentecostal churches (denominations or "concilios") in New York City, that to date from all data available, are also the six major Hispanic Pentecostal churches for the Northeast:

- The Spanish Eastern District of the Assemblies of God
- The Latin American Council of the Pentecostal Church of God
- The Assembly of Christian Churches
- The Church of God, Spanish District Council for the East
- The Damascus Christian Church
- The Defenders of the Faith[145]

Caraballo, besides noting Whitman's first five, lists an additional fifteen Hispanic Pentecostal churches in New York City. These are "concilios" and do not include the hundreds of "Independent" indigenous local churches not affiliated with any "concilio":

- Iglesia Pentecostal de Jesucristo
- Iglesia Pentecostal de Jesucristo Internacional
- Asamblea Pentecostal de Jesucristo

---

[143]José Caraballo, "A Certificate Program for Hispanic Clergy and Lay Leaders In An Accredited Theological Seminary: A Case Study with Projections," (Unpublished D.Min. professional project, Drew University, Madison, New Jersey, 1983), p. 66.

[144]David Traverzo Galarza, "A New Dimension in Religious Education for Hispanic Evangelical Church in New York City," pp.10-11; Traverzo Galarza statement is *contra* Joseph P. Fitzpatrick, whom he quotes, "In view of the total New York population of Puerto Ricans, the Pentecostal basis for community appears to be limited and of short duration," *Puerto Rican Americans: The Meaning of Migration to the Mainland*, p. 129 in *Ibid.*, p. 40.

[145]Frederick L. Whitman, "The New York Spanish Protestants," *The Christian Century*, p. 163.

- Iglesia Cristiana Rehoboth
- Federación de Iglesias y Ministros Pentecostales
- Asambleas de Iglesias Pentecostales el Libano
- La Iglesia de Dios
- Iglesia de Dios de la Profecía
- Asambleas de Iglesias Cristianas Unidas
- Iglesias Pentecostales Gethsemaní
- Movimiento Misionero Mundial
- Iglesia Pentecostal Jardín de Oración
- Iglesia de Dios Pentecostal Movimiento Internacional
- Hermanos Unidos en Cristo
- Iglesias Pentecostal Samaria[146]

In Boston and New England area my personal research has identified, in addition to most of the above, the presence of the following "concilios":

- Iglesia Universal Pentecostal
- Iglesia de Cristo Misionera
- Iglesia Evangélica Samaria
- Iglesia El Buen Samaritano
- Iglesia Cristiana Pentecostal

The number of churches comprising these "concilios" vary. In New York City alone the following statistics are found:

1)	The Spanish Eastern District of the Assemblies of God	-137 churches
2)	The Latin American Council of the Pentecostal Church of God	- 91 churches
3)	The Assembly of Christian Churches	- 67 churches
4)	The Church of God, Spanish District Council for the East	- 78 churches
5)	The Damascus Christian Church	- 35 churches[147]

In Boston in 1988 there were a total of 37 Hispanic Protestant churches; of these 27 were Pentecostals, almost all affiliated with a "concilio."

---

[146]José Caraballo, "A Certificate Program ...," pp. 66-67.

[147]José Caraballo, "A Certificate Program ...," pp. 67-73.

In the Northeast as well as the mainland U.S.A., the largest Hispanic Pentecostal church is the Assemblies of God. There are 1,010 Assemblies of God Hispanic churches in mainland U.S.A.; counting Puerto Rico, the total is 1,189.[148] From 1980 to 1986 the churches increased "a whopping 33.3 percent ... and just as quickly as Hispanics are starting churches, they are training ministers ... during the 1980's the number of Hispanic ministers has increased 20.5 percent to 2,732."[149]

While there are no comprehensive data available tabulating the total numbers of Hispanic Pentecostal churches in the U.S.A., all concede that they are the largest and fastest growing Hispanic churches - a testimony to their aggressive evangelism and sacrificial church planting efforts.

Through the years many outstanding leaders have emerged in Hispanic Pentecostalism, in addition to those previously mentioned one can note the following: Demetrio Bazán, José Girón, Adolfo Carrión, José Caraballo, Aimee García Cortese, Julie Ramírez, Abelardo Berrios, Pablo Figueroa, Luciano Padilla Jr., to name but a few. There is also a cadre of progressive thinking Hispanic Pentecostals that should be noted also. They have contributed and will contribute significantly to the future development of Hispanic Pentecostalism: Jesse Miranda, Esdras Betancourt, Daniel De León, Isaac Canales, Efraín Agosto, Kittim Silva, Samuel Solivan and Pablo Polischuk, to name a few.

Social Role of the Hispanic
Protestant Church

The Hispanic Protestant church is a church of an oppressed ethnic minority, one that lives and works under a dominant church and society. Yet, it is a church that in its most active and socially significant expressions plays for Hispanics, and models for society at-large, the significant roles of: (1) Survival, (2) Signpost, (3) Salvation, (4) Shalom, (5) Secrets of the Reign, (6) Seedbed, and (7) Social Service Provider.

The first four aforementioned "S's" are my alliteration and categorization of Orlando Costas' presentation of the social roles and ethical responses of minority Protestant churches in American society, which I am at present focusing

---

[148]"Hispanics In the Assemblies of God Outpace General U.S. Spanish Population in Rapid Growth," *The Pentecostal Evangel*, 19 July 1987, pp. 14-15.

[149]*Ibid.*, p. 14.

on Hispanics.[150] The final three, "Secrets of the Reign," "Seedbed," and "Social Service Provider" are my additions, expanding on Costas' contribution.

Survival ("A Place of Cultural Survival"):

Costas reminds us that "the minority church is a place of cultural survival. It helps either to preserve or to reconstruct the value systems, language, music, art, costumes, symbols, and myths of its respective communities."[151]

As we noted previously in my "Types of Hispanic Protestant Church Structures - Culture Liberation," it has been, above all, the Hispanic Pentecostal churches (found in types A, C, and D) who have expressed more faithfully their linguistic and cultural heritage in their "repossession of cultural values that were lost in the process of acculturation by their mainline sister churches."[152]

No one can visit today an Hispanic Protestant church (particularly indigenous Pentecostal congregations) without being impressed by the "fiesta" (celebration) expressed in their native instruments - guitar, "maracas," and even "bongos" - and thus savor the depth of the Hispanic soul.

Signpost ("A Signpost of Protest and Resistance"):

To the dominant church the Hispanic congregation is a "foreign enclave," a possible "threat to the unity of the universal church" or a "mission station." This is a paternalistic view at best, one that is shattered by the persistent presence of the Hispanic church, that does not go away, but stands "... as a disturbing sign on the fringes of an unjust society ... a prophetic indictment against the racism, political oppression, economic exploitation and sociocultural marginalization which have been such a constituent part of the American way of life."[153]

---

[150]See Orlando Costas, "Social Justice in the Other Protestant Tradition: A Hispanic Perspective," in Frederick Greenspahn, ed., *Contemporary Ethical Issues in the Jewish and Christian Traditions* (Hoboken, NJ: Ktau Publishing House, Inc., 1986), pp. 205-229.

[151]*Ibid.*, p. 221.

[152]*Ibid.*, p. 222.

[153]*Ibid.*, p. 223.

Costas underlines the ambivalent nature of a dominant church's interpretation and practice of the Gospel - one compromised in its legitimation of the vested interest and institution of the powers that be; but yet compelled to come to terms with the *conditio sine qua non* of gospel faithfulness, namely, commitment to the poor and the oppressed. Thus, the prophetic witness of the Hispanic church: as "a sign of protest not only against an unjust society, but also against the legitimizing role of the majority church and its theological and social betrayal of the gospel."[154]

Salvation ("A Liberated and Liberating Community"):

Literally dotting the many inner city "barrios" of America one can find communities of hope and liberation. Be it a storefront or converted synagogue, or perhaps a traditional church building "abandoned" by its "sister" Anglo church, one finds the proclamation of the Gospel of Jesus Christ and the gathering of God's Church providing "freedom," "dignity," "self-worth," "comfort," "strength," "hope," "joy" - "abundant life."

A liberated community lives out the Gospel both in its life and liberating mission. Though poor by the standards of the world, it witnesses to a richness of faith, hope, and love (1 Cor. 13:13), that can only be an indictment of the dominant church.

Costas is right when he states:

Indeed the prophetic genius of the minority church is that it has learned to "sing the Lord's song in a strange land" (Ps. 137:4). It has been able to give its respective communities a vision of a more fraternal, just, and peaceful world, enabling them to hope even when there seems to be no hope. Its ethic has been clearly one of liberation.[155]

---

[154]*Ibid.*

[155]*Ibid.*, p. 224.

Shalom ("An Agent of Reconciliation"):

The suggestively rich Scripture word "Shalom" (peace) speaks of wholeness, completeness, well-being, welfare, harmony, and reconciliation. It is both a personal and communal expression that is at the heart of the Gospel (Luke 1:79; 2:14; Acts 10:36; Ephesians 4:3, Hebrews 12:14).

The Hispanic church, as a minority church, is singularly called to play both a redemptive and reconciling role in the greater society - an agent of Shalom. "Because it is a liberated community, it is committed to reconciliation. Because it has an ethic of liberation, it can play a major role in bringing about a new, reconciled national church and society."[156]

The uniqueness of the Hispanic *mestizo* culture coupled with its redemptive experience of multiple rejection ("the Galilee principle" of Elizondo) and freedom (Elizondo's "resurrection principle") make of the Hispanic church a powerful agent for reconciliation. The Hispanic church, as a minority church, according to Costas

> ... serves the cause of social reconciliation, and validates thereby its
> personal reconciliation with God, by working for structures that
> make it socially and politically difficult for the strong to oppress the
> weak, for the majority to exploit the minority ... the minority church
> expresses its love toward its majority counterpart by challenging it
> to repentance and restitution and inviting it to join forces in the
> struggle for a new moral order.[157]

Secrets of the Reign ("Hermeneutical Advantage of the Poor"):

The minority church, the Hispanic church in the U.S.A., is the "church of the poor." As noted in chapter I (Hispanic American Reality), theirs is a "Portrait of a 'pueblo' at the periphery of the American metropolis." In view of this reality, Scripture teaches us, as has been made quite clear by contributions of the theology of the Third World, especially from Latin America, that God has a "preferential option for the poor." In the Law, Prophets and the Gospel God's justice is demonstrated in God's preference for those whom society has discarded. Paul says it in no uncertain terms:

---

[156]*Ibid.*, p. 224.

[157]*Ibid.*, p. 225.

> But God chose the foolish things of the world to shame the wise;
> God chose the weak things of the world to shame the strong. He
> chose the lowly things of this world and the despised things - and
> the things that are not - to nullify the things that are (1 Corinthians
> 1:27-28).

This "good news to the poor," which Jesus preached, when taken seriously places
the "non-poor" at a decided disadvantage when it comes to hearing the good news.

The witness of Scripture is clear that while the Gospel is for all, the rich
and powerful (including the religious "powers-that-be") because of their grasping
or dependence ("idolatry") on their financial or religious advantage, hear it as "bad
news." This is part and parcel of the meaning of the "hermeneutical advantage of
the poor."

Ones understanding of the Scripture and of the faith is decidedly influenced
by ones position regarding the "poor." There is a sense in which wealth and power
blind one to see and participate in God's liberating action in history. In another
sense, the "poor" church is at an advantageous position to hear the secrets of the
Reign. Their dependence, their trust, their power is on the mercies of a just,
loving, and speaking God.

Justo L. González states:

> What all this means is that when we understand the significance of
> the poor for the proper understanding of Scripture and of the
> Christian faith, we must come to the conclusion that a church that
> does not have the poor in its midst, a church that does not identify
> with the poor, is at a decided disadvantage.[158]

Seedbed for Community Leaders ("Emerging Leadership...Nurtured"):

In the minority-poor community, especially among Blacks, the church has
been a literal "seedbed" in producing leaders. We know from the history of
African-Americans that it has been the church that provided that context in which
a wholesome self-image, an authentic pride and identity, a solidarity around the

---

[158]Justo L. González, *The Hispanic Ministry of the Episcopal Church in the Metropolitan Area
of New York and Environs* (New York City: Grants Program of Trinity Parish, 1985), p. 7.

critical socio-political issues pressing on the life of the community, has developed and that eventually nurtured that kind of leadership that has served its people.

In the Hispanic community the same phenomenon is developing in the church, though to a lesser degree, given the "options" available to Hispanics in forming and participating in other institutions of society. These options were not historically available to Blacks. Notwithstanding "the crisis in Hispanic leadership"[159] that Dr. José Caraballo reminds us of, it is significant to note the emerging leadership in the Hispanic community that has been nurtured in the Hispanic Protestant church.

Caraballo himself lists a few examples among Pentecostals, such as: former Congressman Robert García; Attorney José R. Erazo, former assistant to former New York City Major Abraham Beame; David Vidal, the first Puerto Rican journalist at *The New York Times*; author Piri Thomas; Rev. Aimee Cortese, first woman prison chaplain in New York State.[160] This list can be easily expanded, since it just covers New York City, adding other key Pentecostals as well as mainline Protestant Hispanics from New York City and other sections of the U.S.A.[161]

According to Ms. Andrea R. Cano, Communications Director, World Council of Churches - U.S. Office, in a study by the Institute of Urban Planning of U.C.L.A., "the majority of Hispanic professionals in Los Angeles county are Protestants." Key leadership roles in the arts, education, the media and business, etc., were being played by Hispanic Protestants.[162]

Few institutions in society provide Hispanics the inter-personal and political skills that are nurtured in the minority church.

---

[159]See José Caraballo, "A Certificate Program for Hispanic Clergy and Lay Leaders In An Accredited Theological Seminary: A Case Study with Projections," pp. 97-100.

[160]*Ibid.*, p. 10.

[161]One of the key Hispanic political leaders in Boston, Mr. Felix Arroyo, was a former Protestant seminary student at the "Seminario Evangélico de Puerto Rico."

[162]Personal conversation with Ms. Andrea R. Cano on June 25, 1987 at Newark Airport, Newark, New Jersey.

Social Service Provider ("Natural Support Systems - Source of Strength"):

Without a doubt the Hispanic Protestant church plays a vital role in providing critically needed social services. Melvin Delgado and Denise-Humn Delgado categorize the natural support systems in the Hispanic communities, which minimize the use of formal resources, into four components: (1) the extended family; (2) folk healers; (3) religious institutions; and (4) merchants and social clubs that function totally or partially to help individuals in distress.[163]

It is noteworthy that in their discussion of the role of religious institutions Pentecostalism warrants the most significant positive description.[164] The following description from Vivian Garrison's "Sectarianism and Psychological Adjustment: A Controlled Comparison of Puerto Rican Pentecostals and Catholics," cited by the Delgados is both typical and cogent:

> Each of these small churches has a missionary society that answers requests of members and nonmembers, visits homes, and cares for the ill and disturbed. In addition to pastoral counseling, the ministries and the missionary societies provide emergency financial aid, go to the airport to meet new arrivals and orient them to the city, and locate housing and employment for members through the Pentecostal grapevine. All of these churches support several Pentecostal programs to rehabilitate drug addicts, prostitutes, and other outcasts of society. Most Pentecostals go to their ministers or members of their church with any problem they might have. Services offered by the church are provided from the resources within the group and within the broader network of Pentecostal affiliations.[165]

The Delgados' appreciation for religious institutions, by which they note and emphasize the "alternative religions" among Hispanics, is supported by their empirical findings. In the twenty (20) criteria of needs served, religious institutions serve sixteen (16), only the extended family registers higher, seventeen (17), (See, Figure 2-4).

---

[163]Melvin Delgado and Denise Humn-Delgado, "Natural Support Systems: Source of Strength in Hispanic Communities," *Social Work* (January 1982), pp. 83-89.

[164]They do note that other "alternative religions" (Seventh-Day Adventist and Jehovah's Witnesses) may play similar roles; *Ibid.*, p. 85.

[165]*Ibid.*, p. 85.

Figure 2-4

**Breakdown of Needs Served by Natural
Support Systems in Hispanic Communities**

Needs Served	Natural Support Systems			
	Extended Family	Folk Healers	Religious Institutions	Merchants & Social Clubs
1. Accessibility to community	X	X	X	X
2. Communication in Spanish	X	X	X	X
3. Continuation of cultural traditions	X	X	X	X
4. Crisis intervention	X	X	X	X
5. Emotional support for interpersonal problems	X	X	X	X
6. Friendship, companionship, trust	X	X	X	X
7. Identification with Hispanic role models, leaders, or experts	X	X	X	X
8. Information and referral	X	X	X	X
9. Care and treatment of the disabled or aged	X	X	X	
10. Financial aid or credit	X		X	
11. Medical care and pharmaceutical products	X	X		X
12. Recreation	X		X	X
13. Translation or interpretation	X		X	X
14. Advocacy	X		X	
15. Physical and emotional rehabilitation		X	X	
16. Religious or spiritual affiliation		X	X	
17. Babysitting, day care, respite care, foster care, or adoption	X			
18. Child rearing and parent education	X			
19. Educational alternative to public school			X	
20. Housing	X			

Source: Melvin Delgado and Denise Humn-Delgado, "Natural Support Systems: Source of Strength in Hispanic Communities," *Social Work* (January 1982), p. 87; Used with permission of *Social Work*

The important role of the Hispanic Protestant church as a service provider in the Hispanic community is the object of increasing number of serious studies. This is in keeping with the Delgados' challenge that "alternative religious groups, and to a lesser extent Catholicism, should be examined from a social service perspective as well as from a religious one in assessing the nature and extent of support in Hispanic communities."[166]   It should be noted that the Hispanic Pentecostal church's role in the delivery of human services was the subject of an extensively researched study by Professor Elba Caraballo-Ireland for Brandeis University.[167]

The Hispanic Protestant church provides a network of informal social services that goes a long way in coping and overcoming in an otherwise hostile and oppressive context.

Hispanic Spirituality and Indigenous Pentecostal Theology

Bibet de fonte putei sui primus ipse.

- St. Bernard of Clairvaux
De consideratione[168]

At the root of every spirituality there is a particular experience that is had by concrete persons living at a particular time. The experience is both proper to them and yet communicable to others. I cited earlier the passage in St. Bernard of Clairvaux in which he says that in these matters all people should drink from their own well. The great spiritualities in the life of the church continue to exist because they keep sending their followers back to the sources.[169]

---

[166]*Ibid.*, p. 85.

[167]Elba Caraballo-Ireland, "The Role of the Pentecostal Church As a Service Provider in the Puerto Rican Community of Boston, Massachusetts: A Case Study," Unpublished Ph.D. dissertation, Brandeis University, Waltham, Massachusetts, 1990.

[168]Cited in Gustavo Gutierrez, *We Drink from our Own Wells: The Spiritual Journey of a People* (Maryknoll, New York: Orbis Books, 1984), p. viii.

[169]*Ibid.*, p. 37.

In this section I will be comparing and contrasting Hispanic Spirituality and that religious self-understanding or understanding of the faith, explicitly and implicitly presented by Hispanic Pentecostals. Thus, the focus will be to look first at the complex synthesis of the parts that make up the Hispanic Spirituality, and then to look at the explicit and the implicit indigenous Pentecostal theology. Though not exhaustive, I will nevertheless paint with broad enough strokes a picture that should prove helpful in understanding that particular Hispanic American "homo religiosus" - the Hispanic Pentecostal.[170]

To speak of Hispanic Spirituality is to speak of that particular or peculiar response of Hispanics to the "mysterium tremendum." It is to speak about a particular "style," form and substance of worship and the obedience of faith. It is ultimately about how an Hispanic acts and is ("doing and being") as a "homo religiosus," and as a person of passion - Unamuno.[171]

All the great spiritual leaders of the Church, as demonstrated by the personalities that were the moving force behind them - the hermits of the East, the monks of the West, Basil, Athanasius, Augustine, Benedict, Dominic, Francis, Ignatius, San Juan de la Cruz and Santa Teresa, to name a few - were a response to the spiritual pilgrimage of a particular people, at a particular time, in a particular context.

The following definition of Spirituality by George A. Lane, S.J. is pertinent:

> In a broad sense spirituality may be described as a way of holiness; but more technically, spirituality is man's possession by God in Christ through the Holy Spirit. There is, then, only one spirituality because there is only one Christ; but when the means of union with God become concretized, various different styles of approach appear. A particular style of approach to union with God is then called a spirituality ... Now this distinction between man's fundamental union with God and the various styles of approach to it has very important ramifications. At any given time and place in history, society challenges men and women differently, and therefore challenges them to respond to God differently. These

---

[170]We are keeping in mind the admonition of Rudolf Otto, "... religion is not exclusively contained and exhaustively comprised in any series of 'rational' assertions," *The Idea of the Holy* (New York: Oxford University Press, 1970 ed.), p. 4.

[171]See Miguel de Unamuno, *Del Sentimiento Tragico de la Vida* (Buenos Aires, Argentina: Editorial Losada, S.A., 1964 ed.).

challenges have brought forth responses from extraordinary men and women.[172]

Characteristics of Hispanic Spirituality

The ideal type or profile of "Homos Hispanicus"[173] provides us eight basic categories which summarize the cultural traits and value orientation of Hispanics. These are ultimately placed at the service or become the means, in an anthropological sense, to that particular style of approach to union with God - Hispanic Spirituality! In its most authentic and significant expressions Hispanic Spirituality coheres with these eight culture traits and value orientations. These are "our own wells" from which we must drink. They are our Hispanic heritage; they are our sources, they are us.

Hispanic Spirituality is the expression of a complex cultural phenomenon. Hispanic Spirituality, thus, must be seen as part and parcel of the creative synthesis of the Hispanic value structure and orientation that has emerged from the three root streams that inform its cultural traits and personality. Hispanic Spirituality responds to the Spanish, Amerindian and African make-up of its "soul." In certain cases the Amerindian influence predominates, in other the African, while in most cases the Spanish influence - whose culture dominance in the Conquest prevailed - is the dominant one. It is important to note that the symbiotic relationship of Hispanic culture and Roman Catholicism is of such a nature that *all* Hispanic Spirituality is deeply influenced by it.

Hispanic Spirituality, while manifested in many forms and through different instrumentalities, in its most *authentic and significant Hispanic expressions* is marked by the following characteristics:

1.   **Passion** - While Hispanic Spirituality is not anti-intellectual or irrational *per se*, it resonates deeply with the passionate nature of the Hispanic "soul." Feelings/emotions are accepted by Hispanics in a wholistic response to life. Passion is at the "heart" of their religious expressions. The emotional fervor noted in the Catholic "holy week;" popular religiosity' passion plays and posadas; the

---

[172]George A. Lane, S.J., *Christian Spirituality - An Historical Sketch* (Chicago: Loyola University Press, 1984) pp. 2-3; my own personal definition of Spirituality synthesizes a theological (trinitarian) and moral thrust: "In obedience to God, the following of Jesus in the power of the Spirit."

[173]See, chapter I, "Hispanic American Reality."

Protestant preacher or Pentecostal worship service (especially its music), all attest to this significant characteristic of Hispanic Spirituality.

2.   **Personalism** - Personal relations are paramount for Hispanics, above abstract principles and institutions. It explains the significant dependence on mediation (e.g., a saint) to reach God in Catholic religiosity.   Fitzpatrick's comment is relevant:

> In Latin America, religious practice is marked by the quality of *personalismo*, the pattern of close, intimate personal relationships which is characteristic of Spanish cultures everywhere. Thus the individual perceives his religious life as a network of personal relationships with the saints, the Blessed Virgin, or various manifestations of the Lord.[174]

It responds to the appeal of the personal *Curandera* or *Curandero* (traditional curer or healer) in the Hispanic communities. The significant role played as a social service provider (in very personal and intimate ways) by these folk healers is noteworthy. Melvin Delgado and Denise Humn-Delgado identify five types of folk healers in the Hispanic community: (1) Spiritist; (2) "Santero" (literally, saint intercessor); (3) Herbalist; (4) "Santiguador" (literally, healer by signing with the cross); and (5) "Curandero" (traditional curer).[175]

The ever-present and quasi-religious "Botanica," the stores where herbs, potions and other remedies are sold - and personal "consultas" (counsel-advice) are dispensed - are finding receptive ears among Hispanics, in an otherwise impersonal society. The Spiritist, with the influential teaching of Allan Kardec and Joaquin Trincado, provide "alternative religious" structures that respond to Hispanic needs in a very personal way.[176]

---

[174]Joseph P. Fitzpatrick, *Puerto Rican Americans*, p. 117; some explain the apparent contradiction of a religiosity that does not attend mass at the institutional church (one Boston study indicated only 31% of Hispanic Catholics attended mass regularly, while 69% considered itself "Catholic but non-practicing") with a "personal" folk religiosity expressed at home - "velorios" (wakes); "imagenes o altares en el hogar" (religious images and altar); "velas" (candles); "rezar el rosario" (pray the rosary).

[175]Melvin Delgado and Denise Humn-Delgado "Natural Support Systems: Source of Strength in Hispanic Communities," *Social Work*, p. 84.

[176]See, June Macklin, "*Curanderismo* and *Espiritismo*:   Complementary Approaches to Traditional Mental Health Services," in Stanley A. West and June Macklin, *The Chicano Experience* (Colorado: Westview Press, 1979).

Personalism also explains the lack of trust for systems or organizations to mediate religious experience. Loyalty is often placed on persons rather than religious institutions or, for that matter, on theological abstract principles distinguishing the different religious confessions. Beyond the socio-political nature or sources of church splits, and the distinct conception of "calling" and ministry in Hispanic Pentecostalism, it would be wise to look seriously at the role played by strong personalities who evoke such loyalty and following. Personalism accounts for bringing to the religious collective life and action a subjective and personal standard.

3.   **Paradox of the Soul** - Realist and Idealist, one can be both without confusion or confinement. The realism and idealism entwined in the "soul" of the Hispanic is indeed a strange paradox that defies neat classification and proves difficult for people to understand. Not infrequently an Hispanic becomes both by turns.

In Hispanic Spirituality this is best seen in the paradox of "El Cristo Español" (The Spanish Christ). The Catholicism that reached Latin America and impacted Spanish cultures everywhere presents a Christ that responds to the "supreme dread" of death and passion for immortality of the Hispanic "soul." John A. Mackay in his classic study of Spanish spirituality notes:

> In Spanish religion Christ has been the center of a cult of death. And yet, paradoxically enough, it was the passion for fleshly life and immortality that created this interest in death. The dead Christ is an expiatory victim. The details of His earthly life are of slight importance and make relatively small appeal. He is regarded as a purely supernatural being, whose humanity, being only apparent, has little ethical bearing upon ours. This docetic Christ died as the victim of human hate, and in order to bestow immortality, that is to say, a continuation of the present earthly, fleshly existence. The contemplation of His passion produces a sort of catharsis, as Aristotle would say, in the soul of the worshipper, just as in the bull-fight, an analogous creation of the Spanish spirit, the Spaniard sees and feels death in all its dread reality in the fate of a victim. The total sensation intensifies his sense of the reality and terribleness of death; it increases his passion for life, and, in the religious realm, makes him cling desperately and tragically to the dead Victim that died to give him immortality.[177]

---

[177]John A. Mackay, *The Other Spanish Christ*, p. 98.

While the above does not exhaust the meaning and significance of the "Spanish Christ," it does reveal the Paradox of the Soul in Hispanic Spirituality. While this interpretation can be challenged at certain points (e.g., Mackay is not as affirming of Catholic Spirituality as I am in this study), it is indicative, nevertheless, of the need for "the development of a more biblical, indigenous and engaged Christology"[178] for Hispanics.

4.   **Community** - Hispanic Spirituality has a deep appreciation for community. The religious experience of Hispanics, particularly first generation - those recently arrived - is often "traumatized" in the religious ethos of North American Society. The symbiotic relationship with its cultural milieu - shot through with its collective/communal religious ethos - in Latin America is often shredded here, producing a spiritual void and often loss of faith.

This is true particularly of Catholics whose sense of identity was tied up to a particular *pueblo* (town or people) that historically created a community. The plaza was the center of community life and the church the main building on the plaza. Public worship and demonstrations and fiestas abounded, reinforcing the sense of community and their sense of being "muy catolico." Joseph P. Fitzpatrick underscores this well:

> In the United States, the *pueblo* in this sense (the community) never worships God. It guarantees to the individual the right to worship God according to his conscience. But practice of the faith in the United States is not a community manifestation; it is a matter of personal choice or commitment. The latin, on the other hand is "Catholic" because he belongs to a Catholic people. This sense of identity, based on religion, which came to penetrate the life of Latin Americans very deeply, was related to a style of Catholicism with which they were familiar - the Catholicism of the *pueblo*, the community of which they were a part.[179]

A deep sense of community also plays no small part in the growth of the "Comunidades de Base" throughout the Spanish-speaking world.

One cannot fathom the growth and the depth of Hispanic Pentecostalism and its Spirituality without coming to terms with the "Quest for Community," that

---

[178]Orlando E. Costas, *Theology of the Crossroads in Contemporary Latin America* (Amsterdam: Editions Rodopi N.V., 1976) p. 97.

[179]Joseph P. Fitzpatrick, *Puerto Rican Americans*, p. 116.

Renato Poblete and Thomas F. O'Dea posit as the key to understanding Hispanic Pentecostalism.[180]

5.   **Romerías** (pilgrimages)/ **Cursillo** (retreat) - The pilgrimages of the Amerindian is manifested in Hispanic religious culture and expresses itself in journeys or travels to holy shrines or holy places. In a contemporary sense the "Spiritual retreat" is its functional equivalent in Hispanic Spirituality.

One is not surprised at the tremendous success and significance of the Catholic "Cursillo Movement" among Hispanics in the United States. The "Cursillo" (retreat), briefly defined by Moisés Sandoval as "a once-in-a-lifetime experience, consists of a three-day series of talks and other activities aimed at achieving an encounter with Christ and renewal in the church."[181] Much of the vitality of the Catholic church in the United States among Hispanics can be attributed to the "Cursillo." It has contributed much toward the "Latinization" (more Hispanic) of the Catholic church and has "laid the basis for a social apostolate contrasting with the individualistic piety in much Latin religious worship."[182]

Sandoval underlines the important role of the "Cursillo" in the following:

> Perhaps no other movement has done more to Latinize the Church in the U.S. than the Cursillo. The movement started in Spain in 1947. Brought to the United States in 1957, it has influenced many leaders and developed others. César Chavez and others prominent in the *Movimiento* are cursillistas. Father José Alvarez, who has long been active in the Spanish apostolate in New York, credits the Cursillo movement with saving the faith of the Hispanic people of New York at a time when they were getting little attention in the church.[183]

In mainline Protestant and Pentecostal circles the "spiritual retreats" continues to play an ever-increasing role in leadership training.

----

[180]Renato Poblete and Thomas F. O'Dea, "Anomie and the 'Quest for Community': The Formation of Sects Among the Puerto Ricans of New York," *American Catholic Sociological Review*, 21:18-36, Spring 1960.

[181]Moisés Sandoval, "The Latinization Process," in Moisés Sandoval, ed. *Fronteras*, p. 452.

[182]Leo Gebler, Joan W. Moore, Ralph Guzmán, *The Mexican American People*, p. 468.

[183]Moisés Sandoval, "The Latinization Process," in Moisés Sandoval, ed. *Fronteras*, p. 451.

6.   **Musical élan** - To speak of a musical élan and Hispanic Spirituality is to speak about that particular quality permeating Hispanic culture, a "gift" from our African heritage, that expresses and impresses all religious experiences with an emotional depth of transcendence, joy and liberation.

Hispanic Spirituality, particularly among Pentecostals, places great value on an emotional musical expression in its liturgy. While its hymnology may not be of "aesthetic grandeur," by some standards of "high" culture, it nevertheless is increasingly an autochthonous expression of the depth of Hispanic anguish and aspirations. On close analysis it reveals both the groans of their oppressed souls and the triumph over anguish and sorrow by their religious faith.

As noted previously, music serves many other functions than to provide joy and a sense of wellbeing: it unites people, transmits social values, denounces injustices, influences human behavior, and puts to sleep or awakens for the struggle.[184]

In the development of Hispanic Spirituality one or more of these functions has also served them well.

7.   **"Fiesta"** (Celebration) - In Hispanic Spirituality there is an ubiquity of and propensity for "fiesta." It is cause and effect of a religious cultural heritage that celebrates and affirms life as a gift. From "Baptismal fiestas" to "fiestas patronales" (patron saint festivals/celebrations) the religious and social calendar of Hispanics marks these and other occasions that celebrate life and community. According to Octavio Paz, "every true fiesta is religious because every true festival is communion."[185]

Whether Catholic, Protestant or Pentecostal "fiesta" characterizes and expresses a deep spirituality, a yearning of the heart, and the heart's response that life is worth living. In the words of Virgilio Elizondo, "the tragedies of their history have not obliterated laughter and joy, fiesta is the mystical celebration of a complex identity, the mystical affirmation that life is a gift and is worth living."[186]

---

[184]See Carlos Rosas, "La Música al Servicio del Reino," *Apuntes* 6 (Spring 1986): 3-6.

[185]Octavio Paz, "Reflections," *The New Yorker*, November 17, 1979, quoted in Ruben P. Armendariz, "Hispanic Heritage and Christian Education," *ALERT* (November 1981): 26.

[186]Virgilio Elizondo, *Galilean Journey: The Mexican-American Promise*, p. 43.

8.   **Family** - The central role of the family is one of the salient characteristics of Hispanic culture. Hispanic Spirituality is imbued deeply by familism. Let me comment briefly on three familistic values: (1) "compadrazgo;" (2) "machismo;" and (3) "la Virgen."

"Compadrazgo" (godparentage) plays the significant role of knitting the community and formalizing informal ties of friendship.[187] The "compadrazgo" system is at heart a religious act of committing godparents to bringing up in the faith the godchild - although it plays other socio-economic roles. It is a formal sacralization of the extended family, so dear to Hispanic culture. It also speaks prophetically of the need to sacralize human ties beyond that of blood.

"Machismo" is a familistic value that has impacted spirituality in an oblique, yet fundamental way. This complex of values known as "machismo" above all speaks of a family structure where authority is vested in the male head of the family, and where a particular definition of masculinity emphasizes physical and sexual prowess. While debate and controversy surround this concept (pro and con), in the final analysis all agree that it has contributed in maintaining Hispanic women in a subordinate role and status.

There are several implications of "machismo" for Hispanic Spirituality. The most obvious one is the marginalization of women from leadership roles in the church (particularly in the Catholic priesthood) and the implicit, and often explicit, assumption that only males can handle, have traffic with, and mediate the "mysterium tremendum."[188]

The seeming paradox, in view of "machismo," is the role of "la Virgen" in Catholic Spirituality. As previously noted in the section "La Morenita: La Virgen de Guadalupe," "la Virgen" is critical for our understanding Catholic Spirituality. Marianism or Mariology describes that movement within the Roman Catholic Church that emphasizes the special veneration of the figure of the Virgin Mary. Catholic spirituality places great emphasis on the Virgin Mother. John A. Mackay, while speaking of the "Spanish Christ," speaks of "La Virgen" as becoming the Queen of Life and Sovereign Lady in Catholic Spirituality:

> A Christ known in life as an infant and in death as a corpse, over
> whose helpless childhood and tragic fate the Virgin Mother

---

[187]Joan W. Moore and Harry Pachon, *Hispanics in the United States*, p. 96.

[188]See, Ada María Isasi-Díaz and Yolanda Tarango, *Hispanic Women, Prophetic Voice in the Church: Toward an Hispanic Women's Liberation Theology* (New York, N.Y.: Harper & Row, 1988).

presides; a Christ who became man in the interests of eschatology, whose permanent reality resides in a magic wafer bestowing immortality; a Virgin Mother who by not tasting death, became the Queen of Life, - that is the Christ and that the Virgin who came to America! He came as Lord of Death and of the life that is to be; she came as Sovereign Lady of the life that now is.[189]

In Protestant and Pentecostal Spirituality the "brothers" and "sisters" in the church become a family, often the only family available to them in the "barrio." It not only provides the psychological and social service support needed, but in a deep religious sense mediates (as the "body of Christ") and sacralizes their spiritual needs.

If we are to understand Hispanic Spirituality, and if we are to nurture an *authentic* and *relevant* Hispanic Spirituality, we must look to and "drink from our own wells." We must see the critical role our cultural heritage plays in our spirituality and affirm those positive characteristics that make up our cultural traits and value orientations; ones that indeed have been hammered out on the anvil of our socio-history and culture.

Hispanic Pentecostal Theology and Spirituality

To speak of indigenous Pentecostal theology is indeed to speak of a project rather than to an accomplished fact, as far as literary production is concerned. On the other hand, to speak of indigenous Pentecostal theology is to speak of a bi-focal universe of discourse. On the one level we are dealing with an explicit theological discourse "received" from the Anglo and used by Hispanic Pentecostals; and on the theological literature (very little) produced by Hispanics.   On another level we are dealing with the implicit theological discourse discerned in its "culto;" "predicacion" (preaching); "testimonio" (testimony/witness), both in word and deed; expressed in actions inside and outside the "community of the Spirit" - the church.

In both cases a comprehensive analysis worthy of such a study cannot be addressed within the scope of this paper. Yet, we will outline some of the salient points vital to and descriptive of an indigenous Pentecostal theology, especially as it relates to Hispanic Spirituality.

In the early years (the first fifteen years), the Pentecostal movement had no distinctive theological or doctrinal shape, given the make-up of its membership

---

[189]John A. Mackay, *The Other Spanish Christ*, p. 102.

from distinct Protestant traditions and the desire of many of its leaders to transcend theological definitions in the interest of maintaining a fellowship bonded by the "experience of the Spirit." Spirituality has always been the interest of Pentecostals, to such a degree that the thinking of many then and even now would agree with the assessment of Vinson Synan:

> As yet a fully developed "Pentecostal" theology does not exist; and many hope that one never does come into existence, since the "letter kills, but the Spirit makes alive." It is not that Pentecostals think theology to be unimportant, but there is concern that theology serve spiritual reality rather than spirituality serve theology.[190]

In time, two particular theological issues interpretive of the Pentecostal experience of the "baptism of the Holy Spirit" brought about division - the issues of sanctification and pneumatology. These two issues received answers reflected in the two main theological traditions which influenced the Pentecostal Movement originally: (1) Wesleyan-Holiness and (2) the Keswickian-Reformed.

A three-fold division that followed can be classified (as noted by Pomerville) as:

1.   Those denominations which hold a Keswick view of sanctification - "that the second experience referred to as 'the baptism of the Holy Spirit' was an 'enduement of power' for service."[191] (Reformed-Baptistic)
2.   Those denominations which hold a Holiness view of "entire sanctification" - that the second experience referred to as the baptism of the Holy Spirit "was a cleansing from sin (Wesleyan eradication - perfectionism)."[192] (Wesleyan)
3.   Those denominations which hold a "Jesus Only" view of the Godhead.[193] (Oneness)

---

[190]Vinson Synan, "Pentecostalism: Varieties and Contributions," p. 18.

[191]Paul A. Pomerville, *The Third Force in Missions: A Pentecostal Contribution to Contemporary Mission Theology*, p. 12.

[192]*Ibid.*, p. 12.

[193]*Ibid.*, p. 12; This unitarian branch of Pentecostalism rejects the traditional doctrine of the trinity, claiming that Jesus is Father, Son and Holy Spirit. It believes that one must be baptized "in Jesus' name," as well as "speak in tongues" as necessary requisites to salvation. It is important to note that in the early Pentecostal development Hispanics were a significant number in the "Jesus Only" division. Victor De León notes that by 1971 there were 220 churches in the United States

These groupings constitute the classical camps of Pentecostalism, ones that Hispanics have been participants in since their inception. With the addition in the 1960's of the "Charismatic Pentecostals," we have the four-fold "major theological camps" of Pentecostalism noted by Synan: (1) Wesleyan Pentecostals; (2) Baptistic Pentecostals; (3) Oneness Pentecostals; and (4) Charismatic Pentecostals.[194]

While Synan may be right in part in stating that "all Pentecostals agree on the presence and demonstration of the charismata in the modern church, but beyond this common agreement there is as much diversity as in all the other branches of Christianity;"[195] there are other theological themes that are common denominators to Pentecostals.

With the possible exception of "Charismatic Pentecostals" one can identify further "four Christological themes defining the basic 'gestalt' of Pentecostal thought and ethos: Christ as Savior, as Baptizer with the Holy Spirit, as Healer and as Coming King."[196] It is important to note that these four christological themes - Pentecostal's "full-gospel" or "four-fold gospel" - constituted the basic theological parameters of the theology of Olazabal and Lugo; both interestingly enough having been instructed in their early Pentecostal pilgrimage by George and Mary Montgomery, former Christian and Missionary Alliance Church leaders.[197]

---

affiliated with the Apostolic Assemblies (Hispanic Oneness); he reminds us that:

> Between 1916 and 1921 the Hispanic Oneness churches were the strongest of the Hispanic Pentecostals on the West Coast. In 1918, however, the great Spirit-filled Trinitarian Methodist evangelist, Francisco Olazabal, came on the scene. He held large evangelistic meetings in major cities of America where the Spanish-speaking people were located. His emphasis was "divine healing, the baptism in the Holy Spirit, and salvation," says Roberto Dominguez. As a result of his ministry the Trinitarian churches grew and were strengthened.

Victor De León, "Growth of Hispanic Pentecostals," *Paraclete* (Winter, 1981), p. 20.

[194]Vinson Synan, "Pentecostalism: Varieties and Contributions," pp. 5-7.

[195]*Ibid.*, p. 5.

[196]Donald W. Dayton, *Theological Roots of Pentecostalism* (Grand Rapids, Michigan: Francis Asbury Press, Zondervan Publishing House, 1987), p. 173; Dayton notes, "These four themes are well nigh universal within the movement, appearing as we have been arguing, in all branches and varieties of Pentecostalism ... This pattern could be traced outside Classical Pentecostalism in the 'Charismatic Movement' or 'Neo-Pentecostalism' and perhaps even in third-world manifestations like certain of the African Independent Churches;" *Ibid.*, pp. 21-22, 31.

[197]Victor De León, *The Silent Pentecostals*, pp. 24-27, 33.

George and Mary Montgomery's former denominational affiliation (Christian and Missionary Alliance) was one of the staunchest members of the Keswick wing of the Holiness Movement. It was natural enough then that the Pentecostal experiences and theological teachings of the Montgomerys would be interpreted through the perspective of Keswickian Pentecostalism. They were affiliated, as well as Olazabal and Lugo, with the Assemblies of God, a movement that in its formative years was deeply influenced by Keswickian and Baptistic theologies.[198]

Olazabal and Lugo, the two foremost Hispanic Pentecostal pioneers and church planters, left a theological legacy, even as they moved away from the Assemblies of God to found indigenous Pentecostal churches throughout the United States and Puerto Rico, based on the four Christological themes of the "full-gospel," interpreted through Keswickian theological perspective.[199]

Hispanic indigenous Pentecostalism in a formal and substantive way has been influenced theologically by classical Pentecostalism, as the case has been with most of Pentecostalism worldwide,[200] albeit filtered through the interpretive nuances of Hispanic culture and history.

As we further focus on indigenous Pentecostal theology, it is of the utmost importance to note and correlate further its theological heritage. As one reads its theological reflection - basically found in Sunday School quarterly, sermon notes and a few published articles, to date - and hears in a somewhat "oral and narrative

---

[198]See William W. Menzies, *Anointed to Serve: The Story of the Assemblies of God* (Springfield, MO.: Gospel Publishing House, 1971) pp. 27-28; Edith L. Waldvogel, "The 'Overcoming' Life: A Study in the Reformed Evangelical Contribution to Pentecostalism" *PNEUMA* (Spring 1979) pp. 7-19.

[199]The strong holiness dimension in Indigenous Pentecostals' practice can be attributed in part to these roots, coupled with the fact of the Wesleyan-Holiness perspective that were the theological inheritance of Olazabal, a former Methodist pastor, and Lugo, whose first pastor Francisco Ortiz, Sr. was a former Methodist.

[200]See especially, Paul A. Pomerville, *The Third Force in Missions: A Pentecostal Contribution to Contemporary Mission Theology*; and Donald W. Dayton, *Theological Roots of Pentecostalism*; It should be further noted that Hispanic Pentecostals' thought and ethos would be significantly impacted after 1937 by the most "popular" and "ubiquitous" theological work among Hispanic Pentecostals, Myer Pearlman's (a converted Jew), *Knowing the Doctrines of the Bible* (Springfield, MO,; Gospel Publishing House, 1937). In Spanish it is known by the more ambitious title of *Teología Bíblica y Sistemática* (Biblical and Systematic Theology).

indigenous culture,"[201] besides the aforementioned Christological themes of the "full-gospel," their theological discourse, one must further confirm their subscription to the four basic principles of the Reformation: *Sola Gracia*, *Solo Cristo*, *Sola Escritura* and *Sola Fe*. Nevertheless, as I previously noted, indigenous Pentecostalism has its "spiritual ancestors" in the left-wing of the Reformation. This is significantly true because of its constituency - the poor and the oppressed - and because of its theological and ethical formulations.

John Thomas Nichols, noting the affinity of the Pentecostal churches in their origins to the left-wing of the Reformation - a fact more indicative of indigenous Pentecostalism *now* than Anglo Pentecostalism and other branches of Pentecostalism today - states:

> ... the emphases which are manifested by the Pentecostals would place them in the radical (left) wing of the Reformation. Like their spiritual ancestors, the Anabaptists, Pentecostals declare (1) that the individual as well as the corporate body of believers should seek for and submit to the leading of the Spirit; (2) that there should be a return to apostolic simplicity in worship; (3) that believers ought to separate themselves from the world; (4) that believer's baptism replaces infant baptism; and (5) that believers should look for the imminent visible return of Christ who will set up his millennial reign.[202]

My own five point pneumatic classification would correlate the above five points as:

    (1)   Spirit's Sovereignty
    (2)   Spirit's Simplicity
    (3)   Spirit's Separation
    (4)   Spirit's Sign
    (5)   Spirit's Sigh

While the above brief survey of the theological roots of Hispanic Pentecostalism is relevant to a correlation with Hispanic Spirituality, it would be much more fruitful and in a real sense closer to its indigenous nature to look at the implicit theology manifested, above all, in the "culto."

---

[201]See, for a somewhat analogous case of "oral and narrative indigenous culture," Walter J. Hollenweger, *Pentecost Between Black and White: Five Case Studies on Pentecost and Politics* (Belfast, Ireland: Christian Journals Limited, 1974).

[202]John Thomas Nichols, *The Pentecostals*, p. 3.

Theology ("theo" - God; "logos" - talk) is "God-talk," basically a dialogue, a discourse. The "culto," "... después de todo se trata en la adoración, de un diálogo con Dios y los hombres."[203] This worship or "culto" is a dialogue with God and men/women, communicated verbally and non-verbally in the many signs and symbols (and sighs) exchanged in the "community of the Spirit" - the church, though not limited to it. Thus, the "culto" is theology and theology is the "culto."

Orlando Costas' comments are apropos:

El culto es el reflejo más claro de la teología de la comunidad de fe. Ello se hace claramente evidente en el N.T., donde los pasajes de mayor profundidad teológica son trozos litúrgicos - himnos, oraciones, confesiones, etc. - tomados directamente de la experiencia litúrgica de las comunidades primitivas. En América Latina ello se hace aún más claro dado el carácter oral de nuestra teología. Nuestra teología ... no es una reflexión lineal, horizontal, escrita. Antes bien, es parte de la vida, que, para bien or para mal, se representa ... por el culto, ya que éste es el punto central de la vida eclesial. De ahí también que sea un índice de las actitudes, el estilo de vida, la cosmovisión y la participación social del pueblo evangélico. Porque refleja un comportamiento psicosocial definido, repleto de imágenes socioculturales, con un contenido ético concreto y con una clara visión de la iglesia y la sociedad.[204]

While a "full blown" indigenous theology could possibly be developed, as implied by the above quotation, having the "locus theologicus" in the "culto," the

---

[203]"after all we deal in worship, with a dialogue with God and men," Carlos A. Valle, "Lo Tradicional y lo Nuevo," in Carlos A. Valle (ed.), *Culto: Crítica y Búsqueda* (Buenos Aires, Argentina: Centro de Estudios Cristianos, Methopress, 1972) p. 14.

[204]"The 'culto' is the clearest reflection of the theology of the community of faith. It is clearly evident in the New Testament, where the passages of the most theological depth are liturgical verses - hymns, prayers, confessions, etc. - taken directly from the liturgical experience of the primitive communities. In Latin America it is even more clearer because of the oral character of our theology. Our theology ... is not a lineal, horizontal, written reflection. It is, however, part of the life which, for good or evil, is represented ... by the 'culto,' since this is the central point of the ecclesial life. From there also it is an index of the attitudes, the style of life, the world vision and the social participation of the evangelical people. Because it reflects a defined psychosocial behavior, filled with sociocultural images, with a concrete ethical content and with a clear vision of the church and the society;" Orlando Costas, *El Protestantismo En América Latina Hoy: Ensayos del Camino* (1972-1974), (San José, Costa Rica: Publicaciones INDEF, 1975), p. viii; see also, J.J. von Allmen, *El Culto Cristiano* (Salamanca, España: Ediciones Sígueme, 1968); Oscar Cullman, *La Fé y El Culto en la Iglesia Primitiva* (Madrid, España: Stadium, 1971).

Figure 2-5 - "Participant Observers -
Iglesia Asambleas Cristianas"

Participant Observers: Iglesia Asambleas Cristianas
                           5 Howard Avenue
                           Dorchester, MA. 02125

A.   COMMUNITY - Describe the community as perceived in terms of socio-economic and
       political reality.

B.   CHURCH BUILDING AND FACILITIES:
       1. Where is the church located
       2. Size and extent of facilities
       3. Parking space
       4. Color or decor of church (outside/inside)
       5. Aesthetic quality (present/absent)
       6. Location of pastor's/church's office
       7. Location of bathrooms
       8. Location and size of classrooms
       9. Microphones, podium, etc. - its usage
       10. Pulpit and backdrop

       Add others:

C.   WORSHIP:
       1. Length of service (total)
       2. Length of devotional part of program
       3. Musical instruments
       4. Singing and music - type/style
       5. Use of Scripture
       6. Use of Hymnal
       7. Creedal Statement - use of/presence
       8. Use of Symbols - verbal/non-verbal
       9. Organized/Disorganized - "open" service
       10. Congregational Participation
       11. Cognitive/emotional "ethos"
       12. Use of pulpit

       Add others:

D.   LEADERSHIP/MEMBERSHIP/MISCELLANEOUS:
       1. Social status
       2. Seating arrangement
       3. Structure of service
       4. Mobility of children/people
       5. Noise level
       6. Testimonies - structure, content, etc.
       7. Preacher/Message - use of Scripture, style,
           homiletical structure, content, etc.

       Add others:

Source: Eldin Villafañe, "hand-out" form, (SE 191) "Sociology of Religion," Gordon-
         Conwell Theological Seminary, November 23,1980.

scope of this paper does not permit it. The balance of this section will focus on
a descriptive analysis of the "culto" of indigenous Pentecostalism. It will compare
and contrast the aforementioned characteristics of Hispanic Spirituality, noting the
implicit theological correlations with the "culto."[205]

The context of Hispanic indigenous Pentecostal spirituality must first be
noted. It is in the inner-city "barrios" store-front churches that one encounters the
dynamic and suggestive "cultos." These are the "barrios" marginal to the power
structures of downtown, inhabited by a disenfranchised and oppressed people. The
store-front churches are, by and large, small, overcrowded, inadequate for
classroom, office, etc., no stained-glass windows, hardly any windows at all - by
most estimation aesthetically unbecoming. In response to whether these storefronts
were *real* churches, Gerald Sheppard, then professor of Old Testament Studies at
Union Theological Seminary, New York City and a Pentecostal, answered:

> Yes, says Sheppard. 'These are authentic expressions of religious
> belief no matter what some people may think. Who's to say that
> just because people are meeting in, for example, an abandoned shoe
> store, that they are not "real" Christians meeting in a "real" church.
> It's the faith that counts, not the setting.'[206]

This is the Church where the believers gather to worship - to celebrate and
proclaim a living Savior.

Costas' statement is true and applicable to these churches dotting our
"barrios," "al celebrar y proclamar al Salvador, la iglesia actua como comunidad
profetica y sacerdotal."[207] Their mere *presence* in the "barrios" is a prophetic
witness to: (1) the principalities and powers, interpreted as either institutions
and/or people who dehumanize God's children; (2) the other churches and
denominations who have left or refuse to enter our "barrios;" (3) the "barrios'"
members themselves, who are challenged and called to forgiveness, hope and

---

[205]Two primary sources will be used: (1) the writer's knowledge based on forty years
participation in the "culto" of indigenous Pentecostalism; and (2) our participant observer notes and
hand-out form from (SE 191) "Sociology of Religion," course taught at Gordon-Conwell
Theological Seminary, see Figure 2-5, "Participant Observers - Iglesia Asamblea Cristiana."

[206]Gerald Sheppard quoted in Charles W. Bell, "New York's Storefront Churches: Pulpits for
the Poor," *New York Sunday News Magazine*, November 21, 1982, p. 8.

[207]"by celebrating and proclaiming the Savior, the church acts as a prophetic and priestly
community," Orlando Costas, "La Realidad de la Iglesia Latinoamericana," from his *El
Protestantismo En America Latina Hoy: Ensayos del Camino* (1972-1974), p. 5.

community; and (4) the believers, too, who are challenged and called not to accept their "status quo."[208]

Their *presence* as a priestly community in a deep and mysterious way sacralizes the "barrios," providing space or context for the gathering of God's people, for intercession, prayer and strength. Piri Thomas speaking about his Tia's Pentecostal church, speaks to this reality:

> It was a miracle how they could shut out the hot and cold running cockroaches and king-size rats and all the added horrors of decaying rotten tenement houses and garbage-littered streets, with drugs running through the veins of our ghetto kids. It was a miracle that they could endure the indignities poured upon our Barrios. I knew that every one of them didn't get weaker. They got stronger. Their prayers didn't get shorter. They got longer.[209]

The presence and location of these churches speaks also theologically of: (1) a missional commitment to the poor; (2) an ecclesiological contextualization, in all dimensions, geographically, physically, etc., (3) and an understanding of spirituality in the life of the church that need not be "limited" by the aesthetic quality of its church building and surroundings.

The indigenous Pentecostals' "culto" is the strongest manifestation and witness to the cultural contextualization of its Spirituality. Songs, "coritos," "testimonios," prayers, offerings, liturgical expressions - open praise: Amen, Hallelujah, Gloria a Dios!, the sermon, all reflect an indigenous Spirituality. Indigenous is understood as that which, in the words of Costas: "... brota o nace, crece, funciona y vive dentro de una situación histórico-cultural específica."[210]

The ethos and infrastructure of the "culto" is permeated by the "barrio culture." There is a "fit" in the linguistic tools used for theology ("God-talk"), praise and all communication, and the "barrio." While the Spanish used may not be the best Castillean, and for that matter neither is the English the proper one

---

[208]In a meeting with Latin American liberation theologians in Pretrópolis, Brazil in January 24, 1991, I raised the question of the role, if any, of the Pentecostal church to Liberation. Leonaldo Boff responded quickly with four positive points, noting the significant role played by the Pentecostal church in the "favelas" of Brazil: (1) "Rescata dignidad mínima"; (2) "Religión de resistencia"; (3) "Liberación espiritual"; y (4) "Lanza un reto al pueblo".

[209]Piri Thomas, *Savior, Savior, Hold My Hand* (Garden City, New York: Doubleday and Company, Inc., 1972), pp. 19-20.

[210]"... emerges, or is born, grows, functions and lives within a specific historical-cultural situation." Orlando Costas, "La Realidad de la Iglesia Evangélica Latinoamericana," p. 6.

used by the bilingual/bicultural new generation, it nevertheless represents an authentic expression of the believer and his/her community. Simple and humble words are spoken that are laden with deep emotion and meaning. A Pentecostal "culto" is an emotional experience.[211] While cognitive signs and symbols are present, it is the emotional or emotive factor that mediates the "mysterium tremendum." The communication of the "true" must be garbed or wrapped emotively in order to resonate effectively and faithfully. It is no surprise that indigenous Pentecostalism's emotional spirituality fits well with and encourages the presence and demonstration of the charismata. There is a real sense in which this emotional spirituality of the "culto" and its charismata foster a true *urban mysticism*.

It is also to be noted that this passionate or emotional "culto" is very personal and existential. The emotions or passions are aroused not by cold, abstract truth or dogma, but by the existential experience of a Person - the Pneumatic Christ! The charismata are very personal and present. Physical signs are seen and touched by the believer, concretely manifested in the "culto." The pastor or leader who has "spiritual authority" and thus commands loyalty does so by virtue of personally embodying and manifesting signs of the Spirit; thus "personal charisma" overrides intellectual, traditional or other cognitive or status-achieved authority.

One example of the "paradox of the soul" of indigenous Pentecostal Spirituality is the effect and function that "Glossolalia"[212] have in the "culto," particularly in relationship to status and leadership. In indigenous Pentecostalism the baptism in the Spirit and the experience of speaking in tongues signals the entrance into a new level of spirituality. The "sense of holiness," closeness to God and the "enduement of power" for service as a function of being "Glossolalic" has a leveling effect in the "culto" with reference to status. In other words, in the "culto" all are equal, for all have equally been or can be "baptized in the Spirit" - given a new Spiritual status by God, above and beyond their present earthly status. The indigenous Pentecostals' "culto" is and can be a true egalitarian expression of community. Yet, paradoxically, this new insight and experience is often blurred

---

[211]Although we are cognizant that an emotional "culto" might have its aberrations, yet, our bias against "emotions" has prevented many from seeing its significant and vital contribution to true Spirituality, not to add theology; see for a positive view and role of the emotions in our lives, Philosopher Robert C. Solomons' *The Passions: The Myth and Nature of Human Emotion* (Garden City, New York: Anchor Press/Doubleday, 1976).

[212]For the finest and most comprehensive study to date on "Glossolalia" please see, H. Newton Maloney and A. Adams Lovekin, *Glossolalia: Behavioral Science Perspectives on Speaking in Tongues* (New York: Oxford University Press, 1985).

by alienating structures of leadership, usually imported from non-glossolalic churches and/or the "mirror image" of the prevailing power structure of the host society. The new status, freedom and boldness is often muted by the placing of the "new wine" into old "wineskins."

Indigenous Pentecostalism thrives in community. The "culto" is at once a "Fiesta" (celebration), as Costas notes, "el culto pentecostal es un culto *espontáneo*, *creativo*, e *intensamente participatorio*,"[213] and an expression of community.

Indigenous musical instruments are used, autochthonous "coritos" are sung, and time is subject to the "event" of the "culto" and not necessarily to a fixed structured time-table. Liturgical expressions (open praises) - Amén, Allelujah, Gloria a Dios! - are expressive of the joy, "fiesta" and experience of liberation found in the "culto." It is a spirituality whose creedal statement is not to be found written and read in the "culto," but one that is verbally given in testimony (given a repetitive structure) and in sermon. Both are in essence authentic creeds and theological confessions of faith.

Renato Poblete and Thomas F. O'Dea are right in underlining the fact that indigenous Pentecostalism, in its "Quest for Community," expresses a Spirituality centered on "a way of life rather than a creed."[214] Whether in the "culto" or outside in the "barrio" or greater society - the world (with its pagan *zeitgeist*) - the communities' religious attitudes and moral standards are defined by parameters that are rigorous and uncompromising. Poblete and O'Dea note:

> They stress a way of life rather than a creed: the emphasis is on intensity rather than universality and they tend to maintain uncompromisingly radical religious attitudes, demanding from their members the maximum in their relationships to God, to the world and to men. The moral standards are very high and there is a genuine austerity about their attitudes and patterns of living. This rigorism often expresses itself in external details: no smoking, no consumption of alcohol drink, no use of cosmetics for women.[215]

---

[213]"The pentecostal 'culto' is a *spontaneous*, *creative*, and *intensely participatory* 'culto'," in Orlando Costas, "La Realidad de la Iglesia Evangélica Latinoamericana," p. 16.

[214]Renato Poblete and Thomas F. O'Dea, "Anomie and the 'Quest for Community': The Formation of Sects Among the Puerto Ricans of New York," p. 21.

[215]*Ibid.*, p. 21.

The contemporary expression for the "Romerías" (pilgrimages) as noted previously is to be found in the spiritual retreats. Indigenous Pentecostalism in its urban setting has placed in the center of its practice for those who seek a deeper spiritual walk with God, "el culto de vigilia" (the vigil "culto"). Rather than retreat to the mountains, for very practical reasons (including financial), in the church or at a member's home believers will gather for an all-night "culto." This "culto de vigilia" will center on prayer and Scripture and it often anticipates spiritual preparations for an evangelistic outreach into the community, a revival in the church, a personal or communal crisis to be confronted, or deep desire to get closer to God.

The Scriptures play an important role in the "vigilia" and in all "cultos." While indigenous Pentecostals have often been caricatured for their handling of Scripture - as fundamentalist, literalist or biblicist - with a certain amount of truth in it for sure, Scriptures, nevertheless, are read in an existential-spiritual manner.[216]

It is important to note the significant role that these "cultos de vigilia" play in leadership development. Not only is attendance expected of would-be spiritual leaders, but many who do attend have often pointed to receiving "the baptism of the Spirit" or their "calling" for ministry at these "cultos de vigilias." Besides prayer and Bible studies, quite frequently the manifestation of the charismata are present - not too infrequently immature and aberrations (of the latter are manifested), providing for the would be leader a "laboratory" (under mentors, of course) to learn how to deal and minister the charismata.

Noteworthy in indigenous Pentecostal Spirituality is the number of "cultos" held during the week. In a great number of cases every day of the week there is a "culto," and at a minimum four "cultos" a week is normal. There is a family quality to the ambiance of the "culto," if for no other reason than for the sheer closeness and amount of contact by the members during the week.

The "machismo" factor is present but somewhat muted given the opportunity for leadership in the "culto" by women. While it is true that women are not as free to occupy, in many but not all churches, the highest rung of authority, yet, in the indigenous Pentecostal's "culto" the women have and exercise their God-given talents, comparable to any other church.

---

[216]More will be said regarding the role of Scriptures in Pentecostalism in my chapter, "Toward an Hispanic American Pentecostal Social Ethic."

Women have played a significant role in the genesis and development of Pentecostalism - as pastors, evangelists, church planters and missionaries.[217] Indigenous Pentecostalism could not have survived without the leadership of women, especially "la misionera" (the local church missionary) ever present in the "culto" and in visitation of homes and hospitals.

There are many other elements in the "culto" that can be descriptively analyzed, but given the scope of this paper, I have noted only those salient elements that demonstrated the rich and vibrant spirituality and implicit theology of indigenous Pentecostalism.

The focus has been on the "culto" as the central expression of indigenous Pentecostals' Spirituality and implicit Theology. It revealed, in summary, the following theological parameters of indigenous Pentecostalism:

A. **A Contextual Theology -** From the Prophetic and Priestly presence in the "barrios" emerges the linguistic tools of "God-talk" responding to the "barrio culture."

B. **A Spiritual Theology -** Emotive and spiritual factors mediate the "mysterium tremendum," rather than cognitive signs or symbols - though these are present and important.

C. **A Personalist and Existential Theology -** The reality of God as a Person, present *now* and not a past or future event impacts all understanding of the faith. The Scriptures truly becomes alive as the "Word of God."

D. **A Liberation Theology -** Identity and solidarity with the poor and oppressed. To experience spiritual freedom from all bondages of the flesh, the devil, and the world; both as experience and goal. *Individualistic* understood in the freedom to be oneself in the "culto" to be authentic, even in the face of oppression in the society.

---

[217]The ambiguous role of women in indigenous Pentecostalism, coupled with the experience of former Catholics (with their religious Spirituality saturated in Mariology or Marianism) played not too small a part in the "Mita Cult." "Mita" (Juanita García Peraza) founded an indigenous Pentecostal cult in Puerto Rico, with branches in New York's West Side, in which she was called "La Diosa" ("The Goddess"). Her followers believed she was the incarnation of the Spirit.

E.   **A Charismatic Theology** - The Glossolalic experiences color all understanding of Spirituality.

F.   **An Egalitarian Theology**- Because of the leveling of the Glossolalic experience, all can receive a "word" from the Lord; "calling," ministry, leadership, as well as theology is not just the province of an elite.

CHAPTER III

SOCIO-THEOLOGICAL INTERPRETATION
OF THE
HISPANIC URBAN PENTECOSTAL REALITY

"Pero tenemos este tesoro en vasos de barro"

- 2 Corinthians 4:7[1]

A basic assumption of this study is its understanding of religion as grounded in the Ultimate (God) and thus not reduced to final psycho-social and/or cultural-economic explanations. Yet, in the words of Otto Maduro,

> No religion exists in a vacuum. Every religion, any religion, no matter what we mayunderstand by "religion," is a *situated* reality - situated in a specific human context, a concrete and determined geographical space, historical moment, and social milieu. Every religion is, in each concrete case, always the religion of these or those determinate human beings. A religion that would not be the religion of determinate human beings would be nonexistent, purely a phantasm of the imagination.[2]

Thus, for the proper understanding of religion as an "earthen vessel" we must undertake an analysis of it as a *situated* reality.

To this point I have been more descriptive. In this chapter I turn to place the Hispanic Pentecostal church, in its recent history, in its socio-theological context. This means I become more analytical and, thus, more critical. In this chapter we lay groundwork for the constructive-reconstructive task that will follow.

---

[1]"But we have this treasure in earthen vessels," 2 Corinthians 4:7.

[2]Otto Maduro, *Religion and Social Conflicts* (Maryknoll, N.Y.: Orbis Books, 1982), p. 41.

The Context of "Person-in-Community"

Homo Socius

Boston Personalism, as noted previously, provides a definition of persons that has affinity with Hispanic personality and value orientations. Notwithstanding the stereotypical portrayal of Hispanic "individualism" in the literature, an authentic and thus a proper understanding of Hispanic culture values and *Weltanschauung* would require a more communal or organic definition of persons; a definition that coheres with Paul Deats' view of the human person, "seen not as an isolate, but as coming to self-awareness and a sense of identity in a community of persons, bound together by value commitments and in purposive activity."[3] It would agree with Walter Muelder "that personality is a *socius* with a *private* center."[4] Peter Berger and Thomas Luckman note well the *socius* nature of the person when they state that:

> Solitary human being is being on the animal level (which, of course, man shares with other animals). As soon as one observes phenomena that are specifically human, one enters the realm of the social. Man's specific humanity and his sociality are inextricably intertwined. *Homo sapiens* is always, and in the same measure, *homo socius.*[5]

"Person-in-Community" defines the reality of the Hispanic. It is a social reality, one that sees persons as social creatures. As such, its understanding of "human nature" is one that posits society as both a product and a producer of persons, thus representing a dialectical anthropological perspective. It is important to note with Peter Berger that:

> ... society is, of course, nothing but part and parcel of non-material culture. Society is that aspect of the latter that structures man's ongoing relations with his fellowmen. As but an element of culture, society fully shares in

---

[3]Paul Deats, "Conflict and Reconciliation in Communitarian Social Ethics," in Paul Deats and Carol Robb, ed., *The Boston Personalist Tradition in Philosophy, Social Ethics, and Theology* (Macon, Georgia: Mercer University Press, 1986), p. 277.

[4]Walter Muelder, "Communitarian Dimensions of the Moral Laws" in *Ibid.*, pp. 244-245.

[5]Peter L. Berger and Thomas Luckman, *The Social Construction of Reality: A Treatise in the Sociology of Knowledge* (New York, N.Y.: Anchor Books, 1967), p. 51.

the latter's character as a human product. Society is constituted and maintained by acting human beings.[6]

A dialectical anthropological perspective can be seen in H. Wheeler Robinson's comments regarding the relations of society and the individual:

> There can never be any ultimate and exclusive antithesis of the two. The individual could not come into existence at all without some form of society, and depends upon it for his growth and development. The society finds articulate expression only through the individuals who constitute it. Human personality is in itself as truly social as individual.[7]

Hispanics are thus found in the web of an ongoing culture and social milieu - American society - one that by and large has preceded them (particularly those in the North East) and/or which they have had little power as a group to "construct" or change. Given their numerical and minority condition, coupled with socio-political powerlessness, it is no surprise to situate them in a marginal and thus dominated status in this society. As an ethnic and religious minority, Hispanic Pentecostals also experience the cultural dominance of the Protestant American culture and that of the Catholic religious culture, as well as socio-economic oppression.

Three Socio-hermeneutical Paradigms

As an interpretive framework three paradigms will be used for understanding Hispanic Pentecostalism, as it relates to its genesis, development and growth, its meaning and function. A corollary emphasis will be given to locating Hispanics, more particularly Hispanic Pentecostals, in American society identifying those forces, both personal and social, which oppress them.

Following Walter Mueldor and Paul Deats' emphasis on multiple and cumulative social causation, in the tradition of Myrdal's *An American Dilemma*,[8]

---

[6]Peter L. Berger, *The Sacred Canopy: Elements of a Sociological Theory of Religion* (New York, N.Y.: Anchor Books, 1969), pp. 6-7; this is significant in order to avoid static hypostatizing thinking regarding social reality, a fact that was often emphasized by Max Weber's methodology.

[7]H. Wheeler Robinson, *Corporate Personality in Ancient Israel*, (Philadelphia: Fortress Press, 1964), p. 21.

[8]Gunnar Myrdal, *An American Dilemma* (New York, N.Y.: Harper and Row, 1944), appendix 3, pp. 1,065-1,070.

the three paradigms will provide a pluralistic and composite portrait of Hispanic Pentecostal reality. Thus the approach also follows Boston Personalism's stress on synoptic integration, as well as critical analysis.

The three paradigms are: (1) Otto Maduro's Conflict Analysis; (2) Renato Poblete and Thomas F. O'Dea's "Anomie and the Quest for Community" Hypothesis; and (3) Luther P. Gerlach and Virginia H. Hine's Functional-structural Analysis.

Otto Maduro's Conflict Analysis[9]

Maduro's conflict analysis provides us with a paradigm in which to situate Hispanic Pentecostalism in the overarching capitalist economy and class nature of American society. He is particularly fruitful in helping us see the relationship of the class struggle and the emergence, maintenance, and/or transformation of religious groups. Religion as both a "product" of society and as a legitimate "producer" of society are critically analyzed by him.

Maduro's informing methodology is Marxist, although he challenges the narrow Marxist theory of religion that would posit the reality of Christianity as purely epiphenomenal. He rather sees "religion as a relatively autonomous terrain of social conflicts"[10] and sees its positive role in the struggle for justice and liberation. Maduro's conflict analysis sets its own parameters by stating its intention to

> pursue the specific problem of religion as *a complex field of mediation of social conflicts*... this definition of religion is, then, a strictly sociological one ... it claims but *one aspect* of the inexhaustible wealth of religious phenomena - the sociologically relevant aspect of these phenomena.[11]

One does not need to fall prey to an economic deterministic view of society to acknowledge the capitalistic mode of production's class emphasis, thus underscoring the class nature of American society. Maduro suggestively posits religion in a classist society as legitimating the existing mode of relationships (the dominant church), escaping in an "apolitical" religious resolution (the oppressed

---

[9]Otto Maduro, *Religion and Social Conflicts.*

[10]*Ibid.*, pp. 79.

[11]*Ibid.*, pp. 6-7; One must note that while Maduro's analysis is set in terms of Latin America, its theoretical constructs are broad enough, and sufficiently insightful, for an analysis of Hispanic Pentecostal reality in North American society.

sect) or serving "a potential revolutionary function." These are dynamic and potentially historic interchangeable roles that religion can play in a society - particularly one embedded in a situation of dominance.

Maduro's progressive Marxist view helps us situate and partially explain the genesis and development of Pentecostalism in general and Hispanic Pentecostalism in particular. As previously noted, Pentecostalism emerged and developed among the disenfranchised, "... ethnically heterogeneous, struggling working class and impoverished unemployed."[12]   Pentecostalism worldwide, and Hispanic Pentecostalism specifically, has remained by and large the "haven of the masses."[13]   Robert M. Anderson's description of Pentecostalism's constituency and the socio-economic milieu prevalent at its beginning is still a relevant description of Hispanic Pentecostal reality:

> The working poor from whose ranks then Pentecostal movement drew the overwhelming bulk of its recruits... were mostly semi-skilled and unskilled workers who made up the urban and rural proletariat of industrial capitalism. They constituted the lowest base of the work force of the nation, and also a free-floating labor reserve. As a class, they were brought into being by the movement of rural Americans to the city and by the influx of masses of immigrants during the period of transition from competitive to monopoly capitalism.[14]

Hispanic Pentecostalism can be viewed as part of that movement of the lower class - the working poor and unemployed - that resolves its economic and class status situation by means of a sectarian religious affiliation. It "may be viewed as one small part of a widespread, long-term protest against the whole thrust of modern urban industrial capitalist society."[15] This correlates well with Charles Y. Glock and Rodney Stark's "deprivation theory."[16] In their deprivation

---

[12]Robert Mapes Anderson, *Vision of the Disinherited: The Making of American Pentecostalism*, p. 122.

[13]See Christian Lalive D'Epinay, *Haven of the Masses: A Study of the Pentecostal Movement in Chile* (London: Lutterworth Press, 1969).

[14]Robert Mapes Anderson, *Vision of the Disinherited: The Making of American Pentecostalism*, p. 225.

[15]*Ibid.*, p. 223.

[16]Charles Y. Glock and Rodney Stark, "On the Origin and Evolution of Religious Groups," in Charles Y. Glock,ed., *Religion in Sociological Perspective: Essays in the Empirical Study of Religion* (Belmont, California: Wadsworth, 1973); Deprivations refer to "any and all of the ways

typology, of which five kinds are noted: economic, social, organic, ethical and psychic, each is resolved by the formation of distinct religious groups. They see the Sect as the religious resolution to economic deprivations.

In a real sense Hispanic Pentecostalism represents in part Karl Marx's description of religion in his *Critique of Hegel's Philosophy of Right*, namely,: "religion is the sigh of the oppressed creature, the heart of a heartless world."[17]

Maduro's conflict analysis not only provides us with a paradigm in which to situate Hispanic Pentecostalism in American society, but it also sets the basic socio-cultural framework for the creative-conflict and confrontation suggested in our subsection, "The Challenge to Confront Structural Sin and Evil," in chapter V, "Toward An Hispanic American Pentecostal Social Ethic." Deats reminds us that "our moral experience includes the experience of conflict, whether we seek to deny or avoid that conflict or we face it head-on ... conflict appears to be inescapable in human experience, despite our efforts to gloss over it, especially in religious groups."[18]   It is important to note that conflict is explicit in the newest formulation of the moral laws tradition of Boston Personalism by Paul K. Deats, Jr.[19]

----

that an individual or group may be, or feel disadvantage in comparison either to other individuals or groups or to an internalized set of standards", *Ibid.* p. 210.

[17]Karl Marx, "Contribution to the Critique of Hegel's Philosophy of Right: Introduction," in Robert C. Tucker, ed. *The Marx-Engels Reader* (New York: W. W. Norton and Company, 1972), p. 12.

[18]Paul Deats, "Conflict and Reconciliation in Communitarian Social Ethics," in Paul Deats and Carol Robb, ed., *The Boston Personalist Tradition in Philosophy, Social Ethics, and Theology*, 281.

[19]*Ibid.*, p. 285: Laws of Praxis: "How shall we respond to conflict and defeat?" Law of Conflict and Reconciliation: All persons, in their own lives and in the lives of groups to which they belong, ought to accept conflict in the course of seeking to formulate and achieve the ideals of personality and of community, and to work through conflict - with others, "friends" and "enemies" alike - toward consensus, justice, and reconciliation. Law of Fallibility and Corrigibility: All persons ought to expect to make - and suffer - mistakes, failures, and defeat, without being overcome by these experiences or losing hope. When mistakes are made, and repentance is acknowledged, and forgiveness asked, the way is opened for resources, human and divine, to be made available.

Poblete and O'Dea's "Anomie and the Quest
for Community" Hypothesis[20]

Utilizing Emile Durkheim's concept of *anomie*, Poblete and O'Dea posit sectarianism as a response to anomie. They state:

> For Durkheim anomie was characterized by two interrelated elements. First of all there is a breakdown of those social structures in which the individual found the psychological support and nurture requisite to personal and psychological security. Secondly, there is a loss of consensus or general agreement upon the standards and norms that previously provided the normative orientations and existential definitions in terms of which individual and group life were meaningful.[21]

Poblete and O'Dea see anomie as a problem engendered by modern urban industrial society. They note the Pentecostal sectarian response by Puerto Rican migrants, in a positive search or quest for community, to be a resolution of this psycho-social phenomena.

The experience of *anomie* by Puerto Ricans and other Hispanics in the North East is abundantly noted in the socio-cultural literature, given the conflictive cultural context, social instability, and the intense "impersonalization of a technological society characterized by urbanism."[22] The cities, especially New York City in this case, receiving the Puerto Rican migration in the 1930's and post war years of 1940's and 1950's, did present a cold and alienating context. Neither language nor culture was affirmed and, typical of uprooted immigrants, small "colonias" were developed.[23] Within these small communities there arose a critical need for values, norms, and cosmization reconstruction given the loss of consensus (Durkheim), loss of moral certitudes (Robert Nesbit),[24] loss of meaning

---

[20]Renato Poblete and Thomas F. O'Dea "Anomie and the 'Quest for Community': The Formation of Sects Among the Puerto Ricans of New York," *American Catholic Sociological Review*, pp. 18-36.

[21]*Ibid.*, p. 21; see Emile Durkeim, *Suicide* (New York: Free Press, 1951, ed.); and Robert K. Merton, *Social Theory and Social Structures* (Glencoe, Ill.: Free Press, 1957) pp. 131-194.

[22]*Ibid.*, p. 23.

[23]See especially, Virginia E. Sanchez Korrol, *From Colonia to Community: The History of Puerto Ricans in New York City, 1917-1948.*

[24]Robert A. Nesbit, *The Quest for Community* (New York: Oxford University Press, 1953).

(Peter Berger).[25]   Given the hostile environment of the metropolis, and the
"remoteness of institutional Catholicism from many of their needs,"[26] a resolution
was found by many in the small, warm, personal, participatory, store-front
Pentecostal churches in their "colonias" - organized and led through their language
and cultural nuances.

The Hispanic Pentecostal Church thus provided Hispanics that social milieu,
cultural affirmation and "cosmization in a sacred mode" (religion)[27] critically
needed to overcome personal and social anomie.[28]

Gerlach and Hine's
Functional-Structural Analysis[29]

Gerlach and Hine's paradigm provides an interpretive or explanatory
scheme that posits that while conditions of deprivation and disorganization may be
causal or "facilitating conditions" in the genesis of a movement, its development
and growth must be sought in the dynamics of the movement itself.

> We do not deny the validity of the theoretical models that seek to explain
> religious movements in terms of such external conditions ... but we do find
> them inadequate as analytical tools without accompanying models for
> understanding the inner structure and processes of a movement itself.

---

[25]Peter L. Berger, *The Sacred Canopy: Elements of a Sociological Theory of Religion* (New York: Anchor Books, 1969).

[26]Renato Poblete and Thomas F. O'Dea, "Anomie and the 'Quest for Community': The Formation of Sects Among Puerto Ricans of New York," p. 28.

[27]Peter L. Berger, *The Sacred Canopy*, p. 25.

[28]See Herve Carrier, *The Sociology of Religious Belonging* (New York: Herder and Herder, 1965).

[29]Luther P. Gerlach and Virginia H. Hine, "Five factors crucial to the growth and spread of a modern religious movement" *Journal for the Scientific Study of Religion* 7 (Spring 1968): 23-40; Used with permission of the Society for the Scientific Study of Religion, copyright 1968. See also, Luther P. Gerlach and Virginia H. Hine, *People, Power, Change Movements of Social Transformation* (Indianapolis: The Bobbs-Merrill Company, Inc., 1970).

Indeed we would prefer to consider these external conditions as 'facilitating' or 'enabling' rather than necessary or sufficient...[30]

Their study of movement dynamics gives us a paradigm which identifies five key factors that were crucial to the growth and development of Pentecostalism:

1. reticulate **organization**
2. fervent and convincing **recruitment** along pre-existing lines of significant social relationships
3. a **commitment** act or experience
4. a change-oriented and action-motivating **ideology**
5. the perception of real or imagined **opposition**.[31]

These five factors, when applied to Hispanic Pentecostalism, are very fruitful for understanding its growth and development. I will look at these five factors, emphasizing very selectively those points that correlate well with the Hispanic experience.

Reticulate and Acephalous Organizational Structure

As previously noted in our section, "Hispanic Spirituality and Indigenous Pentecostal Theology," the "glossolalic" experience has a leveling (egalitarian) effect in the "culto" with reference to status. The "sense of holiness" and the "enduement of power" for service as a function of being "glossolalic" contributes greatly to an understanding of "calling" and ministry/leadership which is no longer the exclusive province of the trained professional or of an elite. One now finds that the most humble member, who has been baptized in the Spirit, has a new spiritual status - so important, given the denial of status by the society at large.

The egalitarian theological praxis of Hispanic Pentecostalism coheres well with Gerlach and Hine's findings in which they note:

---

[30]Luther P. Gerlach and Virginia H. Hine, "Five factors crucial to the growth and spread of a modern religious movement," *Journal for the Scientific Study of Religion*, p. 38.

[31]*Ibid.*, pp. 23-24; They later (1970), in a four year research of movements of social transformation, studied Pentecostals and the Black Power movements utilizing basically the same five factors in a more elaborated and sophisticated fashion, *People, Power, Change Movements of Social Transformation*, p. XVII.

> The concept of individual access to the spiritual source of authority, when taken seriously, tends to prevent organizational solidarity and centralized control...Proliferation through factional splitting, ... organizational spontaneity, even of the denominationally organized sectors of the movement, the remarkable emergence of self-appointed (or God-appointed) indigenous lay leaders and the growth through fission have also been generally noted by students of the movements in Latin America.[32]

The growth and evangelistic thrust in the "barrios" of Pentecostalism owes no small part to this self-understanding and vocational possibilities of the believer.

Gerlach and Hine found in their studies a pattern of inter-relationships and linkages which they called the "infrastructure" of the Pentecostal movement.[33] These too we find very insightful and correlated well with the Hispanic experience. Among the most noteworthy are: (1) personal associations; (2) leadership exchange; and (3) the conceptual commonality and authority of the Spirit/experience.[34]

Regarding *personal associations*, it is worth noting the broad family and friends network and linkages that are established crossing over local groups. There is a cross fertilization process as they visit each other's "culto." This dynamic in the Hispanic Pentecostal churches coheres well with Gerlach and Hine's statement that: "The membership of local groups is hence far from static but rather fluctuates as members come and go from one group to another, thereby forming links between all groups."[35]

The *leadership exchange* within the Hispanic Pentecostal church is great. There is a network of evangelists and leaders who visit each other's churches, crossing community, state and national boundaries. In the Northeast this linkage and network is most noticeable in the continual exchange of evangelists and other leaders with Puerto Rico and the Dominican Republic.

The third element noted is the *conceptual commonality and authority of the Spirit/experience.* By this pattern of interrelationship or infrastructure Gerlach and

---

[32]Luther P. Gerlach and Virginia H. Hine, "Five factors crucial to the growth and spread of a modern religious movement", p. 26.

[33]*Ibid.*, 27.

[34]*Ibid.*, p. 27-30.

[35]*Ibid.*, p. 27.

Hine's finding underscores the common bond that unites those who have been baptized in the Spirit, and whose understanding of ultimate leadership of the Pentecostal movement rests on the Holy Spirit. What is significant here and amply noted in the Hispanic Pentecostal church in the "barrios" is that there is a sense of *unity*, given the above-noted self-understanding of the Spirit, linking groups that are organizationally different.

> (This) core integrating ideology under-girds the capability of the movement to organize diversity ... provides a basis for continuing interaction between resulting splinters. United in core belief, the Pentecostals can then unite against genuine opposition and/or what they believe to be opposition.[36]

Hispanic Pentecostal churches are noted for their "strong" leaders; though a quick and superficial analysis of authority in the Hispanic Pentecostal churches can be misleading. Notwithstanding the emergence of more than their share of "charismatic" (not to say dictatorial) leaders, one must look carefully at the prevailing ethos of leadership empowerment in the "culto" and the mediating structures. One must note that the Pentecostal structure in the local church "culto" especially, and somewhat in organization ("concilio"), provides for a variety of leadership opportunities and developments to match members' emerging gifts. Most importantly all Pentecostal structures are "fueled" by a self-understanding of the Spirit that relativizes all human authority.

As I noted previously, paradoxically, too often this new insight and experience is often blurred by alienating structures of leadership, usually imported from non-glossolalic churches and/or the "mirror image" of the prevailing power structure of the host society. The new status, freedom, and boldness is often muted by the placing of the "new wine" into old "wineskins." Yet, over all, the type of intricate and loosely organized structures of Hispanic Pentecostalism facilitates its appeal and growth.

Fervent and Convincing Recruitment

Without a doubt, the experience of Pentecostals worldwide, and no less Hispanic Pentecostals, has been characterized by evangelistic zeal. L. Grant McClung Jr., in his "Spontaneous Strategy of the Spirit/Pentecostal Missionary Practices" states:

---

[36]*Ibid.*, pp. 29-30.

Evangelism and pentecostalism could be said to be synonymous terms. It is expected, espe-cially in the Third World, that to be a pentecostal Christian one is to be a witness. Pentecostals feel an obligation to reach all men with the gospel ... Pentecostals see aggressive evangelism in the pages of the New Testament and feel that they must respond accordingly.[37]

The baptism of the Spirit with the ensuing power for witness is part of the self-understanding of the Pentecostal believer. This power is validated both in Scripture by such verses as "But ye shall receive power, after that the Holy Ghost is come upon you: and ye shall be witnesses unto me both in Jerusalem, and in all Judea, and in Samaria, and unto the uttermost part of the earth," (Acts 1:8), and in aggressive and effective witness in the "barrios."

While the evangelistic zeal and witness by Hispanic Pentecostals extends to all, it is most noted and effective among friends and family. The extended family values still prevalent in the "barrios" provide the context for a wide impact of "face-to-face recruitment along lines of pre-existing social relationships."[38] Not only father and mother, daughters and sons, but, uncles and aunts, nephews and nieces, grandparents and in-laws, lest we forget - the "compadrazco," (godparents) are often found in the "barrio" family culture. Friends and, above all, relatives are the highest percentage of recruited members in the Hispanic Pentecostal church. This recruitment along lines of relatives is borne out by Gerlach and Hine's study regarding Pentecostal church members. They state, "relatives are responsible for recruiting 71 percent of the established Pentecostal sect members."[39] They add further, that in recruiting relationships, "kinship ties are more significant at the lower end of the socio-economic scale."[40]

Their study thus suggests an observation, which coheres well with this writer's observation of Hispanic Pentecostals, that "while facilitating conditions such as deprivation of various types or social disorganization may predispose

[37]L. Grant McClung, Jr. (ed.), *Azusa Street and Beyond: Pentecostal Missions and Church Growth in the Twentieth Century* (South Plainfield, N.J.: Bridge Publishing, Inc., 1986), pp. 74-75.

[38]Gerlach and Hines, "Five factors...," p. 30.

[39]*Ibid.*, p. 31.

[40]*Ibid.*, p. 31.

people to joining a movement, close association with a committed 'witness' or recruiter is empirically far more explanatory."[41]

A Commitment Act or Experience

Commitment is a crucial factor in movement dynamics. Gerlach and Hines, while not looking into the nature of commitment experience, note well its effect. "We found that commitment in Pentecostalism involved not only a highly motivating religious experience, but often a more objectively observable act."[42] They, thus, divide commitment into two categories: (1) commitment experience and (2) commitment act.

In Pentecostalism such a commitment experience or act "sets the believer apart in some way from the larger social context, cuts him off from past patterns of behavior and sometimes from past associations, identifies him with other participants in the movement, and provides high motivation for change behavior."[43]

The paramount commitment experience in Pentecostalism is personal conversion to Jesus Christ as Lord and Saviour: It is a life-transforming experience. Yet, the *commitment experience* that most distinguishes Pentecostalism, thus markedly setting it apart, is "glossolalia." In Hispanic Pentecostalism this experience can be more radical given the nature of "glossolalic" manifestations and expressions in the Hispanic lower class emotional context and its status granting to recipients - so much more profound and significant since they often have no other status in the "barrio" or larger society.

Within the Hispanic Pentecostal "culto" one can note readily the "symbols of identity" - dress codes and behavior taboos - which serve as "bridge-burning" and "power-generating" *acts of commitment*. They eventually reinforce and set the behavior apart, solidifying the person's involvement/identity in Pentecostalism. Often these can be analyzed as hiding a sexist (machismo) bias against women, to which most dress codes are directed.[44] They also may express status seeking

---

[41]*Ibid.*, pp. 31-32.

[42]*Ibid.*, p. 32.

[43]*Ibid.*, p. 32.

[44]Illustrative of this is the writer's need, through the years, to address this issue under the "five P's": "Pelo" (hair), "Pintura" (cosmetic), "Prenda" (jewelry) y "Pantalones" (pants) = "Pecado"

affirmation of the in-group sectarian church. Ironically, these "symbols of identity" begin to diminish in emphasis and value as the status of the members of the sect begins to increase in the larger society, due largely to educational and socio-economic achievements.

The high commitment expressions and acts cultivated and found in Hispanic Pentecostalism contribute significantly to the presence of "Charisma." According to Gerlach and Hine, "Charisma, that quality traditionally assigned by sociologist and anthropologist only to magnetic leaders of emergent movements, flows freely through the ranks of Pentecostalism."[45] Given the intense and emotional ethos of Hispanic Pentecostal "cultos" and the emergent "Charismatic" leaders, it is no surprise that Pentecostalism in the "barrios" of the Third World (including the U.S.A.) has great appeal and spreading power to the downtrodden and oppressed poor.

Ideology

Gerlach and Hine are careful to remind us that their interest in ideology is not so much with the particular theological or ideological formulations - content - as with the cognitive or restructuring experience of the Pentecostal believer.[46] Among their findings I will highlight the following, which are particularly relevant to Hispanic Pentecostalism: (1) dogmatism or certitude; (2) personal power and personal worth; (3) and rejection of ideal-real gap.[47]

Dogmatism or Certitude

In Pentecostalism Gerlach and Hine agree with Erich Hoffer's remark that "the effectiveness of a doctrine does not come from its meaning but from its

---

(sin)?.

[45]Gerlach and Hines, "Five Factors...," p.32.

[46]"In such an analysis of movement dynamics, there is more to be gained by identifying generic characteristics of movement ideologies - characteristics which may be found in the ideology of any movement - which are functional in terms of the growth of the movement, and which promote personal or social change.", Luther P. Gerlach and Virginia H. Hine, *People, Power, Change Movements of Social Transformation*, p. 159.

[47]for listing of other characteristics see, *Ibid.*, pp. 181-182.

certitude."[48]   The conversion experience and subsequent baptism of the Spirit produce profound cognitive and valuative changes in the believer.   The belief system of the Pentecostal offers "a simple master plan presented in symbolic and easily communicated terms."[49]   What outsiders would label dogmatism, insiders call certitude.   Thus, the authoritarianism or dogmatism present is seen by Gerlach and Hine as having little to do with personality type but more with the certitude resulting from the commitment process - the Pentecostal baptism in the Spirit, and speaking in tongues.   The baptism in the Spirit operates in the believer a cognitive restructuring process that is revelatory in nature.   "There is a sense of finality - of having gotten firm hold on a belief system or a conceptual framework that fully satisfies the human need for explanation and meaning."[50]

In Hispanic Pentecostalism one can appreciate the "certitude factor" that brings along a strong sense of meaning and hope to the believer in an otherwise meaningless and hopeless "barrio".   Yet, the belief system that is "inherited" or presented has often been one of narrow and individualistic piety with little, if any, of the social or political implications that a broader conceptual framework could provide.

The dogmatism or certitude factor is a function of the baptism in the Spirit and not necessarily tied down to a particular theological and/or ethical formulation. Thus, there is a real sense, which we will explore later in this study, in which the codification of the new ideology (theology) can be broadened and/or reconstructed.

Personal Power and Personal Worth

The believer's reported personal experience with an external power at conversion and, most surely, at his/her baptism of the Spirit is a confirmation of the belief in a personal access to a source of transcendent power.   This experience of power engenders in turn in the believer, a "power relationship" manifested in risk-taking (some would say, greater faith), sense of control over personal destiny, and even the destiny of the world.   An apparent passive or fatalistic attitude

---

[48]*Ibid.*, p. 159, quoted from Eric Hoffer, *The True Believer* (New York, N.Y.: Harper & Row, 1951), p. 76.

[49]Gerlach and Hine, "Five factors crucial to the growth and spread of a modern religious movement", p. 24.

[50]Gerlach and Hine, *People, Power, Change Movements of Social Transformation*, p. 161.

towards personal and world events may be noted, though this is best understood within the framework of actively striving to fulfill the will of an omnipotent God.

The baptism in the Holy Spirit profoundly influences the self-worth of the person. In the "barrio" Pentecostal church, the impact is noticeable as believers, "new creatures in Christ," in touch with the power of the universe, find new status and personal worth. Their evangelistic or recruitment zeal owes no small measure to this new self-image and its motivating power.

The missing dimension, which would be the logical extension, is to place this "power relation" in an expanded social conceptual framework (social ethic).

Rejection of Ideal-real Gap

The potential revolutionary nature of the ideological factors (theology) in Pentecostalism becomes quite evident in its intolerance for the ideal-real gap. Gerlach and Hine remind us that:

> A philosophical acceptance of the ideal-real gap is typical in social institutions designed to maintain social stability at the status quo. Fanaticism, the hallmark of movements and revolutionary social change, is in essence a rejection of this gap.[51]

Attitudinal changes resulting from the Baptism experience and strong support from other fellow believers, coupled with the Scriptural assurances of the power at his/her disposal, bridges the gap for the Pentecostal. In other words, their ideology (theology) provides for a method - the power of the Spirit - to overcome the gap between the ideal creedal values of a society and its actual practice.

The aggressive nature of Pentecostalism noted in evangelism and mission, risk-taking, and reinterpretation of any negative feedback as positive affirmation of his/her ideological position, are all indicative of the rejection of the ideal-real gap. Malony and Lovekin state that "Characteristic of movement ideologies like Pentecostalism is the strong and verbalized rejection of this gap and a striving for the ideal."[52]

---

[51]Gerlach and Hine, "Five factors...," p. 34.

[52]H. Newton Malony and A. Adams Lovekin, *Glossolalia: Behavioral Science Perspectives on Speaking in Tongues*, p. 194.

In Hispanic Pentecostalism this is noted most singularly in the attitude towards sickness and holiness. Belief and practice of divine healing and, thus, the power of the Spirit of God to heal physical impairment is crucial. The admonition to practice holiness - because the power is there to do so - is paramount. Gerlach and Hine state it well:

> Christianity's impossible ethic, "Be ye therefore perfect as your Father in heaven is perfect," of little concern to most church goers, is important to the Pentecostal largely because his ideology also provides a method by which the ethic becomes possible.[53]

What is indicative of the above is the narrow framework of the revolutionary insight that rejects the ideal-real gap. The Pentecostal's intolerance for sickness - a physical, not "spiritual" condition - should extend to other non-spiritual areas of life, (i.e., intolerance for bad housing, unemployment, injustice). The potential for radical social change is within the bosom of Hispanic Pentecostals in the "barrio" given the radical experience of the baptism in the Spirit.

Opposition

Liston Pope in his celebrated *Millhands and Preachers* wrote of the possession of a "psychology of persecution" in sectarian groups. The real or perceived opposition by those movements that experience the baptism in the Spirit is well known. The experience of ridicule and rejection from other churches (mainline Protestant and/or Catholic) that Hispanic Pentecostals have lived through in the "barrios," coupled with the racist and classist "benign neglect" of many, have contributed in Hispanic Pentecostals to this "psychology of persecution."

The opposition to Pentecostalism is a historic fact, although it has been ameliorated since the 60's by the "neo-pentecostal revival" in mainline Protestant and Catholic churches. Yet, given the nature of the "glossolalic" experience itself, and the cultural and linguistic differences of Hispanics, it is no surprise to see in the "barrios" a continued opposition. This can take the form of "redlining" by banks, difficulty in securing "space" or a store-front for the church, or actual pejorative and ridiculing statements in the local press. Gone are the days when stone throwing or possible physical harm accompanied participation in an Hispanic Pentecostal service. Opposition by many Hispanic mainline churches, and some Catholics too, takes on more sophisticated and subtle forms.

---

[53]Gerlach and Hine, "Five factors...," p. 34.

The tendency of Hispanic Pentecostals to easily attribute all opposition to their faith experience of "glossolalia," oftentimes hides a deeper opposition and rejection; one rooted on their being a "class church" - a church of the poor - with all the cultural and social baggage which it carries. To be Hispanic, poor, and Pentecostal is to be an easy "scapegoat" target for many in the "barrios."

The phenomenon of opposition, real or perceived, has contributed to the development of Pentecostalism in an oblique but positive way. Gerlach and Hine note "... optimum amounts of opposition, short of effective total suppression, serve to intensify commitment, unify the local group, and provide a basis for identification between groups."[54]

Gerlach and Hine's movement analysis emphasizes the dynamic nature of the five factors identified - factors that feed on each other, interrelating with the others dynamically, thus contributing to the growth and development of the movement. They are instructive and rich in their explanatory power when applied to Hispanic Pentecostalism.

The *situated* reality of Hispanic Pentecostalism is further defined by its self-understanding as the Community of the Spirit. This self-referrence is critical for the understanding of Hispanic Pentecostalism in society, to which I now turn our attention.

The Community of the Spirit in Society

The Church: Community of the Spirit

Without a doubt the church, with its "culto," is the central focus of Hispanic Pentecostalism. It is the locus of the believer's personal liberation and status affirmation within society. It is the locus of the believer's social life - witnessed to by the enormous amount of "cultos" during the week. But above all, it is the locus of the manifestation of the Spirit - she/he meets the Spirit here as no place else.

The self-understanding of the Hispanic Pentecostal church is that it is the community of the Spirit. While such may not be the official articulated definition, it, nevertheless, is reflected in its "culto" and its interpretation. There the believers are incorporated into the body of Christ by the Spirit, are gathered as the people

---

[54]*Ibid.*, p. 37.

of God by the Spirit, and experience the "glossolalic" gifts as the temple of the Holy Spirit.

As the community of the Spirit, "the church is, in the most exact sense, a *Koinonia*, a common sharing in the Holy Spirit."[55] Bishop Newbigin states about the Pentecostal church:

> ... its central element is the conviction that the Christian life is a matter of the experienced power and presence of the Holy Spirit today; that an excessive emphasis upon those immutable elements in the Gospel upon which orthodox Catholicism and Protestantism have concentrated attention may, and in fact often does, result in a church which is a mere shell, having the form of a church but not the life.[56]

Bishop Newbigin defines the nature of the church as it operates in the three major confessions of Christianity, namely: Protestant, Catholic and Pentecostal. His three-fold paradigm sees the church as: (1) "the congregation of the faithful" - Protestant; (2) "the body of Christ" - Catholic; and (3) "the community of the Spirit" - Pentecostal.   As the congregation of the faithful, the church is incorporated in Christ by the preaching of the Word and the sacraments. As the body of Christ, it is incorporated sacramentally into the life of His Church. As the community of the Holy Spirit, it is incorporated in Christ by the power of the Holy Spirit.[57] Each of the noted paradigms brings out the rich and multi-faceted glory and mystery of the Church; all are needed to fully comprehend the nature of the Church and its mission. Each also provides a critique of the other church, noting the missing or least emphasized characteristic of the church.

It is important to note that the Church, as the community of the Spirit, while Scriptural and consistent with its own experience of God, can so isolate its own particular understanding of the truth that it can suffer distortion as it makes its "truth" the sole determinant for its life and mission. This distortion tendency is equally true of the other churches - the genesis of heresy is oftentimes but misplaced emphasis on truth.

In Hispanic Pentecostalism two critical distortions (one internal and the other external) as the community of the Spirit, are to be noted as significant to our

---

[55]Lesslie Newbigin, *The Household of God: Lectures on the Nature of the Church*, p.90.

[56]*Ibid.*, p. 87.

[57]*Ibid.*, pp. 32-110.

study: (1) "the setting of ardour against order",[58] and (2) the setting of the world against culture.

The *setting of ardour against order* speaks of that religious experience - that spirituality - of the faithful that emphasizes the extemporaneous, the spectacular - "the tendency to regard order and organization as antithetical to the life of the Spirit."[59] While it is true that "... where the Spirit of the Lord is, there is liberty" (2 Cor. 3:17), it is equally true that, "God is not a God of disorder but of peace" (1 Cor. 14:33). While one must be careful to "... quench not the Spirit" (1 Thessalonians 5:19), it becomes quite apparent in an Hispanic Pentecostal "culto" that the "ardour" element is dominant. It is true that an underclassed, mostly uneducated and oppressed Hispanic group is bound to be very emotional in its religious expressions. Yet, it is equally true that an orderly and balanced response to the religious life - where the heart and mind embrace - is critically needed and possible. While God's grace utilizes even these very emotional occasions to meet deep spiritual and psychic needs, the life and mission of the church suffers when not enough emphasis, discipline and time is given to rationally consider other aspects of the faith in the gathered community, in the "culto". The tendency to cater to immediate emotional needs, while providing needed psychic catharsis and genuine spiritual blessings, nevertheless can become shortsighted, and ultimately unhealthy. Liturgy, Scripture and Proclamation must be attended to in a reasonable way - providing, thus, disciplined, planned, and systematic exposition and deliberation of critically needed teaching and counsel.

A proper conceptualization (theology) of the Spirit's working would indeed see the Spirit's operation in the supernatural events of the "glossolalic" gifts ("the wind, earthquake and fire") but equally in the quiet ("still small voice") of rational discussion and exposition of His Word (1 Kings 19:12).

The *setting of the world against culture* speaks of a legitimate impulse of Hispanic Pentecostals that "all is not well in human society and its products," but which indiscriminately categorizes most human achievements (culture) as sinful or evil. It is a theological reflection of the world (*kosmos*), in its New Testament understanding, that is too inclusive of human endeavors but equally too excluding of a theology of creation, that should inform it.

It appears that the "vision of the disinherited" (the Hispanic Pentecostals) rejects those persons and institutions, and their informing values, that have rejected

---

[58]A phrase of John MacKay utilized by Newbigin, *Ibid.*, p. 103.

[59]Lesslie Newbigin, *The Household of God*, p. 104.

them in the dominant culture. Thus, they too often project the fulfillment of their own vision of a renewed "heaven and earth" to the *eschaton*. Both the psycho-social dynamics of the oppressed and the disenfranchisement of sectarian groups and their theological formulations must be met and challenged by theological reconstruction. Such reconstruction while taking serious the eschatological hope, brings to bear, nevertheless, an authentic and responsible commitment to the cultural mandate of creation (Genesis 1:26, 28; 2:15) in this present age.

Hispanic Pentecostalism must, I am convinced, see the affirmation and dynamics of the "brooding" of the Spirit in creation, as genesis, continued reality and final consummation (Genesis 1:1-3; John 16:7-15; Romans 8:22-23). Hispanic Pentecostalism must be challenged to see the limitations of their present community ethic and to reconstruct it in terms of a broader social ethic.[60]

Church-Sect Typology

Church-Sect Typology, a legacy of Troeltsch and Weber, has undergone various creative revisions, additions and reconstructions.[61] Yet, the basic portrait still stands, namely, that in society the followers of Christ must decide, as a group - the Church - whether they will "compromise" with the dominant values of their culture or will, through some "restoration" process, follow in the steps of Jesus.

At the heart of Church-Sect Typology is an attempt to identify and classify the different forms the church typically takes in society. As an ideal type, it suffers the same fate as all classifications of religious organizations. In the words of J. Milton Yinger, "Classifications are in one sense arbitrary. They oversimplify the data by disregarding what are held to be minor differences in order to emphasize what are thought to be major similarities. They are constructs of the

---

[60]I will address further the issue of the world and culture in my next chapter, "The Holy Spirit and Social Spirituality: A Pneumatological Paradigm."

[61]See Ernst Troeltsch, *The Social Teaching of the Christian Churches*, trans. by Olive Wyon (London: George Allen and Unwin, 1931), 2 Vols; especially Vol. I, pp. 331-81, and II, pp. 993-1013; Max Weber, *From Max Weber: Essays in Sociology*. Trans. and ed. by H.H. Gerth and C. Wright Mills (New York: Oxford University Press, 1946); Werner Stark, *The Sociology of Religion: A Study of Christendom*, 3 vols. (New York: Fordham University Press, 1967); H. Richard Niebuhr, *The Social Sources of Denominationalism* (New York: Holt, Rinehart, and Winston, Inc., 1929), Walter G. Muelder, "From Sect to Church", *Christendom* (Autumn, 1945), pp. 450-462; Liston Pope, *Millhands and Preachers* (N.Y.: Yale University Press, 1942); Bryan R. Wilson, *Sects and Society* (London: William Heinemann, Ltd., 1961); J. Milton Yinger, *The Scientific Study of Religion* (New York: The Macmillan Company, 1970), pp. 251-281.

mind, not descriptions of total reality."[62]   While some scholars consider the Church-Sect typology as too generalized (at best a low level type of conceptualization, if not useless), others value its insights and contribution as an analytic tool.

Three particular contributions have emerged in my study that constitute in part the essence of its utility and analytical value. They can be summarized by three categories: (1) **The Sectarian Portrait** and its corollary, (2) the **Sectarian Principle**. Along with these two I will discuss what can be called (3) the **Sectarian Fate**, applying them to Hispanic Pentecostal reality.

The Sectarian Portrait

The Church and Sect types reflects two variant interpretations of the Christian tradition. As two independent sociological expressions, their forms in society are ultimately determined by the degree to which they desire to affirm or deny/reject the dominant values of their culture, in relating their Gospel and the world.

Whether one utilizes the constructive refinement of Church-Sect typology of Yinger[63] or others, the emerging and abiding portrait of sectarianism is its adamant rejection of the "world" and/or any compromise with it. It is a repudiation of the posture of that religious group - the Church - which has "recognized the strength of the secular world and, rather than either abandoning the attempt to influence it or loosing its position by contradicting the secular powers directly, accepts the main elements in the social structure as proximate goods."[64]

Hispanic Pentecostalism in our "barrios" represents a sectarian religious expression. It is the "haven of the masses" - the poor and downtrodden.

Hispanic Pentecostalism at this juncture in history can be classified as a "Sect Movement" in Yinger's 10 element refinement and extension of the Church-Sect typology. More specifically, it can be classified as an "Avoidance Sect," a sub-category of Yinger's "Sect Movements," which

---

[62]J. Milton Yinger, *The Scientific Study of Religion*, p. 251.

[63]Yinger's typology moves in a continuum from: Universal institutionalized church, Institutional ecclesia, Diffused ecclesia, Institutional denomination, Diffused denomination, to Established sect, Established lay sect, Sect movement and Charismatic sect; see *The Scientific Study of Religion*, pp. 251-281.

[64]*Ibid.*, p. 253.

devalues the significance of this life, projects its hope into the supernatural world ... occurs among those who have as yet achieved little hope for improvement of their lot, such as some deprived minorities ... their avoidance responses are more symbolic than physical. They seek trances, visions, and the "gift of tongues" - temporary escapes into a world where their standards rule. They struggle with life's problem by transforming the meaning of life, by substituting "religious status for social status", in Liston Pope's meaningful phrase.[65]

Yinger's typology of religious organizations differentiates types of religious groups by three variables that constitute its sorting criteria: (1) Inclusiveness of the religious structures; (2) Extent of alienation from societal values and (3) Extent of organization, complexity and distinctiveness of the religious structures.[66]

Any empirical study of Hispanic Pentecostalism will quickly note that it ranks low regarding *inclusiveness* of all members of a society within its constituency. Its appeal is to the poor and working class who are not at home in the majority culture or its economy. Its members are converted, glossolalic affirming, poor and working class believers in the "barrios" of our inner-cities. The extent of *alienation from societal values* is high. They reject the secular values and structures of society. Although this rejection is real and significant, couched in religious language and other symbols, there is an increasing ambivalence shown as their socio-economic and educational lot is improving in this upwardly mobile American context where they have been marginalized.

The extent of *organizational development* in Hispanic Pentecostalism is still low. The development of professional staff, bureaucracy and other organizational complexity, while incipient in certain "concilios" (i.e., Asambleas de Dios), is by and large minimal.

The Sectarian Portrait is a sociological portrait of the form of the church in society. It is basically a negative assessment of the form of the church in the "world".

The Sectarian Principle

A corollary of the Sectarian Portrait is what I call the Sectarian Principle. The Sectarian Principle reflects, thus, a positive *theological assessment* of certain

---

[65]J. Milton Yinger, *The Scientific Study of Religion*, pp. 277-278.

[66]*Ibid.*, p. 260.

elements of the sociological Sectarian Portrait. Two elements that define the Sectarian Principle are: (1) counter-cultural and (2) prophetic.

The *counter-cultural* element found in sectarianism reflects a *protest* against the prevailing milieu of the dominant culture -manifested in perceived or real linguistic, economic, psychic, social, ethical or cultural oppression. It questions the ruling norms that exists in personal interactions, as well as social relations and structures. It posits its own counter-point, whether by the authority of Scripture, community, charismatic person or the Spirit - thus providing an external and/or transcendent point of reference.

While this element of the Sectarian Principle can be naive, obscurantist, and downright oppressive in extreme cases, it, nevertheless, at its best represents a peculiar insight of sectarianism which implicitly subscribes to Paul Tillich's "Protestant Principle" - the protest (both divine and human) against absolutizing any relative reality. At its best this element of the Sectarian Principle can be thus seen as a critique of the prevailing cultural norms which seek to dictate the terms of the "life and mission" of the church.

The *prophetic* element of the Sectarian Principle is the denouncement of those factors, both personal and social, which are viewed as destructive to life. At its best it puts in operation Tillich's "Protestant Principle." It calls for repentance, righteousness and justice - in personal and systemic terms, in relationship both to God and other persons and communities.

Hispanic Pentecostalism, like many other religious groups that have been classified and situated as a sectarian religious group, have manifested at times the prophetic elements of the Sectarian Principle noted above - often done so not by choice or design.

The counter-cultural protest, expressed by presence and proclamation, while evident in the Hispanic Pentecostal church in the "barrio," I am convinced, needs to move from individualistic terms to a more social systemic framework. It must rightfully discern and affirm those positive elements in culture that are not only conducive to its own "life and mission," but life affirming to all Hispanics, and to society at large. It must be equally discerning and critical of those socio-political and cultural elements which oftentimes it affirms or passively submits to, but which may be ultimately destructive (i.e., economic policies, political disenfranchisement, community or social injustices) to the Hispanic Pentecostal church, Hispanics, and/or other persons and groups in the greater society.

The prophetic element of the Sectarian Principle in Hispanic Pentecostalism needs a broader and deeper conceptual (theological) understanding of the "principalities and powers" - those oppressive demonic elements, both personal and social.[67]

While the Hispanic Pentecostal church provides a liberating context in the "culto" for personal transformation and expressive freedom, it, nevertheless, fails to extend it socially and, thus, fails to provide for a full theological liberation that understands systemic sin and oppression. The believer who encounters a force beyond in the Spirit, that does indeed affect his/her personal life at home and interpersonal relations, nevertheless, has not discerned the depth of the "mystery of iniquity" that is manifested in the structures of oppression found in social, economic, political, and cultural systems. At worst the positive sectarian principle that is present, and often intuitively sensed in Hispanic Pentecostalism, can be so corrupted resulting in a closed and irrelevant self-serving "religious club."

Hispanic Pentecostalism can become more marginal, ineffective and eventually oppressive of its own members, thus dissipating the power found in the Spirit in self and institutional maintenance. Yet, it must be noted that Hispanic Pentecostalism in view of its rejection of the "world" and its liberating theology of the Spirit - although individually interpreted and narrowly defined - is therefore "potentially revolutionary in impulse."[68]

The Sectarian Fate

By Sectarian Fate I refer to the question relating to the present evolution and future development of a sectarian group. It has been the thesis of H. Richard Niebuhr, Liston Pope and others that, given the American socio-economic context and the push-and-pull of other churches in society, that sectarianism is short lived. That transition from sect to church is an expected evolutionary process in our society.[69]

There are historical exceptions to this evolutionary process in the American religious scene. There may be factors in the greater society that may "hold" the evolution or development of a sectarian group, as well as internal dynamic factors in the group itself that may resist the process. The examples of the Quakers and

---

[67]I will address the theological issue of "principalities and powers" in my next chapter, "The Holy Spirit and Social Spirituality: A Pneumatological Paradigm."

[68]Robert Mapes Anderson, *Vision of the Disinherited*, p. 202.

[69]See especially, H. Richard Niebuhr, *The Social Sources of Denominationalism*, and Liston Pope, *Millhands and Preachers*.

Figure 3-1
Liston Pope's 21 factors/variables of the process of transition from Sect to Church

1.   From membership composed chiefly of the propertyless to membership composed of property owners.

2.   From economic poverty to economic wealth, as disclosed especially in the value of church property and the salary paid to ministers.

3.   From the cultural periphery toward the cultural center of the community.

4.   From renunciation of prevailing culture and social organization, or indifference to it, to affirmation of prevailing culture and social organization.

5.   From self-centered (or personal) religion to culture centered religion, from "experience" to a social institution.

6.   From noncooperation, or positive ridicule, toward established religious institutions to cooperation with the established churches of the community.

7.   From suspicion of rival sects to disdain or pity for all sects.

8.   From a moral community excluding unworthy members to a social institution embracing all who are socially compatible within it.

9.   From an unspecialized, unprofessionalized, part-time ministry to a specialized, professional, full-time ministry.

10. From a psychology of persecution to a psychology of success and dominance.

11. From voluntary, confessional bases of membership to ritual or social prerequisites only (such as a certificate of previous membership in another respected denomination, or training in an educational process established by the denomination itself).

12. From principal concern with adult membership to equal concern for children of members.

13. From emphasis on evangelism and conversion to emphasis on religious education.

(Figure 3-1, continued)

14. From stress on a future in the next world to primary interest in a future in this world - a future for the institution, for its members, and for their children; from emphasis on death to emphasis on successful earthly life.

15. From adherence to strict Biblical standards, such as tithing or nonresistance, to acceptance of general cultural standards as a practical definition of religious obligation.

16. From a high degree of congregational participation in the services and administration of the religious group to delegation of responsibility to a comparatively small percentage of the membership.

17. From fervor in worship services to restraint; from positive action to passive listening.

18. From a comparatively large number of special religious services to a program of regular services at stated intervals.

19. From reliance on spontaneous "leadings of the Spirit" in religious services and administration to a fixed order of worship and of administrative procedure.

20. From the use of hymns resembling contemporary folk music to the use of slower, more stately hymns coming out of more remote liturgical tradition.

21. From emphasis on religion in the home to delegation of responsibility for religion to church officials and organizations.

Source: Liston Pope, *Millhands and Preachers*, New Haven,Conn.: Yale University Press, 1942., pp. 122-124; Used with permission of Yale University Press.

Anabaptists are given by Yinger and classified as "Established Sects." Such sects, by reason of the nature of their original protest (more social in nature), coupled with the experience of vigorous persecution and opposition, developed more intense group solidarity and morale and, thus, structures of personal and communal isolation. They have institutionalized somewhat the sectarian principle, even though they have changed and accommodated significantly regarding class status in this society.[70]

The fate of most sects in the American context is extinction or evolution into a church. Hispanic Pentecostalism to date, given the nature of its original sectarian protest - in terms of individual salvation - and its lack of development of doctrine (theology), will, like other Anglo Pentecostal sects of the past (i.e., Assemblies of God), be moving into the classification of a denomination.

It is instructive to note Liston Pope's 21 factors (see Figure 3-1) that show the specific aspects of this dynamic evolutionary movement from sect to church. These are ideal type variables that in the words of Pope, constitutes "a parable rather than designation of religious institutions as organism."[71] Hispanic Pentecostalism, while still a solid "sect movement" in our American social context, is beginning to experience the pressures and tensions of the Sect to Church transition. The trend, thus the fate, of Hispanic Pentecostalism in the American context can be summarized as follows:

A)   It will become part and parcel of American denominationalism (the Church) as it moves into the mainstream, due to the push-and-pull of upward social mobility of its members - thus status achievement and the socio-political power of class.[72]

or

---

[70]J. Milton Yinger, *The Scientific Study of Religion*, pp. 266-268.

[71]Liston Pope, *Millhands and Preachers*, p. 122.

[72]My view of "denominationalism" is informed by critiques such as that given by H. Richard Niebuhr, "Denominationalism in the Christian church is ... an unacknowledged hypocrisy. It is a compromise, made far too lightly, between Christianity and the world ... the evil of denominationalism lies in the conditions which make the rise of sects desirable and necessary: in the failure of the churches to transcend the social conditions which fashion them into caste-organizations, to sublimate their loyalties to standards and institutions only remotely relevant if not contrary to the Christian Ideal, to resist the temptation of making their own self-preservation and extension the primary object of their endeavor," *The Social Sources of Denominationalism*, pp. 6, 21.

B)   It will resist the transition process at various levels and become a biblical Church at the service of the Reign of God. In order to be more than an "Established Sect" in the traditional sense, it must resist the negative elements of upward mobility (i.e., uncritical acceptance of present economic relations, structural racism and sexism, materialism and unresponsiveness to the poor and the oppressed). Its self-understanding as a Church must be defined by a broader theological framework - one that incorporates knowledge of and mission to both personal and social-structural sin. Thus, it will need to develop a social ethic, rather than be satisfied with its present "community ethic" (an ethic for the church). It will then take seriously its call as a church to be a "community of the Spirit" *in* the world and a "community of the Spirit" *for* the world, but not *of* the world.

CHAPTER IV

THE HOLY SPIRIT AND SOCIAL SPIRITUALITY:
A PNEUMATOLOGICAL PARADIGM

> At the end of the "postscript" Barth also told of his
> dream - which he had also occasionally mentioned in
> conversations - that someone, and perhaps a whole
> age, might be allowed to develop a "theology of the
> Spirit," a "theology which now I can only envisage
> from afar, as Moses once looked on the promised
> land." He was thinking of a theology which, unlike
> his own, was not written from the dominant
> perspective of Christology, but from that of
> pneumatology...
>
> - on Karl Barth[1]

   In the previous chapters I have presented a portrait of a "pueblo" at the periphery of the American metropolis - marginalized and oppressed. I have also understood the "Homo Hispanicus" as a deeply religious person. I noted the rich cultural and religious heritage and deep spirituality that informs the life and "quest for community" in the "barrios." The Hispanic Pentecostal church has been presented in its context, noting its significant role in the "barrio." An undeniable force in the "barrio" - a context of hope and community in an otherwise alienating experience. Hispanic Pentecostals, nevertheless, have defined their spirituality too individualistically. There is a need to extend the Hispanic Pentecostals' understanding of spirituality's struggles with the flesh, the world and the devil with their *social correlates* - sinful social structures, the "world" (*kosmos*), and "principalities and powers" - if a social ethic is to emerge. This emerging social ethic must cohere with Hispanic Pentecostals' experience - particularly as it relates to the Spirit.

---

[1]Eberhard Busch, *Karl Barth: His life from letters and autobiographical texts* (Philadelphia: Fortress Press, 1976), p. 494.

The person and ministry of the Holy Spirit is receiving in this latter part of the century its due attention. Above all factors contributing to this focus has been the remarkable renewal movement of worldwide Pentecostalism. The emerging "third force" - Pentecostalism - challenges the "'silence on the Holy Spirit' by Western theologians," one that "reveals the pneumatological bankruptcy of ... scholastic-oriented Western theology."[2]   Among the many reasons for the emergence of Pentecostalism as a worldwide renewal movement at the turn of the century was "its emphasis on the experiential dimension of the Christian faith, the dynamic experience of the Spirit."[3]   Pentecostalism in the U.S.A., as well as worldwide, emerged in the context of the "oppressed of the 'spirit'," reflecting the cold and formal state of Christianity; and in the context of the "'spirit' of the oppressed," reflecting the poor and disinherited. Hispanic Pentecostalism in the "barrios" also participated in this dual oppressive situation: an experience of a "distant" Christianity, and an experience of a "distant" socio-cultural enfranchisement.

The "nearness" of God the Spirit in Pentecostalism - as manifested in the "glossolalic" gifts and other ministries resulted in a rich and vibrant spirituality, Pentecostalism's most significant contribution. This spirituality, especially in its Hispanic apparel, has tended to be privatistic, ecstatic, mystical and/or confined to the four walls of the "culto."[4] A spirituality, understood "as a way of responding to God, a style of living the life of the Holy Spirit,"[5] needs a broader social dimension. Ultimately, it is to understand that every spirituality is social, and that every spirituality should cohere with a proper anthropological, biblical and theological understanding of *spiritual living*.

Paul Pomerville reminds us of the need for fresh theologizing from the Pentecostal viewpoint, given the "underdeveloped nature of pneumatology in general and Pentecostal mission theology in particular."[6] It is from this broader perspective and from Hispanic Pentecostal's spirituality that I address the theological reconstructive task in this chapter. The pneumatological paradigm that I offer will draw from the relevant literature (Scripture, theology, ethics) those

---

[2]Paul A. Pomerville, *The Third Force in Missions*, p. 33.

[3]*Ibid.*, 63.

[4]One important exception has been evangelization, though still defined individualistically.

[5]Frances X. Meehan, *A Contemporary Social Spirituality* (Maryknoll, New York: Orbis, 1982), p. 1.

[6]Paul A. Pomerville, *The Third Force in Mission*, p. 13.

elements which are coherent with the Hispanic Pentecostal experience and informative in building and enriching the same.

A Wholistic Spirituality: An Emerging Need

> Any reflection that does not help in living according to the Spirit is not a Christian theology. When all is said and done, then, all authentic theology is spiritual theology. This fact does not weaken the rigorously scientific character of the theology; it does, however, properly situate it.
> - Gustavo Gutierrez[7]

A spirituality, if it is to be authentic and relevant, should correlate with all of life; for after all the Spirit of the Lord, who leads and empowers, must lead and empower all areas of our life. A spirituality can be defined as "a particular style of approach to union with God" (George A. Lane)[8], "a following of Jesus" (Gustavo Gutierrez)[9], "a style of living the life of the Holy Spirit" (Francis X. Meehan)[10], or my own personal definition, which synthesizes a trinitarian and moral thrust, "in obedience to God, the following of Jesus in the power of the Spirit." Undergirding these various definitions is a self-understanding of a loving heart yearning, seeking and responding as a whole person, in the obedience of faith, to a loving God.

The history of the spiritualities of the church reflects the spiritual pilgrimage of particular individuals and of particular people, at a particular time and in a particular context. One can surely make a case for the emergence at distinct periods throughout the church (both Catholic and Protestant) of what can be termed a wholistic spirituality - covering "the following of Jesus" in both personal transformation/piety (prayer, mystic, contemplation, thus, inner-directed and vertical) and social transformation/piety (justice, advocacy, social action, thus, outer-directed and horizontal). However, from the early hermits of the East and monks of the West to San Juan de la Cruz and Santa Teresa, even to our present age, the inner-directed, contemplative motif has been dominant in the spirituality of the church. It was to the credit of the Spaniard, Ignatius of Loyola and his

---

[7]Gustavo Gutierrez, *We Drink from Our Own Wells*, p. 37.

[8]George A. Lane, *Christian Spirituality - An Historical Sketch*, p. 2.

[9]Gustavo Gutierrez, *We Drink from Our Own Wells*, p. 1.

[10]Frances X. Meehan, *A Contemporary Social Spirituality*, p. 1.

followers to systematize and give concrete instruction for "seeking God in all things,"[11] for the following of Jesus in a volitional thrust "outside" the monastery/wall in a "worldly" social engagement. It was a significant contribution to spirituality that in the words of Meehan "shifted the church away from seeing monastic prayer as the predominant model for spiritual living".[12] While in Ignatian spirituality contemplative prayer is important, its new approach brought a different understanding to spirituality. Gannon and Traub note:

> The revolution in spiritual thinking and practice initiated by Ignatius
> of Loyola consisted, then, in a shift of emphasis in the idea of God
> - where he is, how he acts in the world, and how he might be
> found. It should not be surprising that these notions would lead to
> a new approach to spirituality and a different understanding of the
> relation between prayer and action. To Ignatius, the spiritual life
> was not, first of all, a problem of prayer or activity, but of a fidelity
> to God which demanded fidelity to divine tasks. If previous writers
> conceived of the spiritual life as a union with God principally
> through interior prayer, Ignatius, so impressed with God's
> continuous saving action in the world, was convinced that a person
> could achieve union with God in action ... Casting off the last
> traces of Neo-Platonism and surmounting the prayer-action
> dichotomy of previous Christian spirituality, Ignatius affirms that
> union with God is essentially a union of love ... a union which can
> be achieved no matter what the circumstances.[13]

This union with God in love is basic to our understanding of spirituality, as is the Ignatian insight of the validity of its *locus* in action. It is in the experience of the Holy Spirit in the salvific process that persons first consciously and transformingly encounter the love of God in Jesus Christ. This "trinitarian" encounter notes the seeking Spirit of God as the initiator of the encounter with the divine. It is a contextual and inductive process. The encounter is *contextual* because we are met *subjectively* in the depth of our being in a personal way; and because we are met *objectively* in our given historical, cultural and social reality. It is *inductive* because we begin our spiritual pilgrimage in response to what has happened to "me" or to "us" in the here and now of our earthly life - from the particularity of our being as "persons-in-community." This initial experience of the

---

[11]Thomas M. Gannon and George W. Traub, *The Desert and the City: An Interpretation of the History of Christian Spirituality* (New York: The Macmillan Company, 1969), p. 208.

[12]Francis X. Meehan, *A Contemporary Social Spirituality*, p. 1.

[13]Thomas M. Gannon and George W. Traub, *The Desert and the City*, p. 158-159.

Spirit, that is encountered in the context of the hearing of the Word, in the "culto" - though the Spirit may choose where it pleases (John 3:8) - is first encountered as an experience of the pouring out of the love of God by the Holy Spirit. "God has poured out his love into our hearts by the Holy Spirit, whom he has given us" (Romans 5:5). The Holy Spirit the "binding" person of the trinity - uniting the Father and the Son, a "community of persons" and a "person-in-community" - now unites us to God by God's love. Love becomes the dominant relationship of the believer to God and to other persons. Love becomes the source, motive and power of the living in the Spirit, even our ethical walk.

The above bears much affinity with Augustine's understanding of the role of the Holy Spirit and love in the salvific process. As theologian David F. Wells notes:

> Augustine frequently identified the Holy Spirit with love. This enabled him to see the Spirit as being both the means and the aim of our salvation. The Spirit is the means because he is the one who pours divine love into the hearts of sinful men and women, love that enables them to reach the goal of loving God. Accordingly, Augustine defined grace as the infusion of love into human hearts by the Holy Spirit. ... Because of this infusion of love, sinners are transformed and enabled to become just by becoming lovers of God and their fellow human beings.[14]

Notwithstanding certain limitations in the Augustinian conceptualization of the role of the Holy Spirit and love in the salvific process, it nevertheless is both biblical and relevant in its experiential thrust. Hispanic Pentecostalism's experience of the Holy Spirit coheres with the focus on the Spirit and love in the *Ordo salutis*. The love of God in Jesus Christ in the *metanoe* experienced, initiated and mediated by the Holy Spirit, effects a transformation in the believer, thus commencing the spiritual pilgrimage. It is a transformation in which love becomes the fundamental virtue and fundamental criterion of "being" and "doing" in the believer's spirituality. This transformation experience motivates and challenges the believer to seek "in obedience to God, to follow Jesus in the power of the Spirit."

Jesus Christ, the Anointed One (Luke 4:18; Acts 10:38), is the paradigm "par excellence" of this spirituality. Through *the power of the Spirit* the believer is <u>both</u> "being transformed into his likeness with ever-increasing glory, which comes from the Lord, who is the Spirit" (2 Corinthians 3:18); and challenged to

---

[14]David F. Wells, *God the Evangelist: How the Holy Spirit Works to Bring Men and Women to Faith* (Grand Rapids, Michigan: Wm. B. Eerdmans, 1987), p. 37.

follow Him, "as the Father has sent me, I am sending you ... receive the Holy Spirit" (John 20:21-22). Thus, the double focus and goal of Christian spirituality has: (1) a vertical focus - the continual transformation into the likeness of Jesus, the resurrected Lord; and (2) a horizontal focus - the following of Jesus, in similar obedience of the Father's missional calling (Luke 4:18-19). Both of these foci and goals can only be carried out in the power of the Spirit, and undergirded by God's love. Both have a vertical and horizontal dimension that interrelates them and dynamically "nourishes" them. "Transformation" needs "following" and "following" needs "transformation." Both have a personal and social dimension that equally interrelates them and dynamically "nourishes" them.

The "vertical-transformation" focus and its interrelationship with the horizontal is noted well in 1 John 4:7-13:

> ... let us love one another, for love comes from God. Everyone who loves has been born of God and knows God. Whoever does not love does not know God, because God is love. This is how God showed his love among us: He sent his one and only Son into the world that we might live through him. This is love: not that we loved God, but that he loved us and sent his Son as an atoning sacrifice for our sins. ... since God so loved us, we also ought to love one another. No one has ever seen God; but *if we love each other, God lives in us and his love is made complete in us.* We know that *we live in him* and *he in us*, because he has given us of *his Spirit.*

The "horizontal-following" focus and its interrelationship with the vertical is noted well by Jesus' missional self-understanding (which should also be ours) in Luke 4:18-19:

> The *Spirit of the Lord* is on me; therefore he has *anointed me* to preach good news to the poor. He has sent me to proclaim freedom for the prisoners and recovery of sight for the blind, to release the oppressed, to proclaim the year of the Lord's favor.

This dynamic and dialectical spirituality is to be "worked out" in a social context, one that deeply needs both contemplative and apostolic activity. The brokenness of society (so visible in our "barrios"), the scriptural missional mandate, and the Spirit's love constrain us to feed the hungry, visit the sick and prisoners, shelter the homeless and poor - to express God's love in social concerns. In Matthew 25: 35, 36, 40, Jesus graphically depicts the interrelationship of the vertical and horizontal dimension of worship and social concern, and thus challenges us to a wholistic spirituality:

For I was hungry and you gave me something to eat, I was thirsty and you gave me something to drink, I was a stranger and you invited me in, I needed clothes and you clothed me, I was sick and you looked after me, I was in prison and you came to visit me... I tell you the truth, whatever you did for one of the least of these brothers of mine, you did for me. (Matthew 25: 35-36, 40).

In this century, through the careful reading and re-reading of Scripture (especially from the context of the periphery) and the critical utilization of the analytical tools of the social sciences, we have gained a new understanding of our social reality. The concomitant Pentecostal outpouring of the Spirit, also in this century, has brought to many a critical awareness and discernment of the depth and complexity of sin (the "mystery of iniquity"). Coupled with the dire human predicament of Hispanics in the "barrios," this should challenge the Hispanic Pentecostal churches to acknowledge that an authentic and relevant spirituality must be wholistic, responding to both the vertical and horizontal dimension of life.

I now move to consider elements contributing to a social spirituality, the missing dimension or focus in Hispanic Pentecostal experience. These elements will be presented utilizing two major metaphors: The Spirit's "Grieving," and the Spirit's "Brooding".

The Spirit's "Grieving" - Sin: Personal and Social

And do not *grieve* the Holy Spirit of God... Be imitators of God... live a life of love, just as Christ loved us and gave himself up for us as a fragrant offering and sacrifice to God.

- Ephesians 4:30; 5:1-2

The spiritual pilgrimage of the believer is a pilgrimage of love. Any true spirituality is ultimately the loving of God and the neighbor as oneself (Matthew 19:19) - the integration of the spiritual and the ethical, of worship and service, and of identity and vocation. Love is often easier to acknowledge than to define. What Augustine said of "time" can probably be said of love: "If no one asks me, I know, if I wish to explain it to one that asketh, I know not."[15]   In any

---

[15]Augustine, *Confessions*, Bk. 11 (Edw. Pusey Translation, New York: Random House, 1949), p. 253, quoted in Francis X. Meehan, *A Contemporary Social Spirituality*, p. 1.

description love is deeply personal. The love of God in Christ poured out by the Holy Spirit establishes a loving relationship with God that, as with all love affairs, particularly the human response, is subject to the vacillations, void, and vicissitudes of life.

As mere humans in a spiritual pilgrimage of love, we grieve the object of our love often. Whether the grieving of that object of love be human or divine (in our immediate understanding of the object), it is ultimately a grieving of the Spirit. The "love of the Spirit" (Romans 15:30) can be grieved. A careful exegesis of Paul's admonition in Ephesians chapter four and chapter five places the context of the grieving of the Spirit within an ethico-spiritual relationship with others. These attitudes and actions of the believers that "cut" the relationship of love and thus grieve the Holy Spirit are called sin in Scripture. In the biblical revelation sin can be more broadly described as: *disobedience* to the Lordship of God, *injustice* and alienation, and *unbelief* and idolatry.[16] We sin, thus the Spirit is grieved, when we do not imitate God, sacrificially give up ourselves as Christ, and "live a life of love." (Ephesians 4:30; 5:1-2).

In Hispanic Pentecostals' spirituality in the "barrios" sin and the demonic are ever present in matters of discourse and action relative to pre-conversion life, present struggles in "living the life of love" (sanctification), and obstacles to personal and the church's life and mission. The ubiquity of sin and the demonic in Hispanic Pentecostalism's spirituality is above all heightened by the baptism in the Spirit, which to the believers places them in a new level, if not a new awareness, of spiritual warfare. This new awareness of the ubiquity of sin and the demonic and the ensuing spiritual warfare in Hispanic Pentecostal spirituality is consistent with the history of spirituality of the church.[17] As typical of the contemplative strand of spirituality, this spiritual warfare against the flesh, the world and the devil (Ephesians 2:2-3) tends to be seen in individualistic terms. Thus, there is a critical need for seeing the structural interrelationship of sin - the mystery of iniquity - and the complexity and depth of its manifestation in institutional life.

---

[16]See Orlando Costas, *Christ Outside the Gate*, pp. 21-24; see also, Walter Grundmann: *hamartia*, Gerhard Kittel, editor, trans., Geoffrey W. Bromiley, *Theological Dictionary of the New Testament*, Volume I (Grand Rapids, Michigan: Eerdmans Publishing Company, 1964), pp. 267-316.

[17]See especially, Thomas M. Gannon and George W. Traub, *The Desert and the City: An Interpretation of the History of Christian Spirituality*; and Richard F. Lovelace, *Dynamics of Spiritual Life: An Evangelical Theology of Renewal* (Downers Grove, Illinois: Inter-Varsity Press, 1979).

In this section I propose to consider, in a limited way, first personal sin and then structural/institutional sin within the biblical understanding of the "mystery of iniquity."

Personal Sin

Adam and Eve, the first human couple, as described in the biblical story (Genesis 1-3), enjoyed life and full fellowship with God in the most ideal conditions in the garden of Eden. It was a fellowship that was eventually broken with the entrance of sin upon the occasion of disobedience, and with it came the dire consequence of death (Genesis 3:3, 8 ff.), Death is separation. Separation not only of the physical/corporal from earthly existence, but more radical yet, the separation or "absence of the divine presence from human life."[18]

William Stringfellow in the chapter, "Christ and the Power of Death" in his provocative book, *Free in Obedience: The Radical Christian Life*, speaks powerfully to the presence of death:

> In the fall, every man, every principality, everything exists in a condition of estrangement from his or its own life, as well as from the lives of all other man, powers, and things. In the fall, the whole creation is consigned to death.[19]

Paul clearly teaches that sin is a harsh taskmaster, "for the wages of sin is death" (Romans 6:23a). The predicament of *all* persons is death - separation from God, from others, from themselves, and even from creation. Scripture is quite clear that individual action has marked social implications. It likewise notes that social or corporate action has marked individual implications.[20] Sin, while being deeply personal, is not just individualistic. The person as a *socius* ("person-in-community") is vividly portrayed by Paul's anthropological understanding of "corporate personality" as noted in Romans 5:12: "just as sin entered the world through one man, and death through sin, and in this way death came to all men, because all sinned." Orlando Costas notes, commenting on this verse, that:

---

[18]Orlando Costas, *Christ Outside the Gate*, p. 22.

[19]William Stringfellow, *Free in Obedience: The Radical Christian Life* (New York: The Seabury Press, 1964), p. 62.

[20]In Scripture there are many cases (i.e., Joshua 7; Romans 5:12-21) that illustrate this truth of the interrelatedness of human personality in the web of other persons and actions. For the Hebrew conception of this "corporate personality" see, H. Wheeler Robinson, *Corporate Personality in Ancient Israel*.

The sin of one man affected all, because "all" were represented already in the one. Therefore guilt and condemnation have passed to all. All are guilty of sin, not just because they personally sin, but because they are part of Adam. Thus sin is both personal and social.[21]

Sin and its work is a reality in all human experience. No area of personal and human history is left untouched by its destructive reality. It is ultimately and radically death/separation from God. The response to sin and death is the need for the loving initiative of the Spirit of God to convict of sin, righteousness, and judgement (John 16: 8-11), based on the equally radical answer of "The Crucified God."[22] Paul speaks eloquently of the multifaceted drama of redemption that dealt with sin and death:

> But God, who is rich in mercy, for his great love wherewith he loved us, even when we were dead in sins, hath quickened us together with Christ (by grace ye are saved), and hath raised us up together, and made us sit together in heavenly places in Christ Jesus (Ephesians 2:4-6, KJV).

The power of sin and death is broken. In the Cross of Christ the believer has the resources to overcome its dominion. David F. Wells notes that "the world, the flesh and the devil are not invincible competitors but doomed adversaries. In the work on the Cross, Christ conquered them, and through the work of the Spirit, that conquest is brought into our modern world."[23]

It grieves the Spirit when believers manifest the works of sin. Paul in his letter to the Galatians chapter five notes that sin's work in human nature (*sarx*, "the flesh")[24] is the antithesis of the Spirit's fruit. The Spirit's fruit (love, joy, peace,

---

[21]Orlando Costas, *Christ Outside the Gate*, p. 25; Both Paul and Costas implicitly underline in this passage not just the universality of sin but equally its manifestation in "corporate personality" - as defined by H. Wheeler Robinson's conception, see his *Corporate Personality in Ancient Israel*.

[22]See Jurgen Moltmann, *The Crucified God: The Cross of Christ as the Foundation and Criticism of Christian Theology* (New York, N.Y.: Harper and Row, 1974).

[23]David F. Wells, *God the Evangelist: How the Holy Spirit Works to Bring Men and Women to Faith*, p. 67

[24]Richard Lovelace's words are instructive: "The New Testament designates the total organism of sin by the term *sarx* (flesh), referring to the fallen human personality apart from the renewing influence and control of the Holy Spirit. The flesh is always somewhat mysterious to us, particularly in its effect on our minds and its operation in the redeemed personality. The New

patience, kindness, goodness, faithfulness, gentleness and self-control, Gal. 5:22-23) is the believer-lover's attestation of growth in his/her spirituality. The Spirit's fruits are both sign and substance of "transformation" to Christ's image, and moral virtues needed in the following of Jesus. They are marks of genuine spirituality. The Spirit seeks to restore the fellowship broken by sin and to overcome the separation in a bond of love.

Mystery of Iniquity: The Texture of Social Existence

> For the mystery of iniquity
> doth already work...
> - 2 Thessalonians 2:7

> Our struggle with evil must
> correspond to the geography of
> evil.
> - Stephen C. Mott[25]

In responding to questions concerning the Lord's *parousia* (2:1) Paul in his second letter to the church in Thessalonica notes certain antecedent events. Before the "man of sin" or "man of lawlessness" is revealed (2:3), who incidentally will be destroyed by the Lord (2:8), Paul reminds the Thessalonians of two very important realities already present in the world; the understanding of which is critical for their standing firm in his teaching (2:15). The two realities were the presence of the "mystery of iniquity" already at work in their midst, and the more powerful presence of "the restrainer" (*to katechon*, 2:6, 7). He notes the already presence of a mysterious ungodly force ("mystery of iniquity") that will take concrete shape in a man (2:3,8) before the end. This secret power of iniquity is already at work and has not overwhelmed or "broken out" completely in its heinous destruction due to the presence of "the restrainer" (*to katechon*). While many explanations for "the restrainer" have been given, traditionally, Hispanic Pentecostals and others have identified "the restrainer" as the Holy Spirit.[26]

Testament constantly describes it as something much deeper than the isolated moments of sin which it generates;" *Dynamics of Spiritual Life*, pp. 89-90.

[25]Stephen Charles Mott, *Biblical Ethics and Social Change* (New York, N.Y.: Oxford University Press, 1982), p.16; Used with permission of Oxford University Press, copyright 1982.

[26]For identification of the *to katechon* and relevant exegetical commentaries on this passage of

It is within the framework of the ongoing cosmic conflict between God and Satan, and the restraining power of the Holy Spirit, that any discussion of sin - particularly in its powerful and mysterious (secret) structural or institutional manifestations - must be set.

Social Reality

From the social sciences, particularly the sociology of knowledge, we have learned that the institutions and structures of social life are more than the sum of the individuals that make it up.[27] Society is a dialectic phenomenon that is a human product, as well as producer of the human. Berger and Luckman note that the construction of society is the result of three movements or steps. Berger summarizes the three movements in this dialectic process as follows:

> These are externalization, objectivation and internalization. Only if these three movements are understood together can an empirically adequate view of society be maintained. Externalization is the ongoing outpouring of human being into the world, both in the physical and the mental activity of men. Objectivation is the attainment by the products of this activity (again both physical and mental) of a reality that confronts its original producers as a facticity external to and other than themselves. Internalization is the reappropriation by men of this same reality, transforming it once again from structures of the objective world into structures of the subjective consciousness. It is through externalization that society is a human product. It is through objectivation that society becomes a reality *sui generis*. It is through internalization that man is a product of society.[28]

Scripture see especially, Hermann Hanse, *katecho*, Gerhard Kittel, editor, trans. Geoffrey W. Bromiley, *Theological Dictionary of the New Testament*, Vol. II, pp. 829-830; Fritz Rienecker, Clem L. Rogers, ed. *A Linguistic Key to the Greek New Testament*, 9th edition (Grand Rapids, Michigan: Zondervan Publishing House, 1980), pp. 607-610; and Robert L. Thomas, "2 Thessalonians", *The Expositor's Bible Commentary*, Volume II (Grand Rapids, Michigan: Zondervan Publishing House, 1978), pp. 317-331.

[27]See especially, Peter L. Berger and Thomas Luckman, *The Social Construction of Reality: A Treatise in the Sociology of Knowledge* (New York, N.Y.: Anchor Books, 1967); Peter L. Berger, *The Sacred Canopy: Elements of a Sociological Theory of Religion* (New York, N.Y.: Anchor Books, 1969).

[28]Peter L. Berger, *The Sacred Canopy*, p. 4.

The society that is produced by human beings and confronts individual persons and groups is now a reality *sui generis*, it has a "life" of its own. As such, it impacts persons, has coercive power, and tries to form persons into its image. Society sanctions, directs, and controls us to a greater degree than we care to admit or are cognizant of. As an object reality, society bears the marks of its producers and maintainers. It participates in the human good or evil. Berger, in the interest of protecting against "hypostatizing thinking" and in the interest of a humanized scientific sociology, denies any ultimate ontological status to society. He states that "society is constituted and maintained by acting human beings. It has no being, no reality, apart from this activity."[29]   Yet, it is important to note that biblical and theological research is currently identifying in the make-up of society a quasi-ontological presence,[30] especially in social structures and social institutions, that regulate life. It is important to underline that these quasi-ontological presence have real consequences, regardless of ultimate ontological status.

Social institutions are basically routinized human patterned norms and behaviors for social living (i.e., family, schools, laws, religion, political and social systems).   Some institutions (i.e., family, work, the state...) may even be categorized as a "given," as God's "orders of creation," "divine orders" or "structures of creation."[31]   Thus, they are seen as God's gracious gifts to human beings for social existence in which, "even if only in a fragmentary and indirect way, God's will meets us."[32]

All social structures and institutions "have moral values embedded in them. They can be good or evil."[33]   To speak of sinful structures and institutions is to speak of structures and institutions that have become distorted, misguided, destructive or oppressive.[34]   As such they are in need of liberation - by dismantling, reconstruction, transformation, revolution or "exorcism" - by human

---

[29]*Ibid.*, p. 7.

[30]I will say more on this under "Principalities and Powers."

[31]See especially, Emil Brunner, *The Divine Imperative* (Philadelphia, PA.: The Westminster Press, 1937); and Pedro Arana Quiroz, "Ordenes de la Creación y Responsabilidad Cristiana", in C. René Padilla, ed. *Fé Cristiana y Latinoamérica Hoy* (Buenos Aires, Argentina: Ediciones Certeza, 1974) pp. 169-184.

[32]Emil Brunner, *The Divine Imperative*, p. 291.

[33]Francis X. Meehan, *A Contemporary Social Spirituality*, p. 9.

[34]See Patrick Kerans, *Sinful Social Structures* (New York, N.Y.: Paulist Press, 1974).

and divine power. What is significant to note at this time is that the texture of social existence reveals the presence of institutions and structures that regulate life, that seem to have an objective reality independent of the individual, and thus can become oppressive, sinful or evil. We are all part of this texture of social existence and our spiritual living is impacted by this complex web.[35]

The World

The "world" (*kosmos*) has been a central concern of all spiritualities in the Christian Church in general, and in the sectarian expression in particular. Hispanic Pentecostalism, as an Avoidance Sect, seeks to overcome the world in what Weber called *Weltablehnende Askense* ("world-rejecting ascetism").[36] As noted before, Hispanic Pentecostalism has a legitimate impulse that all is not well in human society, although, the "world" is defined too broadly as inclusive of all human culture. It is important to look closely at the term *Kosmos*[37] for its proper understanding is critical for a social ethic and any authentic spirituality.

In Scripture *Kosmos* has two principal meanings, one positive and the other negative. Its positive meaning refers to all people (John 3:16), and the physical and natural world (Psalms 24:1; Matt. 24:21). Negatively it refers, in the words of C. H. Dodd, to "human society in so far as it is organized on wrong principles."[38] Richard Lovelace's definition is worthy of note:

---

[35]For an early and provocative treatment that deals with sinful and evil social structures, see Walter Rauschenbusch's chapters, "The Super-personal forces of Evil" and "The Kingdom of Evil," in his *A Theology For the Social Gospel* (New York: The Macmillan Company, 1917), pp. 69-94.

[36]See Max Weber, *The Sociology of Religion* (Boston: Beacon Press, 1964 ed.), pp. 166-183; and Max Weber, *From Max Weber: Essays in Sociology*, eds. H. Gerth and C. W. Mills (New York, N.Y: Oxford University Press, 1946); and Max Weber, *The Protestant Ethic and the Spirit of Capitalism* (New York, N.Y.: Scribner's, 1958).

[37]See especially, Hermann Sasse, *Kosmos, Theological Dictionary of the New Testament*, Vol. III, pp. 868-895; H. Richard Niebuhr, *Christ and Culture* (New York: Harper & Row, 1951); Robert E. Webber, *The Church in the World* (Grand Rapids, Michigan: Zondervan Publishing House, 1986); I am indebted in this section on "The World" and the next "Principalities and Powers" to the excellent exposition by Stephen C. Mott's chapter, "Biblical Faith and the Reality of Social Evil" in his *Biblical Ethics and Social Change*, pp. 3-21.

[38]C.H. Dodd, *The Johannine Epistles* (New York, Harper, Moffatt New Testament Commentaries, 1946), pp. 42, quoted in Stephen Mott, *Biblical Ethics and Social Change*, p. 6.

> When world is used in a negative sense in Scripture, what is meant is the total system of corporate flesh operating on earth under satanic control, with all its incentives of reward and restraints of loss, its characteristic patterns of behavior, and its antichristian structures, methods, goals and ideologies ... It involves many forms and agencies of evil which are hard to discern and to contend against on the basis of an individualistic view of sin.[39]

Mott notes that the Greek term basically means *"order, that which is assembled together well,"*[40] and that eventually it "came to be attached to the most important ordering of earthly life, the social order."[41] Thus, in classical Greece *Kosmos* referred to that order of social existence that "protected values and life, but in the apocalyptic thought patterns of first-century Judaism, and particularly of the New Testament, *Kosmos* represents the twisted values which threatened genuine human life."[42] The *Kosmos*, as the legitimate ordering of social life, has itself been corrupted, and, rather than protect values and life, it (the *Kosmos*, the order) "is the intruder bearing immorality."[43] Thus, the theological understanding of *Kosmos*, as used in the New Testament, is the *evil social order* - in whatever form or agency it manifests itself. It refers not to creation, or for that matter to human culture efforts *per se*, but to all elements in the social order which embody "corporate flesh" - social or corporate reality (i.e., structures, systems, institutions, ideologies) which are dehumanizing and in opposition to God and God's redemptive/liberating purposes.

In a theological sense what *sarx* ("the flesh") is to individual, personal existence, the *Kosmos* ("the world") is to social existence. It ultimately means that within the texture of social existence, in our personal life, as well as our corporal life, there is a "principle," a "mystery" of sin or iniquity which is in opposition to human welfare and liberation - even to God.

---

[39]Richard Lovelace, *Dynamics of Spiritual Life*, pp. 93-94.

[40]Stephen C. Mott, *Biblical Ethics and Social Change*, p. 4, his italics.

[41]*Ibid.*, p. 4.

[42]*Ibid.*, p. 5.

[43]*Ibid.*, p. 5.

In the Johannine writings, more than any other New Testament writing, the world is at the center of theological thinking.[44]   In this account redemption and "hence salvation history is a conflict between Christ and the *Kosmos*, or the *Poneros* who rules it."[45]   The evil one (i.e., Satan) is the prince or ruler of this *opposing social order* (*Kosmos*) against God and God's purposes for humanity. Sasse notes that "the *Kosmos* is in some sense personified as the great opponent of the Redeemer in salvation history. It is as it were a powerful collective person which the *harcho tou kosmou* represents."[46]   Jesus' very mission, even his death on the cross, included judgement over the prince of this "evil empire." (John 12:31; 16:11)

As Mott reminds us, "the most characteristic social aspect of *Kosmos* in the New Testament is a system of values which are in opposition to God."[47]   John's exhortation is quite clear on this.

> Do not love the world or anything in the world. If anyone loves the world, the love of the Father is not in him. For everything in the world - the cravings of sinful man, the lust of his eyes and his pride in possessions - comes not from the Father but from the world (1 John 2:15-16).

Thus, it is also quite clear that within the fabric of our social existence there are "systems of values" - manifestations of "corporate flesh" - that militate against our love of God and neighbor, against an authentic spirituality.

It is important to note that the Early Church was not univocal about the "world." Cadoux and Troeltsch show in their treatment of the "world" a more complex scenario - both total rejection and mixed affirmation were present in the Early Church.[48]

---

[44]Hermann Sasse, *Kosmos, Theological Dictionary of the New Testament*, Vol. III, p. 894.

[45]*Ibid.*, pp. 894-895.

[46]*Ibid.*, p. 894.

[47]Stephen C. Mott, *Biblical Ethics and Social Change*, p. 6.

[48]Cecil John Cadoux, *The Early Church and The World* (Edinburgh: T. & T. Clark, 1925); and Ernst Troeltsch, *The Social Teaching of the Christian Churches*.

Principalities and Powers

The "powers," as they are often noted in current biblical , theological and ethical discussions,[49] speak to us that, beyond personal sin and evil, beyond social structures embedded with sinful or evil moral designs, beyond sinful and evil system of values, there exists evil "in the social and political roles of powerful supernatural beings."[50]   The texture of social existence is indeed permeated by "the mystery of iniquity."   Yet, we must note with Mott, that "these biblical concepts relate to phenomena which can be sociologically described and they extend rather than nullify personal responsibility in society."[51]

Contra Berkhoff and others, Mott posits that these "principalities and powers" are angelic powers, not depersonalized social forces or principles. His careful exegesis of Scripture and pertinent Hellenistic and Jewish apocalyptic literature compels him to "stress this background, not to bring the occult into the understanding of institutional evil, but because it shows the political and social significance of the powers."[52]

Our struggle for an authentic and social spirituality must be cognizant that "our struggle is not against flesh and blood, but against the rulers [*archai*], against the authorities [*exousiai*], against the powers of this dark world [*kosmokratores*]" (Ephesians 6:12). These are "powers" who rebelled against God, and, as Yoder reminds us, "were part of the good creation of God."[53] (See, Colossians 1:15-17) Their original power and authority over creation included its social and political life. This authority given by God for providential care has resulted in oppression. They are fallen "powers" with *idolatrous-demonic claims*. Notwithstanding their

---

[49]See, among others, Hendrikus Berkhoff, *Christ and the Powers* (Scottdale, PA.: Herald Press, 1962); Jacques Ellul, *The Subversion of Christianity* (Grand Rapids, Michigan: William B. Eerdmans Publishing Company, 1987) pp. 174-190; Stephen C. Mott, *Biblical Ethics and Social Change*, pp. 3-21; William Stringfellow, *Free in Obedience*, pp. 49-73; Jim Wallis, *Agenda for Biblical People* (New York, N.Y.: Harper and Row, 1976), pp. 38-55; Walter Wink, *Naming the Powers: The Language of Powers in the New Testament* (Philadelphia, PA.; Fortress Press, 184); Walter Wink, *Unmasking the Powers: The Invisible Forces that Determine Human Existence* (Philadelphia, PA.: Fortress Press, 1986); John H. Yoder, *The Politics of Jesus* (Grand Rapids, Michigan (William B. Eerdmans Publishing Company, 1972), pp. 135-162.

[50]Stephen C. Mott, *Biblical Ethics and Social Change*, p. 6.

[51]*Ibid.*, p. 4.

[52]*Ibid.*, p. 8.

[53]John H. Yoder, *The Politics of Jesus*, p. 143.

fallen condition they "cannot fully escape the providential sovereignty of God. He is still able to use them for good."[54] Yoder categorizes the "powers" as religious structures, intellectual structures (-ologies and -isms), moral structures (codes and customs), political structures (the tyrant, the market, the school, the court, race, and nation).[55] The ambivalent status of humanity relative to the "powers," and their manifestations in structures, institutions, and other corporate realities is noted by Yoder under two statements: "we cannot live without them... we cannot live with them."[56] Yoder states that:

> There could not be society or history, there could not be man without the existence above him of religious, intellectual, moral and social structures. *We cannot live without them.* These structures are not and never have been a mere sum total of the individuals composing them. The whole is more than the sum of its parts. And this 'more' is an invisible Power, even though we may not be used to speaking of it in personal or angelic terms.

> But these structures fail to serve man as they should. They do not enable him to live a genuinely free, human, loving life. They have absolutized themselves and they demand from the individual and society an unconditional loyalty. They harm and enslave man. *We cannot live with them.*[57]

What is most significant to note at this time is that the "powers" have been defeated and carried captive by Christ. "And having disarmed the powers and authorities, he made a public spectacle of them, triumphing over them by the cross" (Colossians 2:15). The "powers" have been "disarmed" by Christ, we need not absolutize or respond to their idolatrous-demonic claims. This "good news" is part and parcel of our demonstration and proclamation of the Gospel of Jesus Christ.

---

[54]*Ibid.*, p. 144.

[55]*Ibid.*, p. 145.

[56]*Ibid.*, p. 146.

[57](Italics are Yoder's), *Ibid.*, pp. 145-146; It is interesting to note that Yoder thinks that traditional theologies have sought to describe and treat this theme under the "orders of creation." He finds them wanting, though, in that they were not able to "affirm that it is in Christ that these values all find their meaning and coherence," *Ibid.*, pp. 146-147.

In concluding this section on the "Mystery of Iniquity: The Texture of Social Existence," it is important to note with Steve Mott:

> The existence of an evil order ruled by supernatural beings must either be accepted or rejected on faith, but such reality would not be dissonant with our social experience. Our concern here is not to settle the cosmological question of whether angels and demons should be demythologized but rather to come to terms with social material to which their biblical existence points.

> ... The world-order and the evil presence of the powers are never *synonymous* with the concrete forms of social and institutional life. Institutions function both to enslave and to liberate human existence. The powers are always present along with enslavement and death in small or large degree; but their real existence is behind the scenes in a system of hostile values vying for control of the life of the world.[58]

Any and every spirituality to be authentic and relevant must come to terms with personal and social sin and evil. What is most critical for Hispanic Pentecostalism is to incorporate within its theology and ethics, not to say spirituality, a deeper understanding of the "mystery of iniquity." It must realize that sin and evil goes beyond the individual; that we are all enmeshed in a social living that is complex, dynamic and dialectical; and that our spirituality, and the very Gospel that we preach, needs to be as big and ubiquitous as sin and evil.[59] We will falter in our spirituality and thus grieve the Spirit if "our struggle with evil" does not "correspond to the geography of evil." We are assured in this struggle that

> We are more than conquerors through him who loved us. For I am convinced that neither death nor life, neither angels nor demons, neither the present nor the future, nor any powers, neither height nor depth, nor anything else in all creation, will be able to separate us from the love of God that is in Christ Jesus our Lord (Romans 8:38-39).

---

[58]Italics are Mott's, *Biblical Ethics and Social Change*, pp. 10, 15.

[59]For a provocative and insightful study, that integrates theology with the finding of clinical psychology, in interpreting certain "non-physical realities", see Morton Kelsey, *Discernment: A Study in Ecstasy and Evil* (New York, N.Y.: Paulist Press, 1978).

The Spirit's "Brooding": Signs of the Reign of God

> "En el principio creó Dios los cielos
> y la tierra. Y la tierra estaba
> desordenada y vacía, y las tinieblas
> estaban sobre la faz del abismo, y el
> *Espíritu de Dios aleteaba* sobre la faz
> de las aguas."
>
> - Génesis 1:1-2[60]

The Holy Spirit was present and active in creation. The metaphor used to describe its action is rich and suggestive. "Aleteaba" (hovering) speaks of the fluttering of the wings of a brooding bird, thus conveying both *protection* and *provision* for its young (see, Deut. 32:ll; Isa. 31:5). Leon Wood, commenting on this passage, notes:

> God the Father planned creation. God the Son effected creation
> (John 1:3; Col. 1:16), and God the Holy Spirit brought creation to
> *completion*. Similarly, God the Father planned man's salvation
> (recreation). God the Son effected the plan (incarnation and death),
> and God the Holy Spirit applies the benefit to sinners, thus bringing
> the plan to *completion* once again.[61]

In the economic trinity the Spirit is the "completing" person. The Spirit completes the process of bringing order out of chaos; order out of the "formless and empty" world. The Spirit does more; following our imagery, it protects and provides for the creation. This double mission of the Spirit still continues in the world. The Spirit protects as "the Restrainer" (*To Katechon* - 2 Thess. 2:6, 7), a

---

[60]"In the beginning God created the havens and the earth. Now the earth was formless and empty, darkness was over the surface of the deep, and the *Spirit of God* was *hovering* ["brooding"] over the waters" (Genesis 1:1-2).

[61]Leon J. Wood, *Genesis: A Study Guide Commentary* (Grand Rapids, Michigan: Zondervan Publishing House, 1976), p. 24; italics are mine.

defensive role. The Spirit provides as "the Helper"[62] (*Parakletos* - John 14:16, 26; 15:26; 16:7), an offensive role.

The Holy Spirit as *To Katechon* maintains "order" in our world. It restrains the "powers" from bringing about total oppression and chaos to our world, as noted in our previous section. The Holy Spirit as *Parakletos* is helping to bring God's Reign to completion. It is present in the world to convict of sin, righteousness, and judgement. It is present in the charismatic renewal of the church in and for the world. The Spirit is present as a "Helper" wherever good, love, peace, justice - Signs of the Reign - are manifested in our world.[63]

---

[62]I have chosen to emphasize the "Helper" concept in the "one called alongside" (*Parakletos*) over the Comforter, Counselor or Advocate in view of the "Helper's" more general, positive and inclusive role. The tendency to see the *Parakletos* only in forensic and psychological terms, in contemporary society's obsession with litigation and "mental health", detracts from the more extensive, wholistic and inclusive role as "Helper". There is a legitimate concern to put a distance between the Johannie *Parakletos* being derived from the Gnostic, and more specifically Mandaean world of thought. Yet, this "Helper" concept, though limited in encompassing the richly nuanced *Parakletos*, is quite instructive. Johannes Behm notes that: "The 'helper' concept in Mandaean Gnosis has some of the features of the Johannine Paraclete: sending from the upper world, impartation of revelation concerning part and future by means of the instruction and exhortation of believers, leading to salvation, confirmation in moral conduct." in *Parakletos, Theological Dictionary of the New Testament*, ed. Gerhard Friedrich (Grand Rapids, Michigan: William B. Eerdmans Publishing Co., 1967), p. 808.

[63]The scope of this study does not permit us to enter the *filioque* debate, which in part contributed to the split between the Eastern and Western churches, and whose implications go beyond its trinitarian focus, to the very heart of the Spirit's presence and mission in the world. But it must be noted that Jesus spoke to his disciples about the Spirit coming as *allon parakleton* (another Helper). As George Eldon Ladd states, "This implies that Jesus has already been a paraclete with his disciples, and that the Spirit will come to take his place and continue his ministry with the disciples ... Some commentators go so far as to identify the glorified Christ and the Spirit. However, while there is indeed an identity of function, John maintains a distinction: the Spirit is not Jesus; the Spirit is *another* Paraclete. If John reflected upon it, he would probably say that Christ was present in the Spirit," in George Eldon Ladd, *A Theology of the New Testament* (Grand Rapids, Michigan: Wm. B. Eerdmans Publishing Company, 1974), pp. 294-295. While the function of the glorified Christ can be identified with the mission of the *Parakletos*, it does not exhaust it. While I believe that there is a uniqueness of the Spirit's presence in the church (Rom. 8:23; 1 Cor. 6:19; Eph. 2:14-18), I believe we cannot limit him to it. There is a tendency to a "*practical subordination*, if not an ontological subordination" in the Western church's understanding of the Spirit. See William W. Menzies, "The Holy Spirit in Christian Theology", in Kenneth S. Kantzer and Stanley N. Gundry, editor. *Perspective on Evangelical Theology* (Grand Rapids, Michigan: Baker Book House, 1979), pp. 67-79; and James W. Jones, *The Spirit and The World* (New York: Hawthorn Books, Inc., 1975), especially pp. 78-106.

Gospel of the Reign of God

> But if I drive out demons by the Spirit of
> God, then the Kingdom of God has come
> upon you.
>
> - Matthew 12:28

Eschatology forms the central and essential framework of New Testament theology. The "beginning" of the End, the Reign of God, has broken into our world in the person of Jesus. The message of the New Testament is that God's rule is *already* present in Jesus the Messiah, although it awaits final consummation in the *not yet* of the future. In Jesus Christ we have, in the words of Ladd, the "fulfillment without consummation" of the Reign of God.[64]

The "good-news" of the Reign meant that beyond God's governing through creation and providence God's special reign or rule had broken into history.[65] Jesus Christ himself both proclaimed and embodied the Reign. John Wimber notes, "This explains the two-fold pattern of Christ's ministry, repeated wherever he went: first *proclamation*, then *demonstration*. First he preached repentance and the good news of the Kingdom of God. Then he cast out demons, healed the sick, raised the dead - which proved he was the presence of the Kingdom, the Anointed one."[66]

---

[64]George Eldon Ladd, *The Presence of the Future: The Eschatology of Biblical Realism* (Grand Rapids, Michigan: Wm. B. Eerdmans Publishing Co., 1974), pp. 105-121; Among the many other pertinent works on the Reign, see George Eldon Ladd, *A Theology of the New Testament*; Karl Ludwig Schmidt, *Basileus - Basilikos*, *TDNT*, Vol. l, pp. 564-593; John Bright, *The Kingdom of God* (Nashville: Abington Press, 1953); Herman Ridderbos, *The Coming of the Kingdom* (Philadelphia: Presbyterian and Reformed, 1962); Amos N. Wilder, "Kerygma, Eschatology and Social Ethics," in W.D. Davies and D. Daube, eds. *The Background of New Testament and Its Eschatology* (Cambridge: Cambridge University, 1956), pp. 509-536; C. René Padilla, *Misión Integral: Ensayos Sobre el Reino y la Iglesia* (Grand Rapids, Michigan: Wm. B. Eerdmans Publishing Company, 1986).

[65]It is important to note with Mott that, "the Greek word *basileia*, which is used for *reign* or *kingdom*, means primarily the *act* of reigning rather than the *place* of reigning; thus in most cases it should be translated as *reign, rule, kingship* or *sovereignty*, rather than its usual English rendering, *kingdom*.", in Stephen C. Mott, *Biblical Ethics and Social Change*, pp. 82-83 (italics Mott's).

[66]John Wimber, *Power Evangelism* (San Francisco, California: Harper and Row, Publishers, 1986), p. 6.

The Reign of God in Jesus is one of "spiritual power encounters."[67] Jesus' life and mission were both inaugurated and empowered by the Holy Spirit. Wells states, "so it is that Jesus' birth, baptism, miracles, teaching, sacrifice, and resurrection are all ascribed to the working of the Holy Spirit."[68] Stronstad can thus speak of Jesus' life and mission as that of the Charismatic Christ.[69]

Jesus' own life was demonstrably one of deep spirituality. His life of prayer and obedience to the Father's will are clearly recorded in Scripture. Douglas D. Webster reminds us and challenges us of the need to model such a life of spirituality in his chapter "The Human Spirituality of Jesus."[70]

Jesus' mission is one of the Spirit's anointment for "spiritual power encounters."

> The Spirit of the Lord is on me; therefore he has anointed me to preach good news to the poor. He has sent me to proclaim freedom for the prisoners and recovery of sight for the blind, to release the oppressed, to proclaimed the year of the Lord's favor (Luke 4:18-19).

The powers of the age to come have indeed invaded this age. The "signs and wonders" were a witness to this reality. The Reign of God has come because the "strong man's house" has been invaded by the Charismatic Christ (Matthew 12:28). C. René Padilla states that:

> El reino de las tinieblas que corresponde a este siglo ha sido invadido; el 'hombre fuerte' ha sido desarmado, conquistado y saqueado (Mt. 12:29; Lc. 11:22) ... En otras palabras, la misión histórica de Jesús solo puede entenderse en conexión con el Reino de Dios. Su misión aquí y ahora es la manifestación del Reino como una realidad presente en su propia persona y acción, en su

---

[67]See among others, John Wimber, *Power Evangelism*; Roger Stronstad, *The Charismatic Theology of St. Luke* (Peabody, Mass: Hendrickson Publishers, 1984); and David F. Wells, "Spiritual Power Encounters" in David Wells, *God the Evangelist*, pp. 65-91.

[68]*Ibid.*, p. 29.

[69]Roger Stronstad, *The Charismatic Theology of St. Luke*; He goes on to state that "Jesus is not only anointed by the Spirit, but He is also Spirit-led, Spirit-filled, and Spirit-empowered," *Ibid.*, p. 45.

[70]Douglas D. Webster, *A Passion For Christ: An Evangelical Christology* (Grand Rapids, Michigan: Zondervan Publishing House, 1987), pp. 77-88.

predicación del evangelio y en sus obras de justicia y misericordia.[71]

The Gospel of the Reign is the good news that in the life, death and resurrection of Christ God's reign is manifested in the physical and historical affairs of people - bound and hindered by demonic forces - now able to experience the Spirit's total liberation.[72] God's salvation in Christ affects the whole person - both spiritual and physical - in his/her concrete historical reality. Nothing is exempt from God's reign. While we live in the *not yet* of complete fulfillment of the Reign, that awaits the *parousia* in the future, we nevertheless continue to share in Jesus' mission of liberation through *proclamation* and *demonstration* (See, John 20:21).

The early church's experience of the baptism of the Spirit (Acts 2) was interpreted as a continuation of Jesus' mission in the power of the Spirit. "Signs and wonders" attested their participation in the *now* but *not yet* of the inbreaking of the reign of God. Joel 2:28, 29, was interpreted as the *end* time promise - "the beginning ot the end." The early church saw itself as an eschatological community. The Spirit's outpouring gather in a community of the Reign of God, the community of the Spirit.[73] Roger Stronstad states that,

> If we have interpreted Luke's Pentecostal narrative correctly, then the gift of the Spirit is not salvation, but it is for witness and service. In other words, with the transfer of the Spirit to the disciples on the day of Pentecost, they became a charismatic community, heirs to the earlier charismatic ministry of Jesus.[74]

---

[71]"The kingdom of darkness that pertains to this age has been invaded; the 'strong man' has been disarmed, conquered, and robbed (Matt. 12:29; Lk. 11:22) ... In other words, the historic mission of Jesus can only be understood in connection with the Kingdom of God. His mission here and now is the manifestation of the Kingdom as a present reality in his own person and action, in his preaching of the Gospel and in his works of justice and mercy.", C. René Padilla, *Misión Integral*, p. 182.

[72]Stephen C. Mott, *Biblical Ethics and Social Change*, p. 94.

[73]See James W. Jones, *The Spirit and the World*, pp. 51-76.

[74]Roger Stronstad, *The Charismatic Theology of St. Luke*, p. 62; Stronstad defines the term 'charismatic' in a functional and dynamic sense. By 'charismatic' I mean God's gift of His Spirit to His servants, either individually or collectively, to anoint, empower, or inspire them for divine service," *Ibid.*, p. 13. It is thus devoid of soteriological connotations, emphasizing the prophetic and vocational.

While the church is *not* the Reign, yet, as the community of the Spirit - where the Spirit manifests itself in a unique and particular way (Romans 8:23; 1 Cor. 6:19; Ephesians 2:14-18) - it has the purpose to both reflect and witness to the values of the Reign of God, by the power of the Spirit to the world. Costas states it this way:

> Therefore, the church, which is *not* the Kingdom, is nevertheless its most *visible expression* and its most *faithful interpreter* in our age... as the community of believers from all times and places, the church both *embodies* the Kingdom in its life and *witnesses* to its presence and future in its mission.[75]

The church as the community of the Spirit is also engaged in "spiritual power encounters." It struggles with the forces of sin and death, with the demonic powers that-be, whether individually or institutionally manifested and whether morally, physically or spiritually expressed. The church can depend on the *Parakletos* as it brings the charismatic renewal of the church *in* and *for* the world. "Signs and wonders" are thus legitimate expectations in the Spirit's total liberation. Orlando Costas eloquently states the significance of the cosmic and historic "power encounter" in the following

> The Kingdom is an indication of God's transforming presence in history... a symbol of God's transforming power, of his determination to make "all things new" (Rev. 21:5). The Kingdom of God stands for a new order of life: the new humanity and the new creation which have become possible through the death and resurrection of Jesus. This new order includes reconciliation with God, neighbor and nature, and, therefore, participation in a new world. It involves freedom from the power of sin and death, and, consequently, the strength to live for God and humanity. It encompasses the hope of a more just and peaceful moral order, and thus it is a call to vital engagement in the historical struggles for justice and peace.[76]

---

[75]Orlando Costas, *The Integrity of Mission: The Inner Life and Outreach of the Church* (New York: Harper and Row, 1979), p. 8, (italics Costas').

[76]*Ibid.*, p. 6.

Creation, Culture and History

An authentic spirituality affirms the goodness of God's creation, which includes human culture and its history. While cognizant of the cosmic struggle for God's total creation, a relevant spirituality is nevertheless awed by God's image and likeness in humanity (Genesis 1:26, 27); an *imago Dei* which co-creates, builds, produces and, thus, manifest in its creativity a genuine goodness, a touch of the Divine.[77] This *imago Dei* can be simply stated in the profound words of the Jewish scholar, Abraham Heschel, "there is something in the world that the Bible does regard as a symbol of God. It is not a temple nor a tree, it is not a statute nor a star. The one symbol of God is *man, every man*".[78]

Human responsibility for creation - for nature, culture's development and history - is noted early in the book of Genesis. The so-called culture mandates (Genesis 1:28-31; 2:15), notwithstanding the subsequent Fall (Genesis 3), is not revoked but rather given a new focus and realism - it must contend with sin and evil.

The biblical witness from Genesis to Revelation is that "man has a cultural responsibility toward creation. He is called to unfold its treasure and to build structures that are in harmony with the cycles, the patterns, and the orders of God's creative act."[79]

The culture products of persons in society throughout history - be they material or 'spiritual' - have reflected the imperfections of the Fall (Romans 9:19-22), but they have also reflected the goodness of the *Imago Dei*.

The greatest affirmation of creation, culture and its history, though, is not to be found in the *Imago Dei*, but in the Incarnation. It is the witness of Scripture that, "the Word became flesh and lived for a while among us" (John 1:4); that Christ Jesus, "who being in very nature God ... made himself nothing, taking the very nature of a servant, being made in human likeness and being found in appearance as a man, he humbled himself..." (Philippians 2:6-8); and that, "since the children have flesh and blood, he too shared in their humanity .. for this reason he had to be made like his brothers in every way ..." (Hebrews 2:14, 17). The mystery of the Incarnation cannot be fathomed. The Christological battles of the

---

[77]See Ray S. Anderson, *On Being Human: Essay in Theological Anthropology* (Grand Rapids, Michigan: Wm. B. Eerdmans Publishing House, 1982).

[78]Abraham J. Heschel, *Between God and Man* (New York: Harper and Row, 1959), p. 234.

[79]*Ibid.*, p. 38.

ancient church reveal a portrait of two major schools of thinking that are worth noting in this regard.

The Ebionites of the 2nd century, while affirming the human reality of Jesus, denied his divinity - that God could be present in human form. For the Ebionites, in the words of Justo González, "La distancia entre Dios y el mundo es infranqueable, y todo intento de ver a Dios en el mundo es idolatría".[80]

To the Docetist, who views matter as evil, the human appearance of Jesus Christ was just that - human appearance, not a reality. González's commentary on docetism notes that in this view:

> Dios es un ser espiritual que nada tiene que ver con este mundo físico, ... La materia es mala, y el espíritu es el bien: de modo que es inconceptible que la salvación y la verdad hayan venido a este mundo en un cuerpo material. Al contrario, la salvación consiste en librarse de las ataduras del cuerpo y del mundo físico que nos aprisionan y no nos permiten realizar nuestro destino espiritual.[81]

These two Christological schools ran counter to the teaching of Scripture that in Jesus Christ there is present the divine (against, the Ebionites) as well as the human (against the Docetist). It took the church till the Council of Chalcedon's (451 A.D.) "definition of faith" to finally affirm both the full divinity and full humanity of Jesus. Gabriel Fackre, in reference to the resolutions of both the Council of Nicea (325) and Chalcedon (451), asks,

> Who is Jesus Christ? He is *truly God, truly human, truly one.* This fundamental doctrine of the Incarnation - Deity, humanity, and unity of Jesus Christ - is the Church's effort to be faithful to the figure it

---

[80]"The distance between God and the world is uncrossable and all attempts to see God in the world is idolatry," Justo L. González, "Encarnación e Historia," in C. René Padilla, *Fé Cristiana y Latinoamérica Hoy*, p. 156; see also, Earle E. Cairns, *Christianity Through the Centuries* (Grand Rapids, Michigan: Zondervan Publishing House, 1954), pp. 104-105.

[81]"God is a spiritual being that has nothing to do with this physical world, ... matter is evil, and the spirit is the good: therefore it is inconceivable that salvation and truth have come to this world in a physical body. On the contrary, salvation consists in freeing oneself of the chains of the body and of the physical world that imprisons us and does not permit us to realize our spiritual destiny," Justo González, "Encarnación e Historia", in C. René Padilla, *Fé Cristiana y Latinoamérica Hoy*, p. 155.

met and meets in the pages of the Bible and in its own life with him.[82]

The significance of Chalcedon goes beyond the importance of resolving the issue of Christ's nature, it is a tremendous affirmation of God's creation - the world of humanity, culture and history - and by implication of our attitude to it.

Today many try to "break" the mystery of the Incarnation by not taking seriously either Jesus' divinity or Jesus' humanity. In certain conservative Evangelical and Pentecostal quarters there is the tendency "to emphasize the deity of Christ and minimize or trivialize his genuine humanity."[83] In other so-called "liberal" quarters the tendency is to emphasize the humanity of Christ and minimize or trivialize his genuine deity. A truly biblical view of Christ will emphasize both as critical to a proper understanding of Jesus' life and mission, and to a proper affirmation of creation and history.

The greatness of the Incarnation, which affirms and validates humanity, can be seen in a few verses from a stanza of Unamuno's *El Cristo de Velázquez*:

> ... para ver tu cuerpo blanco que en desnudez al Padre retrataba desnudo. Destapaste a nuestros ojos la humanidad de Dios; con tus dos brazos desabrochando el manto del misterio, nos revelaste la divina esencia, la humanidad de Dios, la que del hombre descubre lo divino...[84]

The Incarnation reveals the humanity of God, and in so doing affirms unequivocally the value and the goodness of creation and culture. Christianity does not reject the world - creation, humanity, and its culture - rather, it can only comprehend its God in Jesus Christ through it. Unamuno teaches us this profound truth about our knowledge of God being understood only *by* and *through* the Incarnation. His *El Cristo De Velázquez* is an expression *of* and commentary *to*

---

[82]Gabriel Fackre, *The Christian Story: A Narrative Interpretation of Basic Christian Doctrine* (Grand Rapids, Michigan: Wm. B. Eerdmans Publishing Company, 1984 ed.), p. 99 (Italics Fackre's).

[83]Douglas D. Webster, *A Passion For Christ*, p. 40.

[84]"... to see your white body that in nakedness the Father you pictured naked. You uncovered to our eyes the humanity of God; with your two arms unbuttoning the mantel of muystery, you revealed to us the divine escence, the humanity of God, by which man discovers the divine" (my translation); Miguel De Unamuno, *El Cristo de Velázquez (Poema)* (Madrid: Esposa-Calpe, S.A., 1967 ed.), p. 24. It has been said by many that Unamuno's poem is one of the greatest treatises on the Incarnation.

the Scripture verse in this book's heading - "*kai ho jurios to somati*" (1 Cor. 6:13).[85]

The "world-rejection" that the church must exercise is that defined by dehumanizing and demonic systemic values and structures, and not the world as God's creation. We are called to discernment; to discern admits a fallen world, the goodness of God's creative act expressed by humanity in and through culture in its history. We are called to discern the Spirit's work not only in the church, the community of the Spirit, but in the world. Beyond the *Spirit's* work in the world of convicting of sin, righteousness and judgement (John 16:8-11), we must see the Spirit's role as *To Katechon* and *Parakletos* wherever we see goodness, love, peace and justice exercised in God's creation - genuine sighs and signs of the Reign of God.

The Reign of God, the Spirit's historical project, takes seriously the world - as humanity, creation and its culture. Present history is affirmed; for history is the arena of the obedience of faith of the reign of God. The clear teaching of Scripture also looks to that future in which all things are made new (Rev. 21:5); where the "dwelling of God is with men, and he will live with them" (Rev. 21:3), in a renewed creation.

---

[85]"and the Lord *for* the body" (1 Cor. 6:13); my italic.

CHAPTER V

TOWARD AN HISPANIC AMERICAN
PENTECOSTAL SOCIAL ETHIC

> Not by might, nor by power, but by my
> Spirit, says the Lord Almighty.
> - Zechariah 4:6

So far, I have understood that the most fruitful approach to developing the theological foundations for a social ethic for Hispanic Pentecostalism rest in the development of a social spirituality. This spirituality must emerge and thus cohere with Hispanic Pentecostal experience - particularly as it relates to the ministry of the Spirit. I have presented those needed elements for a social spirituality, the missing dimension in Hispanic Pentecostal experience. Our pneumatological paradigm coheres with Hispanic Pentecostal experience and seeks to extend its self-understanding as the community of the Spirit *in* the world and *for* the world, but not *of* the world.

In this chapter I will first present under "Ethics as Pneumatology" the implications of our pneumatological paradigm for an Hispanic Pentecostal social ethic. Then I will need to address two significant areas in the development of an Hispanic Pentecostal social ethic, the role of Scripture and the "two pillars" of ethics - Love and Justice. I will conclude this chapter with the implications for the life and mission of the church.

Ethics as Pneumatology

> If we live in the Spirit, let us also
> walk in the Spirit.
> - Galatians 5:25

Ethics in Hispanic Pentecostalism emerges from its experience of the Spirit. The love of God in Jesus Christ poured out by the Spirit begins the spiritual pilgrimage (Rom 5:5). This love becomes the source, motive and power of the living in the Spirit. It is this transforming experience of love that challenges the believer to seek "in obedience to God to follow Jesus in the power of the Spirit." This is both a spirituality and an ethic of the Spirit. Paul in his letter to the Galatians reminds us that both our theological self-understanding and our ethical self-understanding is grounded in the Spirit (Gal. 5:25).

> If we live in the Spirit [theological self-understanding], let us also walk in the Spirit [ethical self-understanding].

> - Gal. 5:25.

It is important to note that the New Testament word for "walk" used by Paul in this verse is *stoichomen* (present active subject of *stoicheo*). As such, it has a military sense in its etymology and has been paraphrased by some as "to follow the marching orders of the Spirit."[1] The New International Version of the New Testament translates the word "walk" as "let us keep in step with." The rich nuances of our "walk" in the Spirit suggest that our ethical conduct, whether personal or social, is a following of the leading of the Spirit.[2]

In the previous chapter I have presented a pneumatological paradigm, a theological foundation focus on the Spirit. The implications from my pneumatological paradigm are many and significant for an Hispanic Pentecostal social ethic. I will consider the ethical implications of three major categories or themes that have emerged from my pneumatological paradigm. These can be schematically presented as follows:

---

[1] See Gerhard Delling, *Stoicheo - Stoicheion*, *TDNT*, Vol. Vii, pp. 666-687; it is very suggestive Delling's notation that, "The military use strictly differentiates *stoichos* for those arranged behind one another from *zugon* for those beside one another," *Ibid.*, p. 666; see also, Fritz Rienecker "Galatians 5:25", *A Linguistic Key to the Greek New Testament*, p. 518.

[2] We may even say a *dancing* after the Spirit - our ethical pilgrimage should be performed in celebration. Ridderbos reminds us that "the word [*stoicheo*] was used for movement in a definite line, as in military formation or in *dancing*." Herman Ridderbos, *The Epistle of Paul to the Church of Galatians: The New International Commentary on the New Testament* (Grand Rapids, Michigan: Eerdmans, 1970), quoted in Fritz Rienecker, *A Linguistic Key to the Greek New Testament*, p. 518, my italics; for a current and insightful presentation that highlights Paul's use of the metaphor of *walking* to describe the moral life of the believer, see, J. Paul Sampley, *Walking Between the Times: Paul's Moral Reasoning* (Minneapolis: Augsbury Fortress Press, 1991).

If we live in the Spirit, [Theological Self- understanding]	let us also walk in the Spirit. [Ethical Self- understanding]
1. The Spirit's histori- cal project	- The challenge to participate in the Reign of God.
2. The Spirit's power encounters	- The challenge to confront structural sin and evil.
3. The Spirit's "charis- matic" empowerment	- The challenge to fulfill the prophetic and vocational role of the "baptism in the Spirit"

The Challenge to Participate in the Reign of God

C. René Padilla reminds us that "el imperativo de la ética cristiana se deriva directamente del indicativo del Evangelio. Lo que *hacemos* es solo la respuesta a lo que *Dios ha hecho*."[3] It can be equally stated that the imperative of Christian ethics - particularly social ethics - is derived directly from the indicative of the Spirit's historical project - the Reign of God. Not only is the framework of New Testament theology eschatological, but equally is its social ethics. The Gospel of Jesus Christ is the Gospel of the Reign of God. In Jesus Christ the Reign was particularized and made efficacious through the Cross. The eternal redemption (Hebrew 9:12) wrought in Calvary was made through the eternal Spirit (Hebrew 9:14). In the Spirit, through whom the risen Christ is mediated to us, the Reign has been universalized.

A proper understanding of the *present reality and scope* of the Reign of God is critically needed by Hispanic Pentecostals. The present *charismata* - glossolalia, divine healing, other manifestations of the Spirit - in Hispanic Pentecostalism can only be biblically and theologically understood if the Reign of God is a present reality. While there may be certain understanding of the relation of the Reign and the Spirit's *charismata* in the Hispanic Pentecostal church, it is the social and political implications that are lacking.

---

[3]"the imperative of Christian ethics is derived directly from the indicative of the Gospel. What *we do* is only the response to what *God has done*," in C. René Padilla, "El Evangelio y la Responsabilidad Social," in C. René Padilla, *El Evangelio Hoy* (Buenos Aires, Argentina: Ediciones Certeza, 1975), p. 79, (Padilla's italics).

The Spirit of God, by whom Christ "went about doing good and healing all that were oppressed of the devil" (Acts 10:38) and through whom Christ "offered himself ... to God" (Hebrews 9:14), *is still* carrying out the Reign task.   To participate in the Reign of God is to participate in the power of the age to come that are present and available to the church by the Spirit. The church must follow the Spirit as Christ. It too must be an "anointed one," the body of Christ thrust in the world to do good and heal all those oppressed of the devil, wherever and however that is manifested. It also must, like Christ, offer itself to God: as a true incarnation in the affairs of the world and as a true cross bearer in social "redemption."[4]

To participate in the Reign of God means to participate in God's rule. It is to take seriously God's call as a church to be a community of the Spirit *in* the world and a community of the Spirit *for* the world. This participation implies that there is no area of life where the rule of God cannot be exercised. While God rules in the Church through the pneumatic (risen) Christ, the church must not see itself as the only *locus* of the Reign of God. Boff reminds us that "the church ... must ... define itself as an instrument for the full realization of the Kingdom and as a sign of a true yet still imperfect realization of this Kingdom in the world."[5] The church is thus challenged not to see itself as an *end* but as a means towards the building of God's Reign.

To participate in the Reign of God is to participate in the political process. Christian participation in the political process is predicated in the understanding that Christ is Lord of the Kingdom of this world, too. Although, the rule of Christ has not been fully manifested - awaiting the *eschaton* - his claim and dominion are to impact all human relations, meaning, the political process. James W. Jones, in speaking about participating in the political process, makes clear the significance of participating in the Spirit's historical project:

> The people of God are still bidden to seek the peace of the city in which they dwell (cf. Jer. 29:7) and to witness to the Lordship of Jesus Christ over the whole of life. Therefore, a total separation from the political Kingdom of this world is probably neither possible nor desirable. The political process can serve the relative peace of the world... The Christian knows that political activity will not bring in the Kingdom of God nor undercut the eschatological

---

[4]In the words of Leonardo Boff, "The church has always understood itself as the continuation of Christ and his mission", Leonardo Boff, *Church: Charism and Power* (New York: Crossroad Publishing Company, 1986), p. 144.

[5]*Ibid.*, p. 146.

tension of the Kingdom of God, which, because it has not yet come, stands over and against the human state of affairs. Therefore, politics is not his ultimate concern. His primary concern must be submission to the plan of God to fill all things with himself through his Spirit. But political activity can serve to fulfill the biblical injunction to seek for peace and to proclaim the Lordship of Christ over all.[6]

The challenge to participate in the Reign of God implies that the Hispanic Pentecostal church must discern the signs of God's reign in the world. While it may be a difficult and often a treacherous task, given the experience of Hispanics being exploited and oppressed in the world-outside-the-church, the need to discern the Spirit's action in the world and unite with the Spirit in the struggle is part of the calling of the church as it witnesses to the full liberation of the Reign. Justo L. González, commenting on the need for Hispanics to develop a political spirituality, notes the importance of discerning the signs of God's reign.

> ... porque la humanidad no tiene otro futuro sino el Reino, los cristianos debemos saber que no tenemos un monopolio sobre toda señal del Reino. Porque Dios es el Rey, su voluntad se hará con nosotros, en nosotros, y hasta a pesar de nosotros ... doquiera se alimenta al hambriento, se viste al desnudo o se visita al cautivo, Dios está presente, y hay señales de su Reino. La espiritualidad que tenemos que desarrollar consiste precisamente en aprender a ver esas señales, aún cuando no vengan de nosotros ni de la iglesia, y a unirnos a Dios en su acción en el mundo, en anticipo de su Reino.[7]

To Hispanic Pentecostals the challenge to participate in the Reign of God also implies reading anew the signs of the Reign present in their own Hispanic culture, religious traditions, and social reality. One finds in these rich resources for ethical reflection that affirm, point to and express genuine signs of the Reign

---

[6]James W. Jones, *The Spirit and the World*, pp. 73-74.

[7]"... because humanity has no other future but the Kingdom, Christians should know that we do not have a monopoly over all signs of the Kingdom. Because God is the King, his will shall be done with us, in us, and even in spite of us ... wherever the hungry are fed, the naked clothed or prisoners visited, God is present, and there are signs of his Kingdom. The spirituality that we must develop consist precisely in learning to see these signs, even when they do not come from us nor the church, and to join God in his action in the world, in anticipation of his Kingdom.", Justo L. González, "Espiritualidad Política", in *Apuntes*, Vol. 3, No. 1 (Primavera 1983), pp. 8-9; see also Justo L. González's "Spirituality and the Spirit of Mañana" in his *Mañana: Christian Theology from a Hispanic Perspective* (Nashville: Abingdon Press, 1990) pp. 157-163.

in their midst. The Hispanic Pentecostal church must learn to see and affirm those signs of the Reign in its midst in the "barrios" if it is to discern those signs outside.   A proper self-understanding (identity) is critical for vocation - for carrying out any missional endeavor.[8] Among the many signs/themes that can be noted we will list five that the Hispanic Pentecostal church needs to acknowledge, reappropriate and share with others - witness to in the greater society.

1.	"Mestizaje"	Hispanics as the *Raza Cósmica*. The Hispanic Pentecostal church reflects this "mixed" constituency - Spanish (white), African (black) and Amerindian stock. It embodies and witnesses to the shalom of the races - signs of the Reign.
2.	"La Morenita"	The significance of the "brown lady" in evangelization in Catholicism has been previously noted. Although, not part of its religious symbols, Hispanic Pentecostals, nevertheless, should be able to affirm with the dominant Hispanic Catholic culture the positive image of womanhood of "La Morenita" in the liberating process.
3.	"Migración"	Since 1848 the migration experience has defined most Hispanics. In a real historical sense they are a pilgrim people. This migration experience has made Hispanics a "pueblo puente" or "pueblo fronterizo."[9] The Hispanic Pentecostal church is challenged to live not only between the "times" (the *now* and *not yet* of the Reign), but also, "must look at 'our'mission as Christian Hispanics in the U.S. Being a *border people*, no matter where we live, we must serve as a means of communication between the rich, over-affluent and misdeveloped world of the

[8]This is a truth that I have learned in matters of race and ethnic relations. It requires an authentic recovery, reappropriation and appreciation of one's history and culture (e.g. identity) before one can properly participate in genuine dialogue with other persons of different culture or race.

[9]"bridge people" or "border people"

North, and the poor, exploited and also misdeveloped world of the South. This, and the mission to other Hispanics, requires that we continue to be a bilingual and bicultural church."[10]

4.   "Menesterosos"
     (the indigent, poor
     and the oppressed)

The Pentecostal church is indeed the, "haven of the poor and the masses" - the poor and the working class. While not "ghettorizing" or locking-out the Hispanics from up-grading their economic conditions, nevertheless the Hispanic Pentecostal church must affirm and see itself as a *locus* where the poor and oppressed can find liberation; where solidarity with the poor and the oppressed can be found in the struggle for a full liberation in the world.

5.   "Modelos Sociales"
     (the significant role
     models by the Hispanic
     Church)

The Hispanic Pentecostal church as it fulfills these the roles in the "barrios" it embodies and witnesses to the Reign of God.
(a) Survival- A Place of Cultural Survival
(b) Signpost- A Signpost of Protest and Resistance
(c) Salvation- A liberated and liberating community
(d) Shalom- An Agent of Reconciliation
(e) Secret of the Reign- Hermeneutical Advantage of the Poor
(f) Seedbed for Community Leaders- Emerging leadership nurtured
(g) Social Service Provider- Natural Support Systems - Source of Strength

[10]Justo L. González, "Hacia un redescubrimiento de nuestra misión," *Apuntes* Year 7, No. 3, Fall, 1987, p. 60 (my italics).

Ultimately, the challenge to participate in the Reign is to understand that the signs of the Reign of God are the Spirit's work in the world to *both* "restrain" evil and "help" establish the conditions for a more just and peaceful moral order in all human affairs. They point to the New Age - the new order that has broken into History. It is a work of grace - God's love reaching out by the Spirit to keep and to make human life human.[11] As Paul Lehmann states,

> Let it be noted that the signs which point to and point up what God is doing in the world are *ethical* signs. What is *indicated* is that the politics of God does make a discernible difference in the world, and the ongoing life of the *Koinonia* is the context within which to come in sight of this difference. The *Koinonia* is the bearer in the world of the mystery (secret) and the transforming power of the divine activity, on the one hand, and on the other, of the secret (mystery) and the 'stuff' of human maturity.[12]

Culture and social institutions and structures must be seen as legitimate arenas where God's grace is manifested to make and keep human life human - thus, the task of the church (the *Koinonia*) is to discern God's presence, and "to follow the marching orders of the Spirit," who goes before us in the struggle. While the church knows that its actions in the world does not bring in the Reign, as a "community of exiles and pilgrims,"[13] it faithfully joins the Spirit in witnessing to its historical task.

The Challenge to Confront Structural Sin and Evil

The Spirit's power encounter defines the cosmic struggle being waged for God's creation. As previously noted, the Spirit as "the restrainer" (*to Katechon*) and as "the Helper" (*Parakletos*) sets the framework for this struggle.[14] In the person and work of Jesus, the "charismatic Christ," this power encounter identified

---

[11]For a provocative and insightful view, see Paul Lehmann's chapter, "What God Is Doing in the World" in Paul Lehmann, *Ethics in a Christian Context* (New York, N.Y.: Harper and Row, Publishers, 1963), pp. 74-101.

[12]*Ibid.*, p. 112, italics are Lehmann's.

[13]See George W. Webber, *Today's Church: A Community of Exiles and Pilgrims* (Nashville, Tennessee: Abingdon, 1979).

[14]Also it is important to note Otto Maduro's conflict analysis as setting the socio-cultural framework for confrontation, creative-conflict.

the Reign of God as present (Matthew 12:28). This spiritual power encounter reached its zenith in Jesus' death on the cross - an apparent victory for sin and evil. Of course, this was followed by the Empty tomb - the Resurrection - thus, the Victory. The Cross, seen both as death and resurrection, signals the triumph over the "powers" (Colossians 2:15). Sin and evil have been conquered. Whether manifested in individual-personal life or in social existence (in structures and institutions) the "powers" have been "disarmed," their idolatrous-demonic claims have been shattered.

Yet, the church is still engaged in a bitter struggle - spiritual power encounters. In the words of John Wimber:

> the final and full establishment of the Kingdom of God, with Christ
> as its head, was assured at the resurrection, but we have yet to
> realize its fullness in these days in which we live ... there is a war
> yet to be fought ... we must equip ourselves by allowing the power
> of the Spirit to come into our lives and work through us to defeat
> the enemy.[15]

The tendency of many, including Wimber, is to see this struggle too individualistically and not see that spiritual warfare must correspond with the geography of evil - the sinful and evil structures of society. The Hispanic Pentecostal church must see itself not only as a *locus* for personal liberation, but also as a *locus* for social liberation. They must see that the texture of social living makes no easy distinctions between the personal and the social. That beyond the security - often more an illusion than a fact - of the "culto," beyond individual-personal struggles and outreach, where there are structures and institutions that must be confronted in the power of the Spirit. The church's mission includes engaging in power encounters with sinful and evil structures.

Our confrontation responds to the nature of the structures themselves. On the one hand, we are aware of their creatureness - they are institutions and structures *by* and *for* humans, although their reality *sui generis*. On the other hand, we are aware of their possible demonic nature - the "powers." On one level of the struggle, it means that the church must bring to bear, through our witness and labors, the power of the Spirit to break the chains of hate, hostility, and injustice embedded in them by introducing the values of the Reign of God (i.e., love, justice, fair play) and setting in place a "chain of change"[16] that immediately

---

[15]John Wimber, *Power Evangelism*, p. 21.

[16]See Mel King, *Chain of Change: Struggles for Black Community Development* (Boston, Mass.: South End Press, 1981).

(thus, radical change - revolution), or gradually (thus, multiple and cumulative amelioration - reformation) humanizes these structures and institutions. On the other level of the struggle, the church must witness to the demonic powers that lie behind the scene, by reminding them of their defeat in Christ and the coming New Age. This witness must be in the power of the Spirit, armed with the "full armor of God" (Ephesians 6: 10-18). Jim Wallis states it well.

> The church demonstrates Christ's victory over the powers by reminding them of their created role as servants, rebuking them in their idolatrous role as rulers, and resisting them in their totalitarian claims and purposes ... We are not asked to defeat the powers. That is the work of Christ, which he has already done and will continue to do. Our task is to be witnesses and signs of Christ's victory by simply standing firmly in our faith and belief against the seduction and slavery of the powers.[17]

The Challenge to Fulfill the Prophetic and
Vocational Role of the Baptism in the Spirit

The Spirit's "charismatic" empowerment has been a singular and distinguishing emphasis in Pentecostalism. Hispanic Pentecostals, as other Pentecostals, have tended to interpret this experience narrowly. While it is true that Pentecostalism has been recognized as a powerful force in evangelism, world missions, church growth and spirituality, it is equally true that their services and prophetic voices against sinful social structures and on behalf of social justice have been missing.

For Pentecostals five episodes in the book of Acts set the biblical precedent of Spirit baptism, thus, building "their distinctive theology regarding the gift of the Spirit."[18] The scope of this study does not permit us to enter the dialogue on the methodological issue of the "normativeness" for theology of Luke's historical record. Be that as it may, it is important to note that Roger Stronstad's *The Charismatic Theology of St. Luke* presents a formidable *apologia* contra Frederick Dale Bruner and James D.G. Dunn, two highly influential works on the baptism

---

[17]Jim Wallis, *Agenda for Biblical People*, pp. 48-49.

[18]Roger Stronstad, *The Charismatic Theology of St. Luke*, p. 5; the Scripture references are: (1) Acts 2:1-13; (2) Acts 8:14-19; (3) Acts 9:17-18; (4) Acts 10:44-46; and (5) Acts 19:1-7.

of the Spirit.[19] Stronstad, in my opinion, not only makes an excellent case for the theological character of Lukan historiography and its theological independence (from Pauline interpretation), but through a careful study of the Old Testament, Intertestamental Period, life and work of Christ (whom he calls the Charismatic Christ), and the primitive church (the charismatic community) he traces the purpose of the baptism in the Spirit distinctively as empowerment for witness and service. He states:

> For Luke, the gift of the Spirit has a vocational purpose and equips the disciples for service. Thus,it is devoid of any soteriological connotations and, contra Dunn, it does not mean that 'it is God's giving of the Spirit which makes a man a Christian'.[20]

Stronstad further underlines the universal potential and objective of the baptism in the Spirit:

> In Old Testament times, and even in the Gospel era, the activity of the Spirit is restricted to chosen leaders. From Pentecost onwards, however,the vocational gift of the Spirit is potentially universal... At His baptism, Jesus becomes the unique bearer of the Spirit, and at Pentecost He becomes the giver of the Spirit... with the qualification that the vocational activity of the Spirit is now potentially universal and *its new object is the ongoing mission of the Messiah*, the gift of the Spirit is in continuity with the way in which God has always poured out His Spirit upon His servants.[21]

What is of critical importance and the *crux interpretum* relative to the baptism of the Spirit is its prophetic and vocational purpose, its universal-egalitarian scope and its missional focus.

---

[19]Frederick Dale Bruner, *A Theology of the Holy Spirit: The Pentecostal Experience and the New Testament Witness* (Grand Rapids, Michigan: Wm. B. Eerdmans, 1970); James D.G. Dunn, *Baptism in the Holy Spirit: A Re-examination of the New Testament Teaching of the Gift of the Spirit in relation to Pentecostalism Today* (London: SCM Press Ltd., 1970); for an excellent exposition contra Dunn see also, Howard M. Ervin, *Conversion - Initiation and the Baptism in the Holy Spirit* (Peabody, Mass.: Hendrickson Publishers, Inc., 1984).

[20]Roger Stronstad, *The Charismatic Theology of St. Luke*, p. 64.

[21]*Ibid.*, p. 79 (my italics). It is important to note that neither glossolalia as "initial evidence" of the baptism of the Spirit, nor as a gift for the church is at issue, rather the baptism of the Spirit's purpose then, and now.

The social ethical implications for Hispanic Pentecostalism are significant. While the universal-egalitarian scope of the baptism of the Spirit is present in the "culto," its greater purpose and missional focus in the service of the Spirit's historical project is not present. The baptism of the Spirit in Hispanic Pentecostalism is rightfully seen as empowerment for service, impacting the believer deeply - giving him/her tremendous boldness, a heighten sense of personal holiness, a new sense of self worth and personal power.[22] Yet, the narrow individualistic focus and purpose implies the dissipation in the "culto," if not elsewhere, of so much energy - spiritual power - that can and should be "tapped" for the broader missional objective of the church. The Hispanic Pentecostal church has the spiritual resources to face the spiritual power encounters of our social struggles. If the "new object [of the baptism of the Spirit] is the ongoing mission of the Messiah",[23] and that cannot be narrowed to Matthew 28:18-21, nor Mark 16:15-18, nor Acts 1:8, then it must, above all, include the Messiah's own missional self-understanding - Luke 4:18-19:

> The Spirit of the Lord is on me; therefore he has anointed me to
> preach good news to the poor. He has sent me to proclaim freedom
> for the prisoners and recovery of sight for the blind, to release the
> oppressed, to proclaim the year of the Lord's favor.

Hispanic Pentecostalism, as most branches of Pentecostalism, must see the bigger picture in the Spirit's economy. The Spirit's "charismatic" empowerment are valid "signs and wonders" of the presence of the Reign. It remains then for the faithful fulfillment of the prophetic and vocational role of the baptism in the Spirit.

> If we live in the Spirit,
> Let us also walk in the Spirit.
>
>   - Galatians 5:25

---

[22]Elements critically needed by all, but especially by the poor and the oppressed in our "barrios"; see, "Gerlach and Hine's Functional-Structural Analysis", Chapter III, "Socio-Theological Interpretation of the Hispanic Urban Pentecostal Reality."

[23]Roger Stronstad, *The Charismatic Theology of St. Luke*, p. 79.

Spirit and Scripture in the Formulation
of the Ethical Norm

> And the sword of the Spirit, which is the
> Word [*rhema*] of God.
> - Ephesians 6:17

> But when he, the Spirit of truth, comes, he
> will guide you into all truth.
> - John 16:13

To speak about the Scripture in Hispanic Pentecostal circles is to speak about "el libro del Espíritu."[24]   While Scripture is held explicitly by Hispanic Pentecostals in what would normally be called a fundamentalist manner, nevertheless, there exists an implicit negation in practice. As noted previously, Hispanic Pentecostals tend to read Scripture in what we called an "existential-spiritual manner." In essence what this means is that the believer approaches the text in an almost sacramental manner.[25]   There is an expectation that the Spirit will speak *now* to him or her. Any and all parts of Scripture from Genesis to Revelation can speak equally the word of the Spirit. There is the confidence that the Spirit of truth will guide into all truth (John 16:13).[26]   What Christian Lalive d'Epinay says of Chilean Pentecostalism is also true of Hispanic Pentecostalism.

---

[24]"the book of the Spirit."

[25]There is some affinity with Donald Bloesch's sacramental understanding of revelation, see Donald G. Bloesch, *Essentials of Evangelical Theology*, 2 vols. (New York, N.Y.: Harper and Row, 1979); among the many works on revelation, see Carl F.H. Henry, ed., *Revelation and the Bible* (Grand Rapids, Michigan: Baker Book House, 1958); Avery Dulles, S.J. *Models of Revelation* (New York, N.Y.: Doubleday and Company, Inc., 1985).

[26]This confidence in the Spirit to lead in all truth resonates with Juan Luis Segundo's response to Cardinal Ratzinger's, "Instruction on Certain Aspect of the 'Theology of Liberation'." Segundo notes the need for a theology of the Spirit in responding to the problem of epistemological conditioning. He states, "Rightly, whoever holds a theology of the Spirit that leads to truth and, little by little, to 'all truth' (John 16:13) does not have any reason to fear that class position may be *determining* his or her mentality and preventing a further approximation to a richer and more correct reading and interpretation of the Word of God," Juan Luis Segundo, *Theology and The Church* (San Francisco, CA.: Harper and Row, Publishers, 1987 ed.), p. 135, italics Segundo.

The fact that certain liberties are taken with the Bible is ... to be ascribed above all to the characteristic belief of Pentecostalism: its faith in the Holy Spirit living and acting today in a spiritual, that is, supernatural way.[27]

Lalive d'Epinay notes that some pastors' "loyalty is not so much to the Biblical word as to the Spirit which gives life to the written word."[28] It is of singular importance to note that Hispanic Pentecostals' understanding of the Spirit is rooted in the Scripture. The Scripture is the Word of God, with full authority for faith and practice (2 Timothy 3:16-17; 2 Peter 1:21). Lalive d'Epinay's comments are apropos.

The importance of the Biblical norm in Pentecostal pneumatology gives one an understanding of why, whatever the liberties taken in regard to the Bible in the name of the Spirit, Pentecostalist prophecies or revelations have never had more than relative or temporary validity and were not treated as a new Revelation, complementary to the Holy Scriptures.[29]

While some of the "liberties" taken can be attributed to lack of sound teaching in biblical exegesis and hermeneutics, the fact of the matter is that implicitly Hispanic Pentecostals subscribe to a view of revelation that is dynamic and continuous in nature. This is in keeping "with the 'ontic' principle of theology and Christian experience. This refers to a view of the faith in which the Christian is seen to confront not only Scripture but also the Holy Spirit."[30] In the ultimate analysis, to Hispanic Pentecostals the compelling evidence for Scripture being the Word of God, and thus authoritative in all areas of life, is what the Reformers called *Testimonium internum Spiritus sancti* (The internal witness of the Holy Spirit).[31]

---

[27]Christian Lalive d'Epinay, *Haven of the Masses: A Study of the Pentecostal Movement in Chile*, p. 194.

[28]*Ibid.*, p. 194.

[29]*Ibid.*, p. 195-196.

[30]Paul A. Pomerville, *The Third Force in Missions*, p. 9.

[31]In this regard it should be noted that, while in certain circles in North America Pentecostalism has joined rank with fundamentalist and mainline Evangelism on the issue of Inerrancy, to Hispanic Pentecostalism it is a non-issue, although *if* asked, they would probably support it.

When we look at the use of Scripture as a source for Christian ethics, we find in Hispanic Pentecostalism a multiplicity of approaches not always appreciated by outsiders, or for that matter, explicitly articulated by the believers themselves. A basic three point typology suggested by Edward LeRoy Long, Jr., and drawn upon by many, is useful.[32] Scripture serves as a source of moral guidance in three ways:

(1)   In **prescriptive** terms by providing moral rules or laws; moral reasoning is seeking a rule to fit a particular moral dilemma;

(2)   In providing guiding ethical ideals and **principles**; Long Jr. calls this approach the *deliberative motif* noting the role of reason as a source of moral judgment;[33] and

(3)   In providing or showing a **pattern of response** for the moral life; Paul D. Simmons summarizes this relational motif by saying that,

> it stresses the response in faith which the believer is to make to the living presence of God. The Bible may certainly provide normative guidance through its specific moral teachings, but the basic consideration is the concrete response of the believer to the action and initiative of God in history. No amount of imitative behavior of the moral directives in Scripture is truly biblical until it is behavior elicited as personal response to the divine activity.[34]

While the prescriptive motif is by far the typical approach to formulating the ethical norm by Hispanic Pentecostals, followed by the deliberative motif, particularly in its explicit pronouncements, one finds again that the implicit practice is different. While still holding a high view of Scripture, as the Word of God - with moral laws and rules and principles binding today - one finds that in fact the

---

[32]Edward LeRoy Long, Jr., "The Use of the Bible in Christian Ethics," *Interpretation* 19 (1965): 149-162; see also his work, *A Survey of Christian Ethics* (New York, N.Y.: Oxford University Press, 1967); for other pertinent works on the Bible and ethics, see Thomas W. Ogletree, *The Use of The Bible in Christian Ethics* (Philadelphia, PA.: Fortress Press, 1983); Walter C. Kaiser, Jr., "The Use of The Bible in Establishing Ethical Norms" (chapter 3), *Toward Old Testament Ethics* (Grand Rapids, Michigan: The Zondervan Corporation, 1983), pp. 39-56; Bruce C. Birch and Larry L. Rasmussen, *Bible and Ethics in The Christian Life* (Minneapolis, Minnesota: Augsbury Publishing House, 1976); James M. Gustafson, "The Place of Scripture in Christian Ethics: A Methodological Study," *Theology and Christian Ethics* (Philadelphia, PA.: United Church Press, 1974), pp. 121-145.

[33]Edward L. Long, Jr., *A Survey of Christian Ethics*, p. 45.

[34]Paul D. Simmons, "The Bible and Bioethical Decision-Making", in his *Birth and Death: Bioethical Decision-Making* (Philadelphia, PA.: The Westminster Press, 1983), pp. 44-45.

relational motif dominates in Hispanic Pentecostals' moral reasoning, especially in those indigenous Hispanic Pentecostal churches where the North American Pentecostals' denominational influence has been minimal.

An analogous example from a different part of the world, that's very instructive, is the way Dr. Paul Yonggi Cho, Pentecostal pastor of the largest local church in the world, the Full Gospel Central Church in Seoul, Korea, distinguishes in Scripture the "word" - as *logos* and as *rhema*. Cho speaks, in what we call the "*rhema* concept,"[35] about differentiating

> between the Word of God [*logos*] which gives general knowledge about God, and the Word of God [*rhema*] which God uses to impart faith about specific circumstances into a man's heart ... *Rhema* is produced out of *logos*. *Logos* is like the pool of Bethesda. You may listen to the Word of God and you may study the Bible, but only when the Holy Spirit comes and quickens a Scripture or Scriptures to your heart, burning them in your soul and letting you know that they apply directly to your specific situation, does *logos* become *rhema* ... The Holy Spirit can take Scripture, the 'said word' of God, and apply it to a person's heart, making it the 'saying word' of God. The *logos* then becomes the *rhema*.[36]

Hispanic Pentecostalism use of the Bible is both "multiple" and "ontic" in moral reasoning. I find this a strength on which to build on, although, there is room for significant development in the deliberative motif. Reason, which is not antithetical to the Spirit or Scripture,[37] needs to play a larger role in the ethical deliberation of Hispanic Pentecostals. The moral laws (rational reflection on experience) tradition of Boston personalism provide a method for moral reasoning

---

[35]While Dr. Cho tries to make a case for a biblically grounded distinction for the meaning and usage of *logos* and *rhema* in the New Testament, it is exegetically questionable, although as a *theological concept*, I find it rich and suggestive.

[36]Paul Yonggi Cho, chapter four "*Rhema*", in his *The Fourth Dimension* (Plainfield, N.J.: Logos International, 1979), pp. 90, 96, 100; it is important to underline that Cho's usage throughout his chapter, with many examples given, is *more* than what we normally call the illumination of the Spirit.

[37]The example of that apostle of the Spirit, Paul, should remind us of the proper role of reason and Scripture in moral discourse. Victor Paul Furnish notes that, "it is unquestionably true that Paul's ethical exhortations, especially those which refer to generally accredited concepts of right and wrong, are often based on the presupposition *that reason* plays a part in the Christian's moral discernment and decision," Victor Paul Furnish, *Theology and Ethics in Paul* (Nashville, Tenn.: Abingdon Press, 1968), p. 79, my italics.

that is not incompatible to the working of the Spirit or the nature and purpose of Scripture.[38] Thus, they should prove useful in Hispanic Pentecostals' deliberation by providing a clear and coherent method and paradigm in developing and testing the "reasonableness" and "moralness" of their ethical pronouncements. As with the over-arching role of Scripture and the church in character formation: shaping the moral Identity, bearer of moral tradition and as a community of moral deliberation, as well as agency of strategy and action,[39] one can see the possibility of having the moral law ethic be so taught (dare we say inculcated) as to provide significant help for the moral reasoning of the Hispanic Pentecostal church. This is consistent with Paul Deats' response to critics of the method of moral laws.

> Some critics have objected that the complicated method of the moral laws lies beyond the capacity of most people and is probably impossible for even the gifted all the time. Here I have been helped by Muelder's comment that he does not begin life *de novo* each morning. He carries or embodies a structure of commitments, loyalties, and moral principles - even habits, which enable him to act with seeming spontaneity in a given situation. It is at this point that the moral law ethic comes closest to an ethic of character.[40]

Just as "personalism recognizes few, if any, 'No Trespassing' signs,"[41] so does Hispanic Pentecostalism's use of the Bible in the formulation of the ethical norm. Its multiple approach (utilizing the prescriptive, deliberative and relational motifs) and the "ontic" principle (the understanding of the "presence," immediacy of the Spirit) should give it the freedom (2 Cor. 3:17) to incorporate the moral law ethic (as method and paradigm) in its ethical formulations; although, it should be noted that there are some conflicts in the inter play of these three motifs.

---

[38]See Edgar Sheffield Brightman, *Moral Laws* (New York, NY.: The Abingdon Press, 1933); Walter G. Muelder, *Moral Law in Christian Social Ethics* (Richmond, VA.: John Knox Press, 1966); and Paul Deats and Carol Robb, (ed.) *The Boston Personalist Tradition in Philosophy, Social Ethics, and Theology.* It should be understood that the transrational or suprarational element in Hispanic Pentecostal experience, in relation to the Spirit and the Scripture, or faith in general, is not to be confused as elements of irrationality or existentialist subjectivism.

[39]Bruce C. Birch and Larry L. Rasmussen, "Bible and Ethics in the Life of the Church," in *Bible and Ethics in the Christian Life*, pp. 185-204.

[40]Paul Deats, "Conflict and Reconciliation in Communitarian Social Ethics," in Paul Deats and Carol Robb, ed. *The Boston Personalist Tradition in Philosophy, Social Ethics, and Theology*, p. 280.

[41]*Ibid.*, pp. 282-283.

The fear of freedom (for heresy and error), that many have when the Spirit is "free" in the church, can be vouchsafed by the understanding of the place of Scripture in the church, and the relation of the Spirit and Scripture as mutually self-validating (i.e. John 16:13). Further, it should be understood that the formulation process' *locus* is the community of the Spirit, the *Koinonia*, which is the bearer of the secret and power of the divine activity (Lehmann), the faithful interpreter of the Reign (Costas), and the sign of a true yet still imperfect realization of the Reign of God in the world (Boff).

It is important to note that in the decision-making process we have the promise of the divine helper (*Parakletos*), to lead us into all truth. This process is best described by the biblical notion of discernment (*dokimazo*, often translated as "proving", "testing", "determining" or "discerning"). Oscar Cullman states,

> The Holy Spirit must lead to the walking in the Spirit ... the working of the Holy Spirit shows itself chiefly in the 'testing' (*dokimazein*), that is, in the *capacity of forming the correct Christian ethical judgment at each given moment*, ... this "testing" is the key of all New Testament ethics.[42]

Discernment within the corporate setting of the church is not antithetical to critical reflection, rather it should include it.[43] Ultimately discernment is a spiritual gift by which the church, as the community of the Spirit, gathers, in a context of critical reflection and the reading of Scripture (in an attitude of prayer and worship), to "dialogue" relative to its "being" and "doing" in the world. It is within such processes that the Spirit "ministers" and the people discerns its responsibility; and thus clarity, consensus and commitment are reached in the deliberation.

---

[42]Oscar Cullman, *Christ and Time: The Primitive Christian Conception of Time and History* (Philadelphia, PA.: The Westminster Press, 1964), p. 228, italics Cullman.

[43]James E. Hug, S.J., "Christian Moral Discernment," in James E. Hug, S.J. (ed.), *Tracing The Spirit: Communities, Social Action, and Theological Reflection* (New York: Paulist Press, 1983), pp. 279-309.

Given the cacophony in the world and amidst the competing claims on the church, it is essential that the community of the Spirit be one that strives to be "characterized by a serious study of the Bible, a careful examination of the social, economic, political and historical forces of our times, and a radical dependence upon prayer and the guidance of the Holy Spirit."[44]

> But when he, the Spirit of truth, comes, he will guide
> you into all truth.
>   -John 16:13

The Spirit's Strategy: Love and Justice

> He has showed you, O man, what is good.
> And what does the Lord require of you? To
> act justly and to love mercy and walk humbly
> with your God.
>
>   - Micah 6:8

I previously have noted that the Reign of God is the Spirit's historical project. Further, we posited the need to participate in this historical project; and to discern the Spirit's action in the world and unite with the Spirit in the struggle, in the faithful witness to the full liberation of the Reign. In addition, I identified the nature of this struggle as "spiritual power encounters" - the confrontation of structural sin and evil - and the entering of the battle equipped by the "charismatic" empowerment of the Spirit, thus fulfilling the prophetic and vocational role of the Spirit's baptism.   The "battle manual"[45] - the Scripture - was discussed, emphasizing the freedom of the Spirit to lead in all moral and ethical formulations, noting the importance of rational reflection on experience. In this section I will

---

[44]Jim Wallis, *Agenda for Biblical People*, p. 76.

[45]It should be noted that the use of "military" metaphors is suggested by Scripture and the history of spirituality, it reflects an action-struggle approach to spirituality and social ethics, and in no way reflects a violent or militaristic position in dealing with conflict. My personal views is best described as a "contingent pacifist," see Paul Deats, "Protestant Social Ethics and Pacifism," in Thomas A. Shannon, ed. *War or Peace?: The Search for New Answers* (Maryknoll, N.Y.: Orbis Books, 1980), p. 89-90.

discuss the Spirit's strategy: Love and Justice. For love and justice are *both* God's grace and means (strategy) in and for God's Reign.

Hispanic Pentecostals understand love and justice as grounded in the grace of God and expressed by God's love in Calvary's cross (John 3:16). In the person and work of Christ, love and justice are defined in concrete and human terms. The Spirit, through whom the love of God has been poured into our hearts, and whose first fruit is love (Gal. 5:22), empowers us *both* to love (*agape*) and to incarnate this love in *just actions* (*dikaioma*, cf. Rev. 19:8; Rev. 22:11; 2 Cor. 9:6-15; 1 John 3:10). Wherever love and justice - "Justice is love rationally distributed (love being the highest personality value)"[46] - are present in society we can discern God's grace and the Spirit's strategy in and for God's Reign.

Love

Agape[47] defines the very nature of God (1 John 4:8,16), manifest what He did ("Grace of God is active in love", John 3:16; 1 John 4:9-11) and is the nature, content and motivation of our ethical response (1 John 4:11, 19). Lewis B. Smedes reminds us that "Jesus' love for us is God's norm for our loving: 'This is my commandment, that you love one another as I have loved you' (John 15:12)." He goes on to add, "Rather than listing rules for the loving life, he made his own life the authoritative model for our loving. So we need ask only one simple question: How did Jesus love us?"[48] Smedes identifies and elaborates Jesus' life of love under four developing statements:

1.   Love moved Jesus to help people.
2.   Love moved Jesus to help all people.
3.   Love moved Jesus to help all people for their sake.

---

[46]Walter G. Muelder, "Communitarian Dimensions of the Moral Laws," in Paul Deats and Carol Robb, ed. *The Boston Personalist Tradition in Philosophy, Social Ethics, and Theology*, p. 251.

[47]See, among the many works, Ethelbert Stauffer. *agapao*, Gerhard Kittel, ed., *TDNT*, Vol. 1, pp. 21-55; Anders Nygren, *Agape and Eros* (New York, NY: Harper and Row, 1953); Victor P. Furnish, *The Love Command in the New Testament* (Nashville: Abingdon, 1972); Soren Kierkegaard, *Works of Love* (New York: Harper and Row, 1963); Lewis B. Smedes, *Love Within Limits: A Realist's View of 1 Corinthians 13* (Grand Rapids,Michigan: Wm. B. Eerdmans Publishing Co., 1978).

[48]Lewis B. Smedes, *Mere Morality* (Grand Rapids, Michigan: Wm. B. Eerdmans Publishing Company, 1983) p. 48.

4.   Love moved Jesus to help all people for their sake without regard for cost.[49]

We are to love as Jesus loved. We are to love the neighbor as ourselves, and even our enemy. The scope and depth of our love is modeled to us by Jesus' life and Cross.

Love's social importance can be seen in various ways, among them the development of human rights. Stephen Mott speaks about the Christian faith's grounding "the perception of human dignity transcendently in the relationship of God to humankind through God's own image [creation] and in the atonement provided for humanity by God through Jesus Christ."[50] Both in creation and in the atonement Mott sees God's love for humankind expressed, and consequently the basis for human rights. In the chapter, "Love and Society" of his *Biblical Ethics and Social Change* he further states:

> A desire for well-being of each person leads to the idea of basic rights for each person. The concept of human rights reflects the three aspects of love ... love as *equality*, in that rights are possessed by all; love as *respect*, in that rights help preserve human dignity; love as *perception of common needs*, in that rights work to protect the minimal conditions for life together.[51]

The close connection of human rights and love helps us in the understanding of love being the basis of justice or justice the necessary instrument of love.[52]

---

[49]*Ibid.*, pp. 48-50.

[50]Stephen C. Mott, "The Contribution of the Bible to Human Rights", in *Human Rights and The Global Mission of the Church*, Boston Theological Institute Annual Series, Vol. 1 (Cambridge, Mass.: Boston Theological Institute, 1985), p. 5.

[51]Stephen C. Mott, *Biblical Ethics and Social Change*, p. 51, my italics.

[52]*Ibid.*, p. 48, 53; for an insightful comparative and cultural perspective on human rights see, Max L. Stackhouse, *Creeds, Society and Human Rights: A Study in Three Cultures* (Grand Rapids: Eerdmans, 1984).

Justice

Justice's (*dikaiosyne*)[53] relation to love has been treated differently by many ethicists and theologians. At one end one can place Paul Tillich for whom love and justice (and power) are inseparable both ontologically and historically.[54] At the other end one can place Emil Brunner for whom there is a marked separation of love and justice.[55] For many who may eschew the ontological ground of justice, and are not willing to make a sharp separation of love and justice, there is the need to maintain both justice and love in immediate relation. Mott makes this connection quite clear.

> Justice is not a different principle, in contradistinction to love; rather it expresses in terms of fixed duty and obligation the appropriate response to love in certain social situations.[56]

When justice is understood as "love rationally distributed," in essence one principle, a certain "wholism" is maintained in socio-political affairs. This prevents the dichotomy that can lead to atomistic realms - thus a negative role for government, and a conservative and status quo political ideology. The implications for Hispanic Pentecostal social-political engagement are significant. The struggle for justice for the poor and the oppressed can be placed at the level of love. It is true that Scripture is quite clear in numerous verses and passages on God's bias for the poor and the oppressed. It is equally clear that service and worship are acceptable only when performed from just human relations. It is when justice is seen as the expression of love that motivations for engagement become possible for many. Actions on behalf of the oppressed in the arena of politics and society at large are actions of love. Love can seek the expansion of the role of government, one that is concerned for social and economic welfare, thus a positive

---

[53]Among the many works see, Gottlob Schrenk, *dikaiosyne*, Gerhard Kittel, *TDNT*, Vol. II, pp. 192-210; Otto Bird, *The Ideas of Justice* (New York, N.Y.: Praeger, 1967); John Rawls, *A Theory of Justice* (Cambridge, Mass.: Harvard University Press, 1971); Paul Tillich, *Love, Power, and Justice* (New York, N.Y.: Oxford University Press, 1954); Emil Brunner, *Justice and the Social Order* (New York, N.Y.: Harper and Row, 1945); *dikaiosyne* in the English Bible is variously translated as righteousness, often bringing ambiguity to the reader, who must determine by the context whether justice should be the better translation. In Spanish "justicia" is used both for righteousness and justice, thus avoiding the possible bias by the translator of the Greek text.

[54]See Paul Tillich, *Love, Power and Justice*.

[55]See Emil Brunner, *Justice and the Social Order*; id., *The Divine Imperative*.

[56]Stephen C. Mott, *Biblical Ethics and Social Action*, p. 54.

and active role for government.[57]   Love can be incarnated in *just action* (*dikaioma*).

The challenge to the Hispanic Pentecostal church is to participate in the Spirit's historical project. The strategy of the Spirit is to empower its people to incarnate its love in *just action* in the world. We must discern the signs and join the Spirit in its action in the world in anticipation of his Reign. Orlando Costas has stated it well:

> The near future is always a foretaste of the distance future. We do not have to wait for the consummation of the Kingdom in order to discern its justice in the social and political sphere and the presence of its liberating power in social structures. The Holy Spirit is showing us already signs of social and political justice and structural liberation in many places and situations. We know that an event is a sign of the justice of God when it enables the poor and oppressed to experience a measure of economic, sociocultural, and political liberation.[58]

---

[57]*Ibid.*, p. 62.

[58]Orlando Costas, *Christ Outside the Gate: Mission Beyond Christendom*, p. 30.

Implication for the Life and Mission of the Church

> The gospel at its best deals with the whole man, not only his soul but also his body, not only his spiritual well-being but also his material well-being. A religion that professes a concern for the souls of men and is not equally concerned about the slums that damn them, the economic conditions that strangle them, and the social conditions that cripple them, is a spiritually moribund religion.
> - Martin Luther King, Jr.[59]

Without a doubt this century, perhaps as no other, the Spirit has been challenging the church in "rethinking identity and vocation."[60]   My study contributes to this process, which sets before the Hispanic Pentecostal church certain vocational tasks based on its identity as the community of the Spirit. In this section I will look briefly at the implications for the life and mission of the church of our social ethical construction. I will follow in part the classical missiological categories of the church's mission: (1) *Koinonia*; the fellowship or community of the Spirit; (2) *Leitourgia*, the worship in the Spirit; (3) *Kerygma*, the proclamation of the "good-news" of the Spirit's historical project; and (4) *Diakonia*, the service in and by the Spirit.

Koinonia

The church is the *Koinonia* of the Spirit. It is the unique *locus* of the Spirit's activity in the world (Rom. 8:23; 1 Cor. 6:19; Ephesians 2:14-18). It is that community which acknowledges Jesus Christ as savior and Lord, and through whom the pneumatic (risen) Christ is mediated by the Spirit. As God's colony in

---

[59]Martin Luther King, Jr., *Strength To Love* (Great Britain: Wm. Collins and Sons, 1963), p. 150.

[60]See, George W. Webber, "Rethink Identity and Vocation", in *Today's Church: A Community of Exiles and Pilgrims*, pp. 26-39; Among the many other works on the mission of the church, and most pertinent to Hispanic Pentecostalism, see, Paul A. Pomerville, *The Third Force in Missions*; James W. Jones, *The Spirit and the World*; Orlando Costas, *Christ Outside the Gate: Mission Beyond Christendom*; id., *The Church and Its Mission: A Shattering Critique from the Third World*; id., *Liberating News: A Theology of Contextual Evangelization* (Grand Rapids, Michigan: Wm. B. Eerdmans, 1989); C. Rene Padilla, *Mision Integral: Ensayos Sobre el Reino y la Iglesia*.

a human world,"[61] it is *both* a model and a sign of redeemed and transformed relationships - It is a *Koinonia* of the Spirit and *Koinonia* with fellow Christians. It witnesses to the Reign of God's reality, by its very existence a "sacrament" in and to the world.

As the community of the Spirit and the Spirit's "tactical unit," its advance in the world is critically affected by living up to its very nature. Minimally, what this implies in the Hispanic Pentecostal church in the "barrios" of the American continent can be categorized as demonstration and denunciation.

By *demonstration* we mean it displays, to the Hispanic community and the world, loving and just structures of relationships. For example, this means that Hispanic Pentecostal churches must exorcise the "machismo" element in their "cultos" - the sexist tendency; although present in other churches, but given the cultural underpinning among Hispanics, it is or may be most destructive. The fact that we have noted previously the significant role of "la misionera" (the local church missionary) and of women in general in Hispanic Pentecostalism does not negate the presence of sexism - nurtured by "machismo."[62]   Another example is the penchant for copying or mirroring other denominations or the "world's" leadership patterns and structures. Loving and just structures mean, if anything, taking the cue from the experience of the baptism in the Spirit - an egalitarian experience and egalitarian producing force for ministerial or leadership self-understanding.   The *Koinonia* will affirm the linguistic and cultural reality of Hispanics. It will be a *locus* for the bilingual-bicultural Hispanic religiosity. As a "pueblo puente" (bridge people), it will provide not only the supporting context for the new immigrants, but also the "space" for the new generation - the English-speaking dominant (second mestizaje) Hispanics.

By *denunciation* we mean that by its very "style of being" or nature the church is prophetic. The implications for Hispanic Pentecostals' life and mission are several. As previously noted, Hispanics are a very family oriented people, in their cultural heritage there are deep roots of community.   Most important is overcoming the pressures of the dominant class-culture of North American Society. The history of Hispanic Pentecostalism in the "barrios" has had much affinity with the primitive church's response to the needy (Acts 2:44-45) - it was one large family. Care must be taken to challenge the inroads of individualism, materialism, classism, racism and sexism in the church.

---

[61]See, George W. Webber, *God's Colony, in Man's World* (Nashville: Abingdon Press, 1960).

[62]See *Against Machismo... interviews by Elsa Tamez* (Yorktown Heights, N.Y.: Meyer-Stone Books, c1987); Ada María Isasi-Diaz and Yolanda Tarango, *Hispanic Women, Prophetic Voice in the Church: Toward an Hispanic Women's Liberation Theology.*

There is an evangelistic cutting edge to the *Koinonia*. Orlando Costas states:

> The communion of the church also has an evangelistic cutting edge. It gives credibility to the message of love that is proclaimed by the community of faith, it offers a model of life that overcomes the barriers that make social peace impossible (selfishness, greed, and alienation), and it makes a prophetic denunciation of human society for its classist, racist, and sexist divisions. When the church fails to live in communion, it not only destroys its credibility in the proclamation of its message but also deprives society of a wholesome and constructive vision of a far better future and of an honest and sincere criticism of its fundamental problems - namely, social and personal sin.[63]

The *Koinonia* is a sign to the world, a true demonstration of the promise and presence of the Reign of God.

Leitourgia

The whole Scripture is a commentary on the worshiping life and vocation of God's people. Jesus reminded the Samaritan woman that worship must be in spirit and in truth (John 4:23-24). Worship in the "cultos" must be complemented by worship *in* the "barrios" of the world.   Hispanic Pentecostalism must reappropriate from its Catholic sacramental past the understanding and challenge that worshiping of Jesus is also accomplished through its ministry and service to and with the poor. Matthew 25 is quite clear that in a mysterious (secret) but profound way our service to the needy - feeding the hungry, clothing the naked, taking in the strangers, visiting the prisoner - is a ministry to Christ. There is great truth in Harvey Cox's statement that:

> Postmodern spirituality begins with the premise that periods of solitude are essential but that one need not meditate in a cell for twenty years to find God. God is present in the confusion and dislocation of the world. One encounters God not by turning one's back on that world but by plunging into it with the faith that the divine-human encounter occurs in the midst of the encounter of

---

[63]Orlando Costas, in "The Basic Evangelizing Community: Contextual Evangelization in the Life and Mission of the Church", *Liberating News! A Theology of Contextual Evangelization*, pp. 139-140.

human with human, especially in the struggle to create signs of the coming of God's reign of peace and justice.[64]

From Amos to Isaiah God's people are challenged to place their worship praxis - offerings, fasting, music, liturgy - within the context of *just action* (*dikaioma*) to the poor and the oppressed. There is a deep spiritual relationship of service (social justice) and solidarity with the oppressed and true worship. The words of Amos still ring true:

> I hate, I despise your religious feasts; I cannot stand your assemblies. Even though you bring me burnt offerings and grain offerings, I will not accept them. Though you bring choice fellowship offerings, I will have no regard for them. Away with the noise of your songs! I will not listen to the music of your harps. But let justice roll on like a river, righteousness like a never-failing stream!
>
> (Amos 5:21-24)

Kerygma

The proclamation of the gospel of Jesus Christ in the power of the Spirit (Acts 1:8) means that the Spirit's historical project is the framework of the good-news we share by word and deed. We preach Christ and Him crucified. Indeed a personal message of redemption and of reconciliation with God (Rom. 5:1) and the neighbor. But the good-news goes beyond the personal and individual dimension. We are to proclaim from the housetop that in Jesus Christ a new order of creation has irrupted in our history; that God through the Spirit is "reconciling the world to himself" (2 Corinthians 5:19). The "principalities and powers" have been disarmed, and thus by our message and just acts we demonstrate that there is no area of human life - personal or social - where this good news is not the power of God.

The Hispanic Pentecostal church in the "barrios" is a vanguard in the proclamation of the *Kerygma*, although its understanding and practice by and large has been confined to the individual. There is genuine enthusiasm in sharing what Jesus Christ means to them in a deep and personal way. Yet, by this very witness and "given" theological conceptualization they have narrowed the scope of the

---

[64]Harvey Cox, *Religion in the Secular City: Toward A Postmodern Theology* (New York: Simon and Schuster, Inc., 1984), pp. 210-211.

Kerygma. The challenge to the Hispanic Pentecostal church is to reappropriate and formulate into theological and ethical praxis those elements of an expanded *Kerygma,* demonstrated by their common life in the "barrios" - the significant social roles they model.

The *Kerygma* has a prophetic cutting edge. This means that the Hispanic Pentecostal church must not be content to preach and witness just to individual-personal sins, but must see the larger spiritual conflict. It must preach from the whole Bible to the whole person. No area is exempt in personal or social life from the *Kerygmatic* task. As the scope and depth of the *Kerygma* is discovered by the Hispanic Pentecostal church, they will join in solidarity with others and bring to bear a clear witness on the many ills that afflict their "barrios" and the world. The issues that the church must deal with in society are many and complex. Among the many issues we list the following: abortion, arms control and disarmament, capital punishment, civil rights, the economy, education, energy, family life, food and agricultural policy, health, housing, human rights, mass media, and regional conflict in the world.[65] Closer to home in our "barrios," among the many issues that are critical are: employment and underemployment (jobs), housing, health, education, drugs, AIDS, immigration, and the undocumented, discrimination and racism.

In confronting these issues the church is cognizant of its weakness too. It must seek the leading of the Spirit as it endeavors to be a faithful witness. The words of Deats are apropos, "This calls for a basic reorientation that takes full account of both resources and obstacles for living out in personal disciplines and corporate responsibilities our obedient response to God's activity in a changing world."[66]

Let there be no mistake, the *Kerygma* is nothing less and nothing more than the full liberation that Jesus Christ brings. We witness to this reality by word and deed in the power of the Spirit.

---

[65]"Political Responsibility: Choice for the 1980s", A Statement of the Administrative Board, United States Catholic Conference, revised edition, March 22, 1984, pp. 8-18; the following statement is worth noting: "A proper understanding of the role of the Church will not confuse its mission with that of government, but rather see its ministry as advocating the critical values of human rights and social justice." *Ibid.,* p. 6.

[66]Paul Deats, *Social Change and Moral Values,* (Washington, D.C.: Board of Christian Social Concerns, Service Department, 1963), p. 36.

Diakonia

The service of the church in, for, but not *of* the world is motivated by the love of God. It is the natural expression of the newness of life found in Christ. The diaconal mission of the church reaches out to all, no human need escapes its concern. To the Hispanic Pentecostal church it means the faithful continuation of its role of social service provider in the "barrios." As noted previously, this has been carefully documented by Melvin Delgado and Denise Humn-Delgado.[67] What was not noted in their study was that the natural support systems in the Hispanic Pentecostal church, that provide so many needed services, are by and large geared to the believers or their immediate family. There is the need to enlarge the scope of the *diakonia*. The Hispanic Pentecostal church must see its diaconal mission in the "barrios," not just for convert-sake, nor for its own members only, but as an authentic expression of love and natural manifestation of the gospel to a hurting humanity.

Whatever form our diaconal mission takes, whatever be its social strategy: social service, social education, social witness, or social action; it ever needs to be reminded that "action really receives its character from prayer."[68]

---

[67]See, "Social Role of the Hispanic Protestant Church," Chapter II, "Hispanic Religious Dimensions."

[68]Jacques Ellul, *Prayer and Modern Man* (New York, N.Y.: Seabury Press, 1979), p. 172.

Conclusion

Overall I have presented a social ethic for Hispanic American Pentecostals, one that coheres with the experience of a poor and oppressed minority-sect church in the U.S.A., with its cultural heritage, and consistent with Hispanic American Pentecostalism's self-understanding of ethics emerging from its experience of the Spirit.

If the Hispanic American Pentecostal church is to faithfully serve its own Hispanic community and beyond, if it is going to survive as an authentic and relevant presence in the "barrios," if it is going to overcome the negative elements of upward social mobility (and become a Church, in Troetsch's sense), *then* it must see itself not just as the community of the Spirit *in* the world, but rather as the community of the Spirit *for* the world, but not *of* the world - a sign of the promise and presence of the Spirit's historical project, the Reign of God.

> "If we live in the Spirit,
> Let us also walk in the Spirit."
> - Galatians 5:25

BIBLIOGRAPHY

Hispanic American Life and Culture

Alba, Victor. *The Mexicans*. New York: Pegasus, 1967.

Albizu Campos, Pedro. *La Conciencia Nacional Puertorriqueña*. Mexico: Siglo Veintiuno Editores, SA, 1974.

Alzaga, Florinda. *Raíces del Alma Cubana*. Miami: Editorial Universal, 1976.

_____. "The Three Roots of Cuban Heritage," *Agenda (A Journal of Hispanic Issues* 10 (January-February 1980): 24.

Anderson, Peter. "A Puerto Rican Family in Boston," a two-part series. *The Boston Globe*. 6 and 13 April 1986.

Arrom, Juan José. *El Mundo Mítico de los Taínos*. Bogotá: Instituto Caro y Cuervo, 1967.

Babin, María Teresa. *The Puerto Ricans' Spirit: Their History, Life, and Culture*. New York: Collier Books, 1971.

Bach, Robert L. "The New Cuban Emigrants: Their Background and Prospects." *Monthly Labor Review* 103 (October 1980): 39-46.

Bean, Frank D., Curtis, Jr., Russell, and Marcum, John P. "Familism and Marital Satisfaction Among Mexican Americans: The Effects of Family Size, Wife's Labor Force Participation, and Conjugal Power," *Journal of Marriage and the Family* 39 (November 1977): 759-767.

Bennett, Philip. "Mexico Losing Professionals: Economic Crisis Spurs Brain Drain." *The Boston Globe*. 28 July 1986.

_____. "Report says Hispanics face barriers in State." *The Boston Globe*. 30 October 1985.

Bloch, Peter. *La-Le-Lo-Lai: Puerto Rican Music and its Performers.* New York: Plus Ultra Educational Publishers, Inc., 1973.

Boorkman, C.J. *Chicano Bibliography.* Bowling Green Station, NY: Gordon Press Pubs., 1974.

Bravo, Enrique, comp. *An Annotated, Selected Puerto Rican Bibliography.* Translated by Marcial Cuevas. New York: The Urban Center, Columbia University Press, 1972.

Castro, Américo. *Iberoamérica: Su Historia y su Cultura.* 4ta. ed. New York: Holt, Rinehart and Winston, 1971.

Cervantes Saavedra, Miguel de. *El Ingenioso Hidalgo Don Quijote de la Mancha.* Madrid: Editorial Espasa - Calpe, S. A., 1981 ed.

Chavez, Lydia. "Striving but Still Lagging: Puerto Ricans Wonder Why." *New York Times.* 5 June 1986.

Colón, Jesús. *A Puerto Rican and Other Sketches.* New York: Mainstream Publishers, 1961.

Cordasco, Francesco and Bucchioni, Eugene. *The Puerto Rican Experience.* Totowa, NJ: Littlefield, Adams and Co., 1973.

Cortes, Carlos E., ed. *Cuban Exiles in the United States: An Original Anthology.* New York: Ayer Co., 1981.

Cullman, Hugh, ed. *A Guide to Hispanic Organizations.* New York, N.Y.: Philip Morris, U.S.A., Public Affairs Department, 1983.

Delgado, Melvin and Humn-Delgado, Denise. "Natural Support Systems: Source of Strength in Hispanic Communities." *Social Work* (January 1982).

de Madariaga, Salvador. *Englishmen, Frenchmen, and Spaniards.* London: Oxford University Press, 1928.

Diaz Soler, Luis M. *Historia de la Esclavitud Negra en Puerto Rico.* Puerto Rico: Editorial Universitaria, Universidad de Puerto Rico, 1970.

Dunn, Lynn P. *Chicanos: A Study Guide and Source Book.* Palo Alto, CA: R. and E. Research Associates, 1975.

Espada, Martin. "Heart of Hunger." The Immigrants Iceboy's Bolero. Natick, Massachusetts: Cordillera Press, 1982.

Estades, Rosa. Patrones de Participación Política de los Puertorriqueños en la Ciudad de Nueva York. Rio Piedras, Puerto Rico: Editorial de la Universidad de Puerto Rico, 1978.

Fernández-Marina, Ramón, Maldonado-Sierra, Eduardo D., and Trent, Richard D. "Three Themes in Mexican and Puerto Rican Family Values," Journal of Social Psychiatry 48 (1958): 167-181.

Fitzpatrick, Joseph P. Puerto Rican Americans: The Meaning of Migration to the Mainland. Englewood Cliffs, NJ: Prentice-Hall, Inc., 1971.

García Mazas, José. "Reflecting on Language." Agenda 10 (May-June 1980): 54.

Glazier, Nathan and Moyniham, Daniel. Beyond the Melting Pot. Cambridge, Mass.: M.I.T. Press, 1963.

Godsell, Goeffrey. "Hispanics in the U.S.: 'Ethnic Sleeping Giant' Awakens," a five-part series, Christian Science Monitor (April 28, 29, 30, and May 1 and 2) 1980.

González, José Luis. El País de Cuatro Pisos. Puerto Rico: Ediciones Huracán, Inc., 1983.

González, Rodolfo. I Am Joaquín. New York: Bantam Books, 1972.

Handlin, Oscar. The Newcomers. Cambridge, MA: Harvard University Press, 1959.

Hanke, Lewis. The Spanish Struggle for Justice in the Conquest of America. Boston: Little, Brown, and Company, 1965.

Haskins, James. The New Americans: The Cuban Boat People. Enslow Publishers, 1982.

Hendricks, Glenn. The Dominican Diaspora: From The Dominican Republic to New York City - Villages in Transition. New York: Teachers College Press, 1974.

Henriquez Ureña, Pedro. Historia de la Cultura en la América Hispana. Mexico-Buenos Aires: Fondo de Cultura Economica, 1947.

"Hispanic Americans, Soon: The Biggest Minority." *Time*, 16 October 1978.

"Hispanics in Massachusetts: A Progress Report." Massachusetts: The
      Commonwealth of Massachusetts, Commission on Hispanic Affairs, 1985.

"Hispanics Make Their Move." *U.S. News & World Report*, 24 August 1981.

Jennings, James and Rivera, Monte. *Puerto Rican Politics in Urban America*.
      Westport, Conn.: Greenwood Press, 1983.

Jordan, Robert A. "Latinos Seeking Political Clout." *The Boston Globe*, 3 August
      1986.

Keyser, Lucy. "English-from Sea to Shining Sea." *Insight*, 20 October 1986.

La Fontaine, Herman, Persky, Barry, and Golubschick, Leonard, eds. *Bilingual
      Education*. Wayne, N.J.: Avery Publishing Group, 1978.

León-Portilla, Miguel. *El Reverso de la Conquista*. Mexico: Editorial Joaquín
      Mortiz, 1970.

Levine, Barry B., *Benjy Lopez: A Picaresque Tale of Emigration and Return*.
      New York: Basic Books, 1980.

Lewis, Gordon K. *Puerto Rico: Freedom and Power in the Caribbean*. New
      York: Harper and Row Pubs., Inc., 1974.

Lewis, Oscar. *La Vida: A Puerto Rican Family in the Culture of Poverty - San
      Juan and New York*. New York: Vintage Books, 1966.

Llanes, José. *Cuban Americans: Masters of Survival*. Cambridge, MA: Abt
      Books, 1982.

Loprete, Carlos A. and McMahon, Dorothy. *Iberoamérica: Síntesis de su
      Civilización*, 2da. ed. New York: Charles Scribner's Sons, 1974.

Luciano, Debra. "Cesar Chavez - Bringing Boycotts to the 1980s." *Agenda* 9
      (July-August 1979): 18-19.

MacKay, John A. *Heritage and Destiny*. New York: The Macmillan Co., 1943.

Macklin, June. *"Curanderismo* and *Espiritismo*: Complementary Approaches to Traditional Mental health Services." in Stanley A. West and June Macklin, *The Chicano Experience.* Colorado: Westview Press, 1979.

Maldonado-Denis, Manuel. *The Emigration Dialectic: Puerto Rico and the U.S.* New York: International Publishing Co., 1980.

——————————. *Puerto Rico: A Socio-Historic Interpretation.* New York: Vintage Books, 1972.

Matthiessen, Peter. *Sal Si Puedes: Caesar Chavez and The New American Revolution.* New York: Random House, 1969.

Meier, Matt S. and Rivera, Feliciano. *The Chicanos: A History of Mexican Americans.* New York: Farrar, Straus, and Giroux, Inc., 1972.

Mirande, Alfredo and Enriquez, Evangelina. *La Chicana: The Mexican-American Woman.* Chicago: University of Chicago Press, 1981.

Moore, Joan W. *Mexican Americans*, 2nd edition. Ethnic Groups in American Life Series. Englewood Cliffs, NJ: Prentice-Hall, Inc., 1976.

Moore, Joan and Pachon, Harry. *Hispanics in the United States.* New Jersey: Prentice-Hall, Inc., 1985.

Morgan, Thomas B. "The Latinization of America," *Esquire*, May 1983.

Murillo, Nathan. "The Mexican Family," in N. Wagner and M. Haug, ed., *Chicanos: Social and Psychological Perspective.* St. Louis: C.V. Mosby, 1971.

Nabokov, Peter. *Tijerina and the Courthouse Raid.* Berkeley, Calif.: Ramparts Press, 1970.

National Conference of Catholic Bishops. *The Hispanic Presence: Challenge and Commitment: A Pastoral Letter on Hispanic Ministry.* Washington, D.C.: U. S. Catholic Conference, 1984.

Negron Montilla, Aida. *Americanization in Puerto Rico and the Public School System: 1900-1930.* Rio Piedras, Puerto Rico: Editorial Universitaria de Puerto Rico, 1975.

"Our Decade in the Sun." *Agenda (A Journal of Hispanic Issues)* 10 (January - February 1980): 2.

Peñalosa, Fernando. "Class Consciousness and Social Mobility in a Mexican-American Community." Unpublished Ph.D. Dissertation, University of Southern California, 1963.

Perusse, Roland I., *The United States and Puerto Rico: Decolonization Options and Prospects.* Lanham, MD.; University Press of America, 1987.

Polischuk, Pablo. "Language Processing in Bilinguals." Unpublished M.A. thesis, San Francisco, California: San Francisco State University, 1975.

"Press Statement of Dr. Harry Pachon, Executive Director of the National Association of Latino Elected and Appointed Officials (NALEO)," September 17, 1986.

Ramos, Samuel. *Profile of Man and Culture in Mexico.* Austin, Texas: The University of Texas Press, 1982.

Rein, Lisa. "Language Debate." *The Tab.* 22 October 1985.

Ribes Tovar, Federico. *Handbook of the Puerto Rican Community.* New York: Plus Ultra Educational Publishers, 1970.

Ricard, Robert. *The Spiritual Conquest of Mexico.* Berkeley: University of California Press, 1966.

Rodríguez, Clara. "Puerto Rican: Between Black and White," in Clara Rodriguez, et al., eds., *The Puerto Rican Struggle.* New York: Puerto Rican Migration Research Consortium, 1980.

Rodríguez, Richard. *Hunger of Memory: The Education of Richard Rodríguez.* New York: Bantam Books, 1982.

Rogg, E., *The Assimilation of Cuban Exiles.* New York: Aberdeen press, 1974.

Samora, Julian and Simon, Patricia V. *A History of the Mexican American People.* Notre Dame, IN: University of Notre Dame Press, 1977.

Sánchez Korrol, Virginia E. *From Colonia to Community: The History of Puerto Ricans in New York City, 1917-1948.* Wesport, Connecticut: Greenwood Press, 1983.

Santos, Ricardo. "Missionary Beginnings in Spanish Florida, the Southwest, and California." in Moises Sandoval, ed., *Fronteras: A History of the Latin American Church in the USA Since 1513*. San Antonio, Texas: Mexican American Cultural Center, 1983.

Seda, Eduardo. "Bilingual Education in A Pluralistic Context." *The Rican: Journal of Contemporary Puerto Rican Thought* I (May 1974): 19-26.

Sedillo, Pedro. "The Forum of National Hispanic Organizations - First Steps Towards Unity." *Agenda (A Journal of Hispanic Issues* 10, January-February 1980: 6.

Selby, John. *En La Brega: Economía política popular para trabajadores Latinos: El Caso de Massachusetts*. Boston: Red Sun Press, 1985.

Senior, Clarence. *The Puerto Ricans: Strangers - Then Neighbors*. Chicago: Quadrangle Books, 1965.

Servin, Manuel P. *Mexican Americans*, 2nd edition. New York: Macmillan Publishing Co., Inc., 1974.

Sexton, Patricia Cayo. *Spanish Harlem: Anatomy of Poverty*. New York: Harper & Row, Inc., 1965.

Sotomayor, Marta. "Language, Culture, and Ethnicity in Developing Self-Concept." *Social Casework* 58 (April 1977): 195.

Tennenbaum, Frank. "Toward an Appreciation of Latin America," in Herbert L. Matthews, ed. *The United States and Latin America*. New York: Columbia University, The American Assembly, 1959.

Thomas, Piri, *Down These Mean Streets*. New York: Vintage Books, 1974.

Tovar, Frederico Ribes. *The Puerto Rican Heritage Encyclopedia*, 3 Vols. New York: Plus Ultra Educational Publishers, Inc., 1970.

_____. *The Puerto Rican Woman*. New York: Plus Ultra Educational Publishers, Inc., 1972.

Ugarte, Francisco. *España y su Civilización*. New York: Odyssey Press, 1952.

United Press International. "Poverty on rise for Hispanics, says Policy Group." *The Boston Globe*. 3 September 1986.

U.S. Commission on Civil Rights. *Puerto Ricans in the Continental United States: An Uncertain Future.* Washington, D.C.: U.S. Commission on Civil Rights, 1976.

Vasconcelos, José. *La Raza Cósmica.* Barcelona: Espasa Calpe, 1925.

Vivo, Paquita. "The Puerto Ricans-Two Communities, One Culture." *Agenda* 10 (January-February 1980).

Wagner, Nathaniel M., and Hang, Marsh J., ed. *Chicanos: Social and Psychological Perspectives.* St. Louis: C.V. Mosby, 1971.

West, Woody. "Bilingual Education in Plain English." *Insight.* 23 June 1986.

Westfried, Alex H. *Ethnic Leadership in a New England Community: Three Puerto Rican Families.* Cambridge, MA: Schenkman Pub. Co., 1980.

Wilson, John M. "Hispanic Images Finally Reach the Big Screen." *The Boston Globe.* 2 January 1986.

Hispanic Americans and Christianity

"A New Mission Field: The Hispanic Population of America." *Christian Marketing Perspective* (A Publication of the Barna Research Group). September-October 1986.

Aragon, Rafael J., "El Movimiento de Refugio." *Apuntes* 5 (Fall 1985): 65-67.

Armendariz, Ruben P., "Hispanic Heritage and Christian Education," *ALERT.*(November 1981): 26.

Arrastía, Cecilio, "The Eucharist: Liberation, Community, and Commitment," *Apuntes.* Vol. 4 (4), Winter 1984, p. 75-81.

_____. *Itinerario de La Pasión: Meditaciones Para la Semana Santa.* El Paso, Tex.: Casa Bautista de Publicaciones, 1978.

Avila, Yiye. *La Ciencia de la Oracion.* Camuy, Puerto Rico: Yiye Avila, 1979.

Betancourt, Esdras. *Manual Comprensivo de Psicologia Pastoral.* San Antonio, Texas: Editorial Evangelica, 1980.

Brackenridge, R. Douglas and Garcia-Treto, Francisco O. *Iglesia Presbiteriana: A History of Presbyterians and Mexican Americans in the Southwest.* San Antonio, Texas: Trinity University Press, 1974.

Caraballo, José, "A Certificate Program for Hispanic Clergy and Lay Persons in an Accredited Theological Seminary: A Case Study with Projections," Unpublished D.Min. professional project, Drew University, Madison, New Jersey, 1983.

Chavez, César E.   "The Mexican American and the Church," in Octavio I. Romano, ed. *Voices: Readings from El Grito.* Berkeley, Calif.: Quinto Sol Publications, 1971.

Cortez, Carlos E., ed. *Church Views of the Mexican American.*   The Mexican American Series.   Salem, N.H.: Ayer Co., 1974.

Costas, Orlando, ed. *Predicación Evangélica y Teología Hispana.* San Diego, California: Publicaciones de las Americas, 1982.

_____. "Hispanic Theology in North America." (B.T.I., Liberation Theology Consultation, Andover-Newton Theological School), October 25, 1986 (Typewritten).

_____. "Evangelizing An Awakening Giant: Hispanics in the U.S." in *Signs of the Kingdom in the Secular City*, comps. David J. Frenchak and Clinton E. Stockwell, ed. Helen Ujvarosy. Chicago: Covenant Press, 1984.

_____. "Social Justice in the Other Protestant Tradition: A Hispanic Perspective." in Frederick Greenspahn, ed., *Contemporary Ethical Issues in the Jewish and Christian Traditions.*   Hoboken, NJ: Ktau Publishing House, Inc., 1986.

_____. *El Protestantismo En América Latina Hoy: Ensayos del Camino (1972-1974).* San José, Costa Rica: Publicaciones INDEF, 1975.

Curti, Josafat. "The Chicano and the Church," *Christian Century* (March 12,1975), pp. 253-57.

DeLeón, Victor. *The Silent Pentecostal: A Biographical History of the Pentecostal Movement Among Hispanics in the Twentieth Century.* Taylors, South Carolina: Faith Printing Company, 1979.

_____. "Growth of Hispanic Pentecostals." *Paraclete* (A Journal Concerning the Person and Work of the Holy Spirit) 15 (Winter 1981): 18.

Domínguez, Roberto. *Pioneros de Pentecostés: En el Mundo de Habla Hispana.* Miami, Florida: Literatura Evangélica. 1971.

Elizondo, Virgilio P. *Christianity and Culture: An Introduction to Pastoral Theology and Ministry for the Bicultural Community.* Huntington, IN: Our Sunday Visitor, Inc., 1975.

_____. *The Future is Mestizo: Life Where Cultures Meet.* Bloomington, Ind.: Myer Stone Books, 1988.

_____. *Galilean Journey: The Mexican American Promise.* Maryknoll, NY: Orbis Books, 1983.

_____. *Mestizaje: The Dialectic of Cultural Birth and the Gospel.* San Antonio, Tex.: MACC., 1978.

_____. *La Morenita: Evangelizer of the Americas.* San Antonio, Tex.: MACC., 1980.

_____. "Toward an American-Hispanic Theology of Liberation in the U.S.A." in Virginia Fabella and Sergio Torres, eds. *Irruption of the Third World: Challenge to Theology.* New York: Orbis Books, 1983.

Espinoza, Marco A. "Pastoral Care of Hispanic Families in the United States: Socio-Cultural, Psychological, and Religious Considerations." Unpublished D. Min. Project, Newton, Massachusetts: Andover Newton Theological School, May 1982.

Falcón, Rafael. *The Hispanic Mennonite Church of North America, 1932 - 1982.* Scottdale, Pennsylvania: Herald Press, 1986.

Fenton, Jerry. *Understanding the Religious Background of the Puerto Rican.* Cuernavaca: Sondeos, 1969.

Figueroa, Deck, Allan. *The Second Wave: Hispanic Ministry and the Evangelization of Culture.* New York: Paulist Press, 1989.

Galvan, Elias Gabriel. "A Study of the Spanish-Speaking Protestant Church and her Mission to the Mexican American Minority." Rel. D. Dissertation, Claremont School of Theology, 1969.,

Garrison, Vivian. "Sectarianism and Psychosocial Adjustment: A Controlled Comparison of Puerto Rican Pentecostals and Catholics," in I. Zeretsky and I. Leone, eds. *Religious Movements in Contemporary America*, Princeton, NJ: Princeton University Press, 1974, 298-329.

Gibson, Lee. "Protestantism in Latin American Acculturation." Unpublished Ph.D. Dissertation, University of Texas, 1959.

Gimenez, John. *Up Tight!* Waco, Texas: World Books, 1967.

González, Justo L., "The Apostles' Creed and The Sanctuary Movement", *Apuntes: Reflexiones Teológicas desde el Margen Hispano.* Vol. 6 (1), Spring 1986, p. 12-20.

_____. *The Theological Education of Hispanics*, a study commissioned by The Fund for Theological Education, New York, N.Y., 1988.

_____. "Two Faces of Hispanic Christianity." *The Judson Bulletin* Vol. VI, No. 1. Newton Center, Mass.: Andover Newton Theological School, 1987.

_____. *The Hispanic Ministry of the Episcopal Church in the Metropolitan Area of New York and Environs.* New York City: Grants Program of Trinity Parish, 1985.

_____. "Hacia un redescubrimiento de nuestra misión," *Apuntes* Year 7, No. 3, Fall, 1987.

_____. *Mañana: Christian Theology from a Hispanic Perspective.* Nashville: Abingdon Press, 1990.

González, Justo and Catherine. *Liberation Preaching: The Pulpit and the Oppressed.* Nashville, Tenn.: Abingdon., 1980.

Guerrero, Andrés. *A Chicano Theology.* New York: Orbis Books, 1987.

Haselden, Kyle. *Death of a Myth: New Locus for Spanish American Faith.* New York: Friendship Press., 1964.

"Hispanics In the Assemblies of God Outpace General U. S. Spanish Population in Rapid Growth." *The Pentecostal Evangel.* 19 July 1987.

Holland, Clifton L. *The Religious Dimension in Hispanic Los Angeles: A Protestant Case Study.* Pasadena, CA: William Carey Library, 1974.

Hurtado, Juan. *An Attitudinal Study of Social Distance between the Mexican American and the Church.* San Antonio: M.A.A.C., 1975.

Illich, Ivan, et. al. eds. *Spiritual Care of Puerto Rican Migrants.* Hispanics in the United States Series. Salem, N.H.: Ayer Co., 1970, 1981 (reprint).

Isasi-Díaz, Ada María and Tarango, Yolanda. *Hispanic Woman, Prophetic Voice in the Church: Toward a Hispanic Women's Liberation Theology.* New York, Harper and Row, 1988.

Lara-Braud, Jorge. *Our Claim on the Future.* New York: Friendship Press, 1970.

Lennon, John J. *A Comparative Study of the Patterns of Acculturation of Selected Puerto Rican - Protestant and Roman Catholic Families in an Urban Metropolitan Area.* Palo Alto, CA: R. and E. Research Associates, Inc., 1976.

Lucas, Isidro. *The Browning of America.* Chicago: Fides/Claretian, 1981.

Lugo, Juan. *Pentecostés en Puerto Rico: La Vida de un Misionero.* San Juan, Puerto Rico: Puerto Rico Gospel Press, 1951.

MacKay, John A. *The Other Spanish Christ: A Study in the Spiritual History of Spain and South America.* New York: The Macmillan Co., 1933.

Maust, John. "The Exploding Hispanic Minority: A Field in our Back Yard." *Christianity Today* (August 1980).

Montoya, Alex D. *Hispanic Ministry in North America.* Grand Rapids, Mich.: Zondervan Publishing House, 1987.

Morales, Adam. *American Baptist with a Spanish Accent.* Valley Forge, PA: The Judson Press, 1964.

National Conference of Catholic Bishops. *The Hispanic Presence: Challenge and Commitment: A Pastoral Letter on Hispanic Ministry.* Washington, D.C.: U.S. Catholic Conference, 1984.

Northeast Catholic Pastoral Center for Hispanics. *A Report: The Hispanic Community, the Church and the Northeast Center for Hispanics*. New York: Northeast Catholic Pastoral Center for Hispanics, Inc., 1982.

Ortegon, Samuel M. "Religious Thought and Practice Among Mexican Baptists of the U.S., 1900-1947." Ph.D. Dissertation, University of Southern California, 1950.

Orozco, E.C. *Republican Protestantism in Aztlan*. Glendale, Calif.: Petereins Press., 1981.

Oxnam, G. Bromley. "Mexicans in Los Angeles from the Standpoint of the Religious Forces of the City." *Annals of the American Academy of Political and Social Science* 93 (January 1921): 130-133.

Parvin, Earl. "Hispanics in the United States," *Missions USA*. Chicago: Moody Press. 1985., pp. 107-128.

Paz, Octavio, "Reflections," *The New Yorker*. November 17, 1979.

Pazmiño, Robert W. "Double Dutch: Reflections of An Hispanic-North American on Multicultural Religious Education." Newton Centre, Massachusetts, 1987 (Typewritten).

Poblete, Renato and Thomas F. O'Dea. "Anomie and the 'Quest for Community': The Formation of Sects Among the Puerto Ricans of New York." *American Catholic Sociological Review*, 21: 18-36, Spring 1960.

Polischuk, Pablo. "Personality Characteristics and Role Preferences Among Hispanic Protestant Ministers." Ph.D. dissertation, Fuller Theological Seminary, 1980.

Protestant Council of the City of New York, Mid-Century Pioneers and Protestants: *A Study of the Protestant Expression Among Puerto Ricans of New York City*. New York: Department of Church Planning and Research of the Protestant Council, 1954.

Recinos, Harold J. *Hear the Cry!: A Latino Pastor Challenges the Church*. Louisville, Kentucky: Westminster/John Knox Press, 1989.

Rembao, Alberto. "Gloria a lo Trivial." *Meditaciones Neoyorkinas*. Buenos Aires: Librería "La Aurora," 1939.

"A Report on the Protestant Spanish Community in New York City." New York:
    Protestant Council of the City of New York, Dept. of Church Planning,
    1960.

Rivera-Pagán, Luis N. "La Cristianización de América: Reflexión y Desafío."
    Apuntes 7 (Primavera 1987): 16-17.

Rodríguez, Daniel R. *La Primera Evangelización Norteamericana en Puerto Rico
    1898-1930.* Mexico, D.F.: Ediciones Borinquen, 1986.

Rodríguez-Bravo, Enrique. *Origen y Desarrollo del Movimiento Protestante en
    Puerto Rico.* Ph.D. Dissertation, The George Washington University, 1972.

Romero, Juan, with Moisés Sandoval. *Reluctant Dawn: Historia del Padre A.J.
    Martínez, Cura de Taos.* San Antonio: Mexican Cultural Center, 1975.

Romo, Oscar. "Ministering with Hispanic Americans," in *Missions in the Mosaic*,
    ed. M. Wendell Belew. Atlanta, Ga.: Home Mission Board, Southern
    Baptist Convention, 1974.

Rosas, Carlos. "La Música al Servicio del Reino," *Apuntes: Reflexiones
    Teológicas desde el Margen Hispano* 6 (Spring 1986): 3-6.

Rycroft, W. Stanley. *Religion and Faith in Latin America.* Philadelphia: The
    Westminster Press, 1958.

Sánchez, Ramon. *Ricardo Tañon: "El Poder y La Gloria de Dios."* San Juan,
    Puerto Rico: Romualdo Real, 1980.

Sandoval, Moisés, ed. *Fronteras: A History of the Latin American Church in the
    USA Since 1513.* San Antonio, Texas: Mexican American Cultural Center,
    1983.

Sandoval, Moisés. *On the Move: A History of the Hispanic Church in the United
    States.* Maryknoll, N.Y.: Orbis, 1990.

Santillana, Fernado. "Refugiados económicos, o víctimas?" *Apuntes* 5 (Winter
    1985): 83.

Solivan, Samuel. "Puerto Rico, A History of Struggle for Liberation" (paper).
    New York City: Symposium on the Self-determination of Puerto Rico, the
    Inter Church Center, 1981.

Soto, Antonio R. *Chicano and the Church*. Denver: Marfel, 1975.

Soto Fontanez, S. *Mission At the Door: A History of Hispanic Baptist Work in New York*. Santo Domingo, Republica Dominicana: Editora Educativa Dominicana, 1982.

Sotomayor-Chavez, Marta. "Latin American Migration." *Apuntes* 2 (Primavera 1982): 18-14.

Stevens Arroyo, Antonio M. "The Religion of Puerto Ricans in New York." In *Puerto Rican Perspectives*, pp. 119-130. Edited by Edward Mapp. Metuchen, NJ.: Scarecrow Press, 1974.

_____. *Prophets Denied Honor: An Anthology of the Hispanic Church in the United States*. Maryknoll, NY: Orbis Books, 1980.

_____. "Puerto Rican Migration to the United States," in Moisés Sandoval, ed., *Fronteras: A History of the Latin American Church in the USA Since 1513*.

Sumner, Margaret L. "Mexican American Minority Churches, U.S.A." *Practical Anthropology* 10 (1963): 115-121.

Sylvest, Jr., Edwin E. "Rethinking the 'Discovery' of the Americas: A Provisional Historico-Theological Reflection." *Apuntes*. 7 (Primavera 1987): 6.

_____. "Hispanic American Protestantism in the United States," Moisés Sandoval, ed. *Fronteras: A History of the Latin American Church in the USA Since 1513*.

Thomas, Piri. *Savior, Savior, Hold My Hand*. Garden City, New York: Doubleday and Company, Inc., 1972.

Traverzo-Galarsa,David. "A New Dimension in Religious Education for the Hispanic Evangelical Church in New York City." Unpublished M.A. thesis. New Brunswick, NJ.: New Brunswick Theological Seminary, 1987.

Unamuno, Miguel de. *El Cristo de Velázquez (Poema)*. Madrid: Esposa-Calpe, S.A., 1967.

Valle, Carlos A. (ed.), *Culto: Crítica y Búsqueda*. Buenos Aires, Argentina: Centro de Estudios Cristianos, Methopress, 1972.

Villafañe, Eldin. "An Approach to Winning Ethnic Minorities in the City," *New England Journal of Ministry*, Vol. 2 (2), Spring 1982, pp. 54-60.

_____. "An Evangelical Call to a Social Spirituality: Confrontring Evil in Urban Society", *Apuntes* II (Verano, 1991): 27-38.

_____. *The Holy Spirit and Wholistic Ethnic Ministry.* Unpublished Manuscript (162 page transcript), delivered as a five (5) part Seminar at National Home Missions Conference, Assemblies of God, Springfiled, Missouri, June 17-29, 1985.

_____. "The Role of the Church in the Preservation of Hispanic Culture: A Puerto Rican Perspective." Unpublished paper, Harvard Divinity School. Cambridge, 1975.

Wagner, John A. "The Role of the Christian Church." in *La Raza: Forgotten Americans*. Notre Dame: University of Notre Dame Press, 1966.

Weigert, Andrew J.; William V. D'Antonio; and Arthur J. Rubel. "Protestantism and Assimilation Among Mexican Americans: An Exploratory Study of Minister's Reports." *Journal for the Scientific Study of Religion* 10 (1971); 219-232.

Whitam, Frederick L. "New York's Spanish Protestants," *Christian Century*. February 7, 1962.

Pentecostals and Related Studies

Butler Flora, Cornelia. *Pentecostalism in Colombia: Baptism by Fire and Spirit.* Cranbury, New Jersey: Associated University Presses, Inc., 1976.

Caraballo-Ireland. "The Role of the Pentecostal Church As a Service Provider in the Puerto Rican Community, Boston, Massachusetts: A Case Study," Unpublished Ph.D. dissertation, Brandeis Unviersity, Waltham, MA. 1990.

Christenson,Larry A. *A Charismatic Approach to Social Action.* Minneapolis: Bethany Fellowship, 1974.

Dayton, Donald W. *Theological Roots of Pentecostalism.* Grand Rapids, Mich.: Francis Asbury Press, Zondervan Publishing House, 1987.

Dearman, Marion. "Christ and Conformity: A Study of Pentecostal Values," *Journal of the Scientific Study of Religion*, 13 (1974): 437-53.

Du Plessis, David J. *The Spirit Bade Me So*. Oakland, Cal.: David J. Du Plessis, 1960.

Fahey, Sheila Macmanus. *Charismatic Social Action*. New York: Paulist Press, 1977.

Gerlach, Luther P. and Hine, Virginia. "Five Factors Crucial to Growth and Spread of a Modern Religious Movement." in *Journal of the Scientific Study of Religion*, 1968, 7, 1. Spr. 23-40.

_____. *People, Power, Change Movements of Social Transformation*. Indianapolis: The Bobbs-Merrill Company, Inc., 1970.

Glazier, Stephen D. *Perspective On Pentecostalism: Case Studies from the Caribbean and Latin America*. Washington, D.C.: University Press of America, 1980.

Hollenweger, Walter J. *The Pentecostals: The Charismatic Movement in the Churches*. Minneapolis: Augsburg Publishing House, 1972.

Lalive D'Epinay, C. *Haven of the Masses: A Study of the Pentecostal Movement in Chile*. London: Lutterworth Press, 1969.

Maloney, H. Newton and Lovekin, A. Adams. *Glossolalia: Behavioral Science Perspectives on Speaking in Tongues*. New York: Oxford Unviersity Press, 1985.

Mapes Anderson, Robert. *Vision of the Disinherited: The Making of American Pentecostalism*. New York: Oxford University Press, 1979.

Martin, David. *Tongues of Fire: The Explosion of Protestantism in Latin America*. Oxford, UK: Basil Blackwell, 1990.

McClung, Jr., L. Grant (ed.). *Azusa Street and Beyond: Pentecostal Missions and Church Growth in the Twentieth Century*. South Plainfield, N.J.: Bridge Publishing, Inc., 1986.

McGee, Gary B. *This Gospel Shall Be Preached: A History and Theology of Assemblies of God Foreign Missions to 1959*. Springfield, Missouri: Gospel Publishing House, 1986.

Menzies, William W. *Annointed to Serve: The Story of the Assemblies of God.*
Springfield, MO.: Gospel Publishing House, 1971.

Nichol, John Thomas. *The Pentecostals.* Plainfield, New Jersey: Logos
International, 1966.

Paris, Arthur E. *Black Pentecostalism: Southern Religion in an Urban World.*
Amherst, Mass.: The University of Massachusetts Press, 1982.

Pomerville, Paul A. *The Third Force in Missions: A Pentecostal Contribution to
Contemporary Mission Theology.* Peabody, Mass.: Hendrickson Publishers,
1985.

Synan, Vinson. *The Holiness-Pentecostal Movement in the U.S.* Grand Rapids,
Michigan: Eerdmans, 1971.

_____, ed. *Aspects of Pentecostal-Charismatic Origins.* Plainfield,
New Jersey: Logos International, 1975.

_____. "Pentecostalism: Varieties and Contributions." Unpublished
lecture presented at the consultation on Confessing the Apostolic Faith from
the Perspective of the Pentecostal Churches. Pasadena, CA.: Fuller
Theological Seminary, 1986.

Tinney, James S. and Short, Stephen N., eds. *In The Tradition of William J.
Seymour.* Washington, D.C.: Spirit Press, 1978.

Van Dusen, Henry P. "The Third Force in Christendom," *Life.* June 9, 1958.

Villafañe, Eldin. "Toward An Hispanic American Pentecostal Social Ethic, with
Special Reference to North Eastern United States", Ph.D. dissertation,
Boston University, Boston, Massachusetts, January 1989.

Wagner, C. Peter. *Look Out! The Pentecostals Are Coming.* Carol Stream, Ill.:
Creation House, 1973.

Willems, Emilio. *Followers of the New Faith: Social Change and the Rise of
Protestantism in Brazil and Chile.* Nashville: Vanderbilt University Press,
1967.

Ethics, Theology and Other Related Studies

Abell, Aaron Ignatius. *The Urban Impact on American Protestantism, 1865-1900*. Cambridge, Mass.: Harvard University Press, 1943.

Alvarez, Carmelo E. *Santidad y Compromiso: El Riesgo de Vivir El Evangelio*. Mexico, D.F.: Casa Unida de Publicaciones, S.A., 1985.

Alves, Ruben. *Protestantism and Repression*. New York: Orbis Books, 1985.

Anderson, Ray S. *On Being Human: Essay in Theological Anthropology*. Grand Rapids, Mich.: Eerdmans, 1982.

Arana Quiroz, Pedro. "Ordenes de la Creación y Responsabilidad Cristiana." in C. René Padilla, ed. *Fe Cristiana y Latinoamérica Hoy*. Buenos Aires, Argentina: Ediciones Certeza, 1974.

Arias, Esther and Mortimer. *The Cry of My People: Out of Captivity in Latin America*. New York: Friendship Press, 1980.

Barbour,Ian G. *Myths, Models, and Paradigms: A Comparative Study in Science and Religion*. New York: Harper and Row, 1974.

Barth, Karl. *Dogmatics in Outline*. New York: Harper & Row, 1959.

Behm, Johannes. *Parakletos*. Gerhard Kittel and G. Friedrich, eds. *Theological Dictionary of the New Testament*, Vol. VI. Grand Rapids, Michigan: Eerdmans Publishing Company, 1964.

Berger, Peter. *The Sacred Canopy*. Garden City, New York: Doubleday, 1969.

Berger, Peter and Thomas Luckmann. *The Social Construction of Reality*. Garden City, New York: Doubleday, 1966.

Berkhof, Hendrikus. *The Doctrine of the Holy Spirit*. Atlanta: John Knox Press, 1982.

_____. *Christ and the Powers*. Scottdale, PA.: Herald Press, 1962.

Bidney, David. *Theoretical Anthropology*. New York: Schocken Books, 1967.

Birch, Bruce C. and Larry L. Rasmussen. *Bible and Ethics in the Christian Life*. Minneapolis: Augsburg, 1976.

Bird, Otto. *The Ideas of Justice*. New York, N.Y.: Praeger, 1967.

Bloesch, Donald G. *Essentials of Evangelical Theology*, 2 vols. New York, N.Y.: Harper and Row, 1979.

Boff, Leonardo. *Church: Charism and Power*. New York: Crossroad Publishing Company, 1986.

Bonhoeffer, Dietrich. *Ethics*. New York: MacMillan, 1955.

Bright, John. *The Kingdom of God*. Nashville: Abingdon Press, 1953.

Brightman, Edgar S. *Moral Laws*. New York: The Abingdon Press, 1933.

Brockmuehl, Klaus. *Evangelicals and Social Ethics*. Downers Grove, Illinois: Inter-Varsity, 1979.

Brown, Robert McAfee. *Theology in a New Key*. Philadelphia: Westminster Press, 1978.

Bruce, F.F. *Commentary on the Book of The Acts*. Grand Rapids, Michigan: Wm. B. Eerdmans Publishing Co., 1980.

Brunner, Emil. *The Divine Imperative*. Philadelphia: Westminster, 1947.

_____. *Justice and the Social Order*. London: Lutterworth Press, 1946.

Brunner, Frederick Dale. *A Theology of the Holy Spirit: The Pentecostal Experience and the New Testament Witness*. Grand Rapids, Michigan: Wm. B. Eerdmans, 1970.

Busch, Eberhard. *Karl Barth: His life from letters and autobiographical texts*. Philadelphia: Fortress Press, 1976.

Cadoux, Cecil John. *The Early Church and The World*. Edinburgh: T. & T. Clark, 1925.

Cairns, Earle E. *Christianity Through the Centuries*. Grand Rapids, Michigan: Zondervan Publishing House, 1954.

Carrier, Herve. *The Sociology of Religious Belonging*. New York: Herder and Herder, 1965.

Cho, Paul Yonggi. *"Rhema"* in *The Fourth Dimension*. Plainfield, N.J.: Logos International, 1979.

Cone, James H. *A Black Theology of Liberation*. Philadelphia: Lippincott, 1970.

_____. *God of the Oppressed*. Minneapolis: Seabury Press, 1975.

_____. *The Spirituals and the Blues: An Interpretation*. Minnesota: The Seabury Press.

Costas, Orlando. *Christ Outside the Gate: Mission Beyond Christendom*. New York: Orbis Books, 1982.

_____. *The Church and Its Mission: A Shattering Critique from the Third World*. Wheaton, Illinois: Tyndale, 1974.

_____. *The Integrity of Mission: The Inner Life and Outreach of the Church*. New York: Harper and Row, 1979.

_____. *Theology of the Crossroads in Latin America*. Amsterdam, Netherlands: Editions Rodopi, 1976.

_____. *Liberating News: A Theology of Contextual Evangelization*. Grand Rapids: William B. Eerdmans, 1989.

Cotham, Perry C., ed. *Christian Social Ethics*. Grand Rapids, Michigan: Baker Book House, 1979.

Cox, Harvey. *Religion in the Secular City: Toward A Postmodern Theology*. New York: Simon and Schuster, Inc., 1984.

Cullman, Oscar. *La Fe y El Culto en la Iglesia Primitiva*. Madrid, Espana: Stadium, 1971.

_____. *Christ and Time: The Primitive Christian Conception of Time and History*. Philadelphia, PA.: The Westminster Press, 1964.

Davis, John Jefferson. *Evangelical Ethics: Issues Facing the Church Today*. Phillipsburg, N.J.: Presbyterian and Reformed Publishing Co., 1985.

Deats Jr., Paul, ed. *Toward A Discipline of Social Ethics: Essays in Honor of Walter G. Muelder.* Boston: Boston University Press, 1972.

_____. "Protestant Social Ethics and Pacifism," in Thomas A. Shannon, ed. *War or Peace?: The Search for New Answers.* Maryknoll, N.Y.: Orbis Books, 1980.

_____. *Social Change and Moral Values.* Washington, D.C.: Board of Christian Social Concerns, Service Department, 1963.

_____. and Robb, Carol. *The Boston Personalist Tradition in Philosophy, Social Ethics, and Theology.* Georgia: Mercer University Press, 1986.

_____. and Stotts, Herbert E. *Methodism and Society: Guidelines for Strategy.* New York: Abingdon Press, 1962.

de Jesus-Marie, Pere Bruno, ed. *Satan.* New York: Sheed and Ward, 1952.

Delling, Gerhard. *Stoicheo-Stoicheion. Theological Dictionary of the New Testament*, Vol. VII. Grand Rapids, Michigan: Eerdmans Publishing Company, 1964.

Dulles, S.J., Avery. *Models of Revelation.* New York, N.Y.: Doubleday and Company, Inc., 1985.

Dunn, James D.G. *Baptism in the Holy Spirit: A Reexamination of the New Testament Teaching on the Gift of the Spirit in Relation to Pentecostalism Today.* Philadelphia: The Westminster Press, 1970.

Durkeim, Emile. *Suicide.* New York: Free Press, 1951, ed.

Dussel, Enrique. *History and the Theology of Liberation.* Maryknoll, N.Y.: Orbis Books, 1976.

Ellul, Jacques. *The Subversion of Christianity.* Grand Rapids, Michigan: William B. Eerdmans Publishing Company, 1987.

_____. *Prayer and Modern Man.* New York, N.Y.: Seabury Press, 1979.

Ervin, Howard M. *Conversion - Initiation and The Baptism in The Holy Spirit.* Peabody, Mass.: Hendrickson Publishers, Inc., 1984.

Escobar, Samuel. *Responsabilidad Social de la Iglesia.* Cochabamba, Bolivia: Publicaciones A.G.U.E.B., 1971.

Escobar, Samuel and Driver, John. *Christian Mission and Social Justice.* Scottdale, Pennsylvania: Herald Press, 1978.

Fackre, Gabriel. *The Christian Story: A Narrative Interpretation of Basic Christian Doctrine.* Grand Rapids, Michigan: Wm. B. Eerdmans Publishing Company, 1984 ed.

Fanon, Frantz. *The Wretched of the Earth.* New York: Ballantine Books, 1963.

Fishman, Joshua. "Language Maintenance." in Stephen Thernstrom ed. *Harvard Encyclopedia of American Ethnic Groups.* Cambridge, Mass.: Belknap Press, 1980.

Forell, George W. *Christian Social Teachings.* Minneapolis: Augsburg, 1971.

Francis, E.K. "The Nature of Ethnic Group." *American Journal of Sociology* 52 (March 1947): 393-400.

Frankena, William K. *Ethics.* 2nd ed. Englewood Cliffs, N.J.: Prentice-Hall, 1973.

Frazier, E. Franklin. *The Negro Church in America.* New York: Shocken, 1973.

Furnish, Victor. *Theology and Ethics in Paul.* Nashville: Abingdon, 1968.

_____. *The Love Command in the New Testament.* Nashville: Abingdon, 1972.

Gannon, Thomas M. and Traub, George W. *The Desert and the City: An Interpretation of the History of Christian Spirituality.* Macmillan Company, 1969.

Gardner, E.C. *Biblical Faith and Social Ethics.* New York: Harper and Row, 1960.

Gee, Donald. *Pentecostés.* Miami, Florida: Editorial Vida, 1970.

Geertz, Clifford. "Ritual and Social Change: A Javanese Example," in William A. Lesa and E.Z. Vogt, ed., *Reader in Comparative Religion: An Anthropological Approach.* New York: Harper and Row, 3rd ed., 1972.

246   The Liberating Spirit

_____. *The Interpretation of Cultures*. New York: Basic Books, Inc., 1973.

Gerth, H.H. and Mills, C. Wright. *From Max Weber: Essays in Sociology*. New York: Oxford University Press, 1946.

Gibellini, Rosino. *Frontiers of Theology in Latin America*. Maryknoll, N.Y.: Orbis Books, 1979.

Gish, Arthur. *Living in Christian Community*. Scottdale, PA.: Herald Press, 1979.

Glock, Charles Y. and Stark, Rodney. "On the Origin and Evolution of Religious Groups." in Charles Y. Glock, (ed.) *Religion in Sociological Perspective: Essays in the Empirical Study of Religion*. Belmont, California: Wadsworth, 1973.

González, Justo L. *The Story of Christianity, Vol. l: The Early Church to the Dawn of the Reformation*. New York: Harper and Row, 1984.

_____. "Encarnación e Historia," in C. René Padilla. *Fe Cristiana y Latinoamérica Hoy*. Buenos Aires, Argentina: Ediciones Certeza, 1974.

_____. "Espiritualidad Política," in *Apuntes*, Vol. 3, No. l (Primavera 1983).

Gordon, A.J. *The Ministry of the Spirit*. Philadelphia: Judson, 1949.

Gordon, Milton M. *Assimilation in America Life: The Role of Race, Religion and National Origins*. New York: Oxford University Press, 1964.

Grounds, Vernon C. *Evangelicalism and Social Responsibility*. Scottdale, PA.: Herald Press, 1969.

Grundman, Walter. *hamartano*. Gerhard Kittel and G. Friedrich, eds. *Theological Dictionary of the New Testament*, Vol. l. Grand Rapids, Michigan: Eerdmans Publishing Company, 1964.

Gustafson, James M. *Christ and the Moral Life*. New York: Harper and Row, 1968.

_____. *The Church as Moral Decision-Maker*. Philadelphia: Pilgrim, 1970.

_____. "The Place of Scripture in Christian Ethics: A Methodological Study," *Theology and Christian Ethics*. Philadelphia, PA.: United Church Press, 1974.

Gutierrez, Gustavo. *A Theology of Liberation*. Maryknoll, N.Y.: Orbis, 1973.

_____. *We Drink from Our Own Wells: The Spiritual Journey of a People*. Maryknoll, N.Y.: Orbis Books, 1984.

Hanse, Hermann. *katecho*. Gerhard Kittel and G. Friedrich, eds. *Theological Dictionary of the New Testament*, Vol. II. Grand Rapids, Michigan: Eerdmans Publishing Company, 1964.

Hendry, G.D. *The Holy Spirit in Christian Theology*. Philadelphia: Westminster Press, 1956.

Henry, Carl F.H. *Christian Personal Ethics*. Grand Rapids, Michigan: Eerdmans, 1957.

_____. *The Uneasy Conscience of Modern Fundamentalism*. Grand Rapids, Michigan: Eerdmans, 1947.

_____. *Aspect of Christian Social Ethics*. Grand Rapids, Michigan: Baker Books.

_____, ed. *Baker's Dictionary of Christian Ethics*. Grand Rapids, Michigan: Baker, 1973.

_____, ed. *Revelation and the Bible*. Grand Rapids, Michigan: Baker Book House, 1958.

Heron, Alasdair. *The Holy Spirit*. Philadelphia: The Westminster Press, 1983.

Heschel, Abraham J. *Between God and Man*. New York: Harper and Row, 1959.

Hessel, Dieter. *Social Ministry*. Philadelphia: Westminster, 1982.

Hodges, Melvin L. *El Espíritu Santo y El Evangelismo Universal*. Miami, Florida: Editorial Vida, 1979.

Holland, Joe and Peter Henriot. *Social Analysis: Linking Faith and Justice*. Maryknoll, N.Y.: Orbis, 1983.

Hollinger, Dennis P. *Individualism and Social Ethics*. Landham, MD.: University Press of America, 1983.

Hopkins. Charles Howard. *The Rise of the Social Gospel in American Protestantism, 1865-1915*. New Haven: Yale University Press, 1940.

Horton, Stanley M. *What The Bible Says About The Holy Spirit*. Springfield, Missouri: Gospel Publishing House, 1976.

Hostos, Eugenio Maria de, *Moral Social*. Argentina: Eudeba Editorial Universitaria de Buenos Aires, 1968 ed.

Hug, S.J., James E. "Christian Moral Discernment," in James E. Hug, S.J. (ed.) *Tracing The Spirit: Communities, Social Action, and Theological Reflection*. New York: Paulist Press, 1983.

Johnson, Joseph A. *The Soul of the Black Preacher*. Philadelphia: A Pilgrim Press Book, 1971.

Jones, James W. *The Spirit and The World*. New York: Hawthorn Books, Inc., 1975.

Kaiser, Jr., Walter C. "The Use of The Bible in Establishing Ethical Norms." *Toward Old Testament Ethics*. Grand Rapids, Michigan: The Zondervan Corporation, 1983.

Kelsey, Morton. *Discernment: A Study in Ecstasy and Evil*. New York, N.Y.: Paulist Press, 1978.

Kerans, Patrick. *Sinful Social Structures*. New York: Paulist, 1974.

Kierkegaard, Soren. *Works of Love*. New York, N.Y.: Harper and Row, 1963.

King Jr., Martin Luther. *Stride Toward Freedom*. New York: Harper and Row, 1958.

_____. *Strength To Love*. Great Britain: Wm. Collins and Sons, 1963.

King, Mel. *Chain of Change: Struggles for Black Community Development*. Boston, Mass.: South End Press, 1981.

Kirk, Andrew. *Liberation Theology: An Evangelical View from the Third World.* Richmond: John Knox Press, 1979.

Kraft, Charles H. *Christianity in Culture: A Study in Dynamic Biblical Theologizing in Cross-Cultural Perspective.* Maryknoll, N.Y.: Orbis Books, 1980.

Ladd, George Eldon. *A Theology of the New Testament.* Grand Rapids, Michigan: Wm. B. Eerdmans Publishing Company, 1974.

_____. *The Presence of the Future: The Eschatology of Biblical Realism.* Grand Rapids, Michigan: Wm. B. Eerdmans Publishing Co., 1974.

Lane, S.J., George A. *Christian Spirituality - An Historical Sketch.* Chicago: Loyola University Press, 1984.

Lehman, Paul. *Ethics in a Christian Context.* New York: Harper and Row, 1963.

Lincoln, C. Eric ed. *The Black Experience in Religion.* Garden City, New York: Doubleday Anchor Books, 1974.

Long, Edward, Jr. *A Survey of Christian Ethics.* New York: Oxford University Press, 1967.

_____. "The Use of the Bible in Christian Ethics." *Interpretation* 19 (1965): 149-162.

Lovelace, Richard F. *Dynamics of Spiritual Life: An Evangelical Theology of Renewal.* Downers Grove, Illinois: Inter-Varsity Press, 1979.

Lovin, Robin W. *Christian Faith and Public Choices: The Social Ethics of Barth, Brunner, and Bonhoeffer.* Philadelphia: Fortress Press, 1984.

Maduro, Otto. *Religion and Social Conflicts.* Maryknoll, N.Y.: Orbis Books, 1982.

Magnusson, Paul. "Rich getting Richer, taking bigger share of US wealth, Study says." *The Boston Globe.* 19 July 1986.

Mannheim, Karl. *Ideology and Utopia: An Introduction to the Sociology of Knowledge.* New York: Harvest Book, 1936.

Marx, Karl. "Contribution to the Critique of Hegel's Philosophy of Right: Introduction." in Robert C. Tucker, ed. *The Marx-Engels Reader*. New York: W.W. Norton and Company, 1972.

Matson, T.B. *Christianity and World Issues*. New York: MacMillan, 1957.

Meehan, Frances X. *A Contemporary Social Spirituality*. Maryknoll, New York: Orbis, 1982.

Memmi, Albert. *The Colonizer and the Colonized*. Boston: Beacon Press, 1965.

Menzies, William W. "The Holy Spirit in Christian Theology." in Kenneth S. Kantzer and Stanley N. Gundry, editor. *Perspective on Evangelical Theology*. Grand Rapids, Michigan: Baker Book House, 1979.

Merk, Frederick. *Manifest Destiny and Mission in American History: A Reinterpretation*. New York: Vintage, 1963.

Merton, Robert K. *Social Theory and Social Structures*. Glencoe, Ill.: Free Press, 1957.

Miguez Bonino, José. *Doing Theology in a Revolutionary Situation*. Philadelphia: Fortress, 1975.

Miranda, Jesse. *The Christian Church in Ministry*. Brussels, Belgium: International Correspondence Institute, 1980.

Moberg, David. *Inasmuch: Christian Social Responsibility in the 20th Century*. Grand Rapids, Michigan: Eerdmans, 1965.

Moltmann, Jurgen. *The Crucified God: The Cross of Christ as The Foundation and Criticism of Christian Theology*. New York, N.Y.: Harper and Row, 1974.

Mott, Stephen C. *Biblical Ethics and Social Change*. New York: Oxford University, 1982.

_____. "The Contribution of the Bible to Human Rights," in *Human Rights and The Global Mission of the Church*. Boston Theological Institute Annual Series, Vol. 1. Cambridge, Mass.: Boston Theological Institute, 1985.

Muelder, Walter G. *Moral Law in Christian Social Ethics*. Richmond: John Knox, 1966.

_____. *The Ethical Edge of Christian Theology*. New York: E. Mellen Press, 1983.

_____. "From Sect to Church," *Christendom*. Autumn, 1945.

Myrdal, Gunnar. *An American Dilemma: The Negro Problem and Modern Democracy*. New York: Harper and Row, 1962.

Nee, Watchman. *The Ministry of God's Word*. New York: Christian Fellowship Publishers, Inc., 1971.

Nesbit, Robert A. *The Quest for Community*. New York: Oxford University Press, 1953.

Newbigin, Lesslie. *The Household of God*. New York: Friendship Press, 1954.

Nicholls, Bruce J. ed. *In Word and Deed: Evangelism and Social Responsibility*. Grand Rapids, Michigan: Wm. Eerdmans Publishing Co., 1985.

Niebuhr, Reinhold. *Moral Man and Immoral Society*. New York: Scribner's Sons, 1932.

Niebuhr, H. Richard. *The Responsible Self*. New York: Harper and Row, 1963.

_____. *Christ and Culture*. New York: Harper and Row, 1951.

_____. *The Social Sources of Denominationalism*. New York: H. Hott and Company, 1929.

Nygren, Anders. *Agape and Eros*. New York, NY: Harper and Row, 1953.

O'Dea, Thomas. *Sociology of Religion*. Englewood Cliffs, N.J.: Prentice-Hall, 1966.

O'Donovan, Oliver. *Resurrection and Moral Order: An Outline for Evangelical Ethics*. Grand Rapids, Michigan: Wm. B. Eerdmans, 1986.

Ogletree, Thomas W. *The Use of The Bible in Christian Ethics*. Philadelphia, PA.: Fortress press, 1983.

Otto, Rudolf. *The Idea of the Holy: An Inquiry into the Nonrational Factor in the Idea of the Divine and its Relation to the Rational.* New York: Oxford University Press, 1965.

Padilla, C. René. *Misión Integral: Ensayos Sobre el Reino y la Iglesia.* Grand Rapids, Michigan: Wm. B. Eerdmans Publishing Company, 1986.

_____. "El Evangelio y la Responsabilidad Social," in C. René Padilla, *El Evangelio Hoy.* Buenos Aires, Argentina: Ediciones Certeza, 1975.

Pasquariello, Ronald D., Shriver, Donald W., and Geyer, Alan. *Redeeming the City: Theology, Politics and Urban Policy.* New York: The Pilgrim Press, 1984.

Pearlman, Myer. *Knowing the Doctrines of the Bible.* Springfield, MO.: Gospel Publishing House, 1937.

"Pentecostalismo y Teología De La Liberación." *Pastoralia*, Año 7, Num. 15, Diciembre 1985.

Perkins, John. *And Justice for All.* Regal Books, 1982.

"Political Responsibility: Choice for the 1980s." A Statement of the Administrative Board, United States Catholic Conference, revised edition, March 22, 1984.

Pope, Liston. *Millhands and Preachers.* New York: Yale University Press, 1942.

Ramsey, Paul. *Basic Christian Ethics.* New York: Scribner's Sons, 1950.

Rauschenbusch, Walter. *A Theology for the Social Gospel.* New York: Macmillan, 1917.

Rawls, John. *A Theory of Justice.* Cambridge, Mass.: Harvard University Press, 1971.

Rich, Spencer. "Divisions of Race Mark Gap in Wealth." *The Boston Globe.* 19 July 1986.

Ridderbos, Herman. *The Coming of the Kingdom.* Philadelphia: Presbyterian and Reformed, 1962.

_____. *The Epistle of Pual to the Church of Galatians: The New International Commentary on the New Testament.* Grand Rapids, Michigan: Eerdmans, 1970.

Rienecker, Fritz, Rogers, Clem L., ed. *A Linguistic Key to the Greek New Testament,* 9th edition. Grand Rapids, Michigan: Zondervan Publishing House, 1980.

Robinson, H. Wheeler. *Corporate Personality in Ancient Israel.* Philadelphia: Fortress Press, 1964.

Sampley, J. Paul. *Walking Between the Times: Paul's Moral Reasoning.* Minneapolis: Augsbury-Fortress Press, 1991.

Sasse, Hermann. *Kosmos.* Gerhard Kittel and G. Friedrich, eds. *Theological Dictionary of the New Testament,* Vol. III. Grand Rapids, Michigan: Eerdmans Publishing Company, 1964.

Schlesinger, A.M. *The Rise of the City, 1878-1898.* New York: Macmillan Company, 1933.

Schmidt, Karl Ludwig. *Basileus - Basilikos.* Gerhard Kittel and G. Friedrich, eds. *Theological Dictionary of the New Testament,* Vol. 1. Grand Rapids, Michigan: Eerdmans Publishing Company, 1964.

Schneider, Louis, ed. *Religion, Culture and Society: A Reader in the Sociology of Religion.* New York: John Wiley, 1964.

Schreiter, Robert J. *Constructing Local Theologies.* Maryknoll, N.Y.: Orbis Books, 1985.

Schrenk, Gottlob. *dikaiosyne.* Gerhard Kittel and G. Friedrich, eds. *Theological Dictionary of the New Testament,* Vol. II. Grand Rapids, Michigan: Eerdmans Publishing Company, 1964.

Schweizer, Eduard; (et.al.) *Pneuma, pneumatikos.* Gerhard Friedrich, ed. *Theological Dictionary of the New Testament,* Vol. 6, . Grand Rapids, Michigan: Eerdmans, 1967.

Segundo, Juan Luis. *The Liberation of Theology.* Maryknoll, N.Y.: Orbis Books, 1976.

_____. *Theology and The Church*. San Francisco, CA.: Harper and Row, Publishers, 1987.

Sider, Ronald. *Rich Christians in an Age of Hunger: A Biblical Study*. Downers Grove, Illinois: Inter-Varsity, 1977.

_____, ed. *The Chicago Declaration*. Carol Stream, Illinois: Creation House, 1974.

Simmons, Paul D. "The Bible and Bioethical Decision-Making," in his *Birth and Death: Bioethical Decision-Making*. Philadelphia, PA.: The Westminster Press, 1983.

Smedes, Lewis B. *Mere Morality*. Grand Rapids, Michigan: Eerdmans, 1983.

_____, ed. *Ministry and the Miraculous: A Case Study at Fuller Theological Seminary*. Pasadena, Cal.: Fuller Theological Seminary, 1987.

_____. *Love Within Limits: A Realist's View of 1 Corinthians 13*. Grand Rapids, Michigan: Wm. B. Eerdmans Publishing Co., 1978.

Snyder, Howard. *Liberating the Church*. Downers Grove, Illinois: Inter-Varsity, 1983.

Solomons, Robert C. *The Passions: The Myth and Nature of Human Emotion*. Garden City, New York: Anchor Press/Doubleday, 1976.

Stackhouse, Max L. *Creeds, Society and Human Rights: A Study in Three Cultures*. Grand Rapids: Eerdmans, 1984.

Stark, Werner. *The Sociology of Religion: A Study of Christendom*. 3 vols. New York: Fordham University Press, 1967.

Starkey, L.M. *The Work of the Holy Spirit*. Nashville: Abingdon, 1962.

Stauffer, Ethelbert. *agapao.*, Gerhard Kittel and G. Friedrich, eds. *Theological Dictionary of the New Testament*, Vol. 1. Grand Rapids, Michigan: Eerdmans Publishing Company, 1964.

Stott, John. *Christian Mission in the Modern World*. Downers Grove, Illinois: Inter-Varsity, 1975.

Stringfellow, William. *An Ethic for Christians and Other Aliens in a Strange Land*. Waco, Tex.: Word Books, 1973.

_____. *Free in Obedience: The Radical Christian Life*. New York: The Seabury Press, 1964.

Stronstad, Roger. *The Charismatic Theology of St. Luke*. Peabody, Mass.: Hendrickson Publishers, 1984.

Swete, H.B. *The Holy Spirit in the Ancient Church*. London: Macmillan, 1912.

Tamez, Elsa. *Against Machismo... interviews by Elsa Tamez*. Yorktown Heights, N.Y.: Meyer-Stone Books, 1987.

Teselle, Sallie, ed. *The Rediscovery of Ethnicity*. New York: Harper and Row, 1973.

Thomas, Robert L. "2 Thessalonians." *The Expositor's Bible Commentary*, Volume II. Grand Rapids, Michigan: Zondervan Publishing House, 1978.

Thurman, Howard. *Jesus and the Disinherited*. New York: Abingdon Press, 1949.

Thrupp, Sylvia L., ed. *Millennial Dreams in Action: Studies in Revolutionary Religious Movements*. New York: Schocken Books, 1970.

Tillich, Paul. *Love, Power, and Justice*. New York, N.Y.: Oxford University Press, 1954.

Troeltsch, Ernst. *The Social Teachings of the Christian Church*. 2 vols. New York: Harper and Row, 1960 (1911).

Unamuno, Miguel de. *Del Sentimiento Trágico de la Vida*. Buenos Aires, Argentina: Editorial Losada, S.A., 1964.

von Allmen, J.J. *El Culto Cristiano*. Salamanca, España: Ediciones Sigueme, 1968.

Wallis, Jim. *Agenda for Biblical People*. New York, N.Y.: Harper and Row, 1976.

Webber, George. *God's Golony in Man's World*. Nashville: Abingdon Press, 1960.

_____. *Today's Church: A Community of Exiles and Pilgrims*. Nashville, Tennessee: Abingdon, 1979.

Webber, Robert E. *The Church in The World: Opposition, Tension, or Transformation?* Grand Rapids, Michigan: Zondervan Publishing House, 1986.

_____. *The Secular Saint: A Case for Evangelical Social Responsibility*. Grand Rapids, Michigan: Zondervan, 1979.

Weber, Max. *The Protestant Ethic and the Spirit of Capitalism*. New York: Scribner's Sons, 1958.

_____. *From Max Weber: Essays in Sociology*. Trans. and ed. by H.H. Gerth and C. Wright Mills. New York: Oxford University Press, 1946.

_____. *The Sociology of Religion*. Boston: Beacon Press, 1964.

Webster, Douglas D. *A Passion For Christ: An Evangelical Christology*. Grand Rapids, Michigan: Zondervan Publishing House, 1987.

Weinberg, Albert K. *Manifest Destiny: A Study of National Expansion in American History*. Chicago: Quadrangle Books, 1963.

Wells, David F. *God the Evangelist: How the Holy Spirit Works to Bring Men and Women to Faith*. Grand Rapids, Michigan: Wm. B. Eerdmans, 1987.

White, R.E.O. *Biblical Ethics*. Richmond: John Knox Press, 1979.

Wilder, Amos. *Keryma, Eschatology, and Social Ethics*. Philadelphia: Fortress, 1966.

Wilkerson, David. *The Cross and The Switchblade*. Westwood, N.J.: Fleming H. Revell Company, 1963.

Williams, Robin M. *American Society: A Sociological Interpretation*. New York: Alfred A. Knopf, 1970.

Wilmore, Gayraud S. *Black Religion and Black Radicalism*. New York: Doubleday Anchor Books, 1972.

_____, and Cone, James, eds. *Black Theology: A Documentary History, 1966-1979*. Maryknoll, N.Y.: Orbis Books, 1979.

Wilson, Bryan R. *Sects and Society*. London: William Heinemann, Ltd., 1961.

Wimber, John. *Power Evangelism*. San Francisco, California: Harper and Row, Publishers, 1986.

Wink, Walter. *Naming the Powers: The Language of Powers in the New Testament*. Philadelphia, PA.: Fortress Press, 1984.

_____. *Unmasking the Powers: The Invisible Forces that Determine Human Existence*. Philadelphia, PA.: Fortress Press, 1986.

Winter, Gibson. *The Suburban Captivty of the Churches: An Analysis of Protestant Responsibility in the Expanding Metropolis*. New York: MacMillan, 1962.

Wogaman, J. Philip. *A Christian Method of Moral Judgement*. Philadelphia: Westminster, 1976.

Wood, Leon J. *Genesis: A Study Guide Commentary*. Grand Rapids, Michigan: Zondervan Publishing House, 1976.

Yinger, J.M. *The Scientific Study of Religion*. New York: MacMillan, 1970.

Yoder, John Howard. *The Christian Witness to the State*. Newton, Kansas: Faith and Life Press, 1964.

_____. *The Politics of Jesus*. Grand Rapids, Michigan: Eerdmans, 1972.

_____. *The Priestly Kingdom: Social Ethics as Gospel*. Notre Dame, Indiana: University of Notre Dame Press, 1984.

Eldin Villafañe is Professor of Christian Social Ethics at Gordon-Conwell Theological Seminary. He was the founding director (1976-1990) of the Center for Urban Ministerial Education (CUME) in Boston and former Associate Dean of Urban and Multicultural Affairs at Gordon-Conwell Theological Seminary.

He is an ordained minister with the Hispanic Eastern District of the Assemblies of God and served as the first president of La Comunidad of Hispanic Scholars of Theology and Religion. He earned his Ph.D. in Social Ethics from Boston University.

Dr. Villafañe was named one of the nation's ten most influential Hispanic religious leaders and scholars by the *National Catholic Reporter* (September 11, 1992).